How can we deal with pl........
of views) in promoting our missions
program? *See page 195.*

Can we trust the "bureaucrats" to run our
missions program? *See pages 175 & 200.*

Why are current denominational budgets
being cut back? *See page 189.*

What is the "two track" system of
funding? *See page 193.*

Who is evaluating the work of our present
mission professionals? *See page 158.*

Who is checking on the effectiveness of
our present mission program? *See pages
157–158.*

Are we tinkering with our structures and
neglecting mission? *See pages 155–156.*

How can the church use modern management techniques? *See page 155.*

What's so unique about managing the
church's business? *See page 11.*

Is there a difference between a leader and a manager? What is the pastor supposed to be? *See page 167.*

Who controls (runs) the "connectional" church? *See page 180.*

How can the individual be a responsible steward in a goal-setting denomination? *See page 180.*

WHEEL WITHIN THE WHEEL:

CONFRONTING THE MANAGEMENT CRISIS OF THE PLURALISTIC CHURCH

RICHARD G. HUTCHESON, JR.

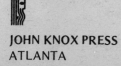

JOHN KNOX PRESS
ATLANTA

Direct mail orders for *Wheel Within the Wheel* are available at $2.95 each postpaid when check accompanies order.

From: William Carey Library, Publishers
    1705 N. Sierra Bonita Avenue
    Pasadena, California 91104

Scripture quotations are from the Revised Standard Version of the Holy Bible, copyright, 1946, 1952, and 1971, 1973 by the Division of Christian Education, National Council of the Churches of Christ in the U.S.A. and used by permission.

Portions of this book represent a further development of ideas first presented in an article, "Pluralism and Consensus: Why Mainline Church Mission Budgets Are in Trouble," *The Christian Century* (July 6-13, 1977). Appreciation is expressed to *The Christian Century* for permission to repeat and elaborate these themes.

Library of Congress Cataloging in Publication Data

Hutcheson, Richard G   1921-
    Wheel within the wheel.

    Includes index.
    1. Church management. 2. Holy Spirit. I. Title.
BV652.H83   658'.91'25   79-11481
ISBN 0-8042-1886-2
ISBN 0-8042-1887-0 pbk.

CONTENTS

5

PREFACE

This book is about the use of management techniques and organizational methods in the church. It is a subject in which I have been deeply immersed for four years, as chairman of the Office of Review and Evaluation of the Presbyterian Church in the United States — the denomination's organizational watchdog.

I came into the organizational management business through the back door, courtesy of the U.S. Navy. Most of my ministry has taken place in a classic bureaucracy, as a Navy chaplain. I was fortunate enough to be promoted "up the ladder" and as is inevitable in a bureaucracy, that meant assignment to administrative and managerial responsibilities. I served as Senior Chaplain, Supervisory Chaplain, and in a succession of "top management" positions on the Washington chaplaincy staff. As one with a lifelong affinity for study and for writing, I began to do my best to learn what organizations are all about, and how to "manage" them. The Navy, with its high commitment to technological education and training, paid my way to several management courses, both on and off duty.

I was fortunate enough in this period to be influenced by three extraordinarily talented people. One of them, Chaplain Edward Hemphill, initiated me into the then-new and still developing Human Relations movement. As a minister of fairly orthodox views, I resisted its secular humanism. Ed practically dragged me, kicking and screaming, into an appreciation of its enormous contribution to contemporary management. Later, when I completed my doctorate (with the help of the Navy), I wrote my dissertation on that fascinating movement.

My second mentor, Professor Robert Worley of McCormick Theological Seminary, introduced me to the world of organizational sociology. His Center for Church Organizational Studies at McCormick was pioneering the task of teaching the church to understand itself as an organization, and to deal with its organizational problems. The seminary's unique Doctor of Ministry program, which Bob directed, was concentrated in its early stages among Southern Presbyterians.

It has had a great influence on many ministers of that denomination. Under his tutelage I developed and coordinated one Doctor of Ministry group made up exclusively of Navy chaplains. I probably got more out of it than the degree candidates did.

My third mentor in the organizational management field was William Fogelman, a synod executive and a manager par excellence of "church systems." In 1968, long before my retirement from the Navy, I was fortunate enough to be asked to serve on my General Assembly's Ad Interim Committee on Restructuring Boards and Agencies, of which Bill was chairman. My three years of working with that committee constituted almost a graduate course in church organization, and was one of my truly formative professional experiences.

In 1974 I retired from the Navy with the rank of Rear Admiral. I was fortunate enough to be asked by the Chief of Army Chaplains to become a consultant assigned to conduct an evaluative study of the Army Chaplaincy, which, subsequently, led me into a modest amount of other organizational consulting. In spite of my jaundiced view of experts I became what passes for one these days without even realizing it. By the time I was called to my present position as Chairman of my denomination's Office of Review and Evaluation, a creation of the organizational restructuring in which I had previously participated, I had become a specialist of sorts in the field of church organizational management.

This string of "fortunate" occurrences I regard, out of my own theological perspective, as my personal experience of the working of the Holy Spirit. For me, this was sufficient evidence that God was shaping my professional life to constitute a "calling." And I so regarded the invitation to become the denominational bureaucracy's resident "expert" in organization and management. From the beginning, however, I had been troubled by the lack of any clear relationship between my two fields of "expertise" — management and ministry. My two hats seemed to have been cut by totally unrelated people. My early discomfot with the secular humanism of the Human Relations movement was matched by discomfort with the difference between the presuppositions of business management (out of which management science comes) and the presuppositions of Christianity.

I was clearly not alone with my feelings of dissonance — or at least the sense that my two selves were not easy to connect. The search committee, which recommended me to the General Assembly for election to my present office, questioned me at length. They wanted to be sure that I was committed not only to good management procedures, but also to the concept of the church as a unique human organization. Although the committee and I were probably equally unable to articulate just what we meant, we were conscious of the gap between organizational management presuppositions and theological presuppositions, and convinced of the need for bridging that gap.

In many ways, my professional pilgrimage, during these years in the Office of Review and Evaluation, has been a continuing attempt to find the manner by which these two fields might not just mutually coexist in the church, but be organically related. It would be inaccurate to say that no one else has given attention to this problem during these years that have seen modern management systems becoming such a prominent concern of the church. Many have done so.

One of the most thorough jobs of relating the theology of the church to the social sciences in general was done by James

Gustafson in his 1961 book, *Treasure in Earthen Vessels: The Church as a Human Community* (Harper, 1961). Gustafson analyzed the church in terms of the "natural processes" it shares with other human communities. He suggested that to a considerable extent, "principles from the social sciences and social philosophy can account for that which also can be accounted for in doctrinal language." But while he examined a number of human processes that take place within the church, he did not deal directly with organizational and management theory, with specific management techniques, nor with any possible conflicts between the two. He saw theology and social science as two different ways of explaining the same natural processes.

The literature dealing specifically with management technology as applied within the church is for the most part newer than Gustafson's theoretical work. Moreover much of this literature has reflected some particular theological perspective. In *The Problem of Wineskins*, for instance, Howard A. Snyder has dealt with church structures (though not with management) from a strongly evangelical position, in a way many have found helpful.

Probably the most prolific writer on organizational and management concerns of the local church is Lyle E. Schaller. His numerous books of down-to-earth advice for pastors and congregations have been widely read. He frequently begins books with brief statements of his theological presuppositions. Theological reflection, however, is not Schaller's purpose. Once his assumptions are stated, he confines himself to the treatment of practical problems.

Perhaps the most consistently theological approach to organizational methods and management techniques has been that of Robert Worley, to whom I have previously referred. He has written three books dealing with church organizational concerns. The first, *Change in the Church: A Source of Hope* (Westminster, 1971) was written from an avowedly Presbyterian confessional perspective. Although his writings are generally more practical than reflective in purpose, his book *A Gathering of Strangers* (Westminster, 1976) contains a reflective chapter entitled: "Thinking about the Church and Ministry." While explicitly "not a theology for congregational life," it is nevertheless "intended to provide categories of thought which

10

may be helpful." Worley, however, like other church organizational thinkers, steers away from formal theology.

The church as a concrete, social, and historical reality is the first hurdle for both ministers and lay persons. It needs a practical theology that enables church people to deal with the church as it is and with the relationships between church and community. It is not possible at this time to write *a* practical theology, nor is it desirable to write one. *Doing* practical theology is a more hopeful and appropriate way to inquire about common life in the church (p. 90).

Systematic theology is not the style of the times. Now many prefer that theology be acted out rather than thought through. Furthermore, theological pluralism is more evident in the church today than in any previous period. Certainly this is true in the mainline Protestant denominations. A normative faith perspective such as pervaded the Catholicism of Aquinas and in a similar manner undergirded Calvin's Geneva, furnishing a base for theological thought, does not now exist. It may be, then, that a commonly accepted "theology of management" is neither possible nor desirable today.

In any event, this book does not pretend to offer one. It is rather, the product of my attempt, as a Presbyterian with an irrepressible tribal concern for theology, to wrestle with the apparent theological contradictions between my two areas of "professional expertise;" and to deal practically with the application of management techniques in the church from my particular theological perspective.

The key, for me, is the uniqueness of the church, which is centered in the active presence of the Holy Spirit. If we take that Presence seriously, the organizational and managerial implications are truly awesome.

In an era characterized by "organizational wheel-spinning," a strikingly apt metaphor comes from the old black spiritual, which interprets one of Ezekiel's visions in terms of the wheel within the wheel. The big wheel of church organization runs by faith. The little wheel within it — its uniqueness and its source of power — runs by the grace of God. "A wheel in a wheel, way in the middle of the air."

I am indebted to many people for help in the preparation of this book. My two colleagues in the Office of Review and Evaluation, Beverly Myres and James Womack, who, though they disagree with me about some of my conclusions, have nevertheless helped me enormously to formulate them as we have struggled together with the issues. The Committee on Assembly Operations authorized the leave of absence during which much of this was written. Barbara Bowers contributed by typing two drafts of the manuscript.

I am most deeply indebted to my wife, Ann Rivers, and my daughters, Libby and Susan, for their emotional support, patience, and love. It is to them that I dedicate the book.

Atlanta, Georgia
September, 1978

Part I

The Organization-Mindedness of the Contemporary Church

Ezekiel saw a wheel
Way up in the middle of the air;
A Wheel in a wheel,
Way in the middle of the air;
And the big wheel ran by faith,
And the little wheel ran by the grace of God;
A wheel in a wheel
Way in the middle of the air.

Old Spiritual

CHAPTER ONE

OD, MBO AND PPBS IN THE CHURCH

Joe Johnson is the minister of Grace Church in Farmington. He was called to be a preacher of the Word and a pastor of the flock. But he has also come to see himself as a "manager" of a "successful organization."

He acquired his new self-image at a three-day Management Skills Workshop for Small Church Pastors, sponsored by an ecumenical agency representing fourteen denominations. According to the brochure sent to him by his own denomination, "effective management is the key to any successful organization. *The minister has a management job to do* in addition to that of a preacher, a teacher, a leader of worship, and a pastor."[1]

Joe is by no means alone with his new managerial self-image. The Management Seminar has become one of the most popular forms of continuing education for ministers. Pastors all over are busily applying MBO (Management by Objective) in their congregations. The organization-mindedness of the contemporary church can be seen everywhere.

A congregation calls in a management consultant, analyzes its "priority goals," and organizes itself into "mission units." A vestry, making an annual retreat for spiritual renewal, spends the weekend in "team-building" and "goal-setting" exercises. The Chief of Chaplains of the United States Army employs a firm of OD (Organization Development) consultants to analyze the ministry of chaplains; the consultants then meet with groups of chaplains throughout the Army over a two-year period, teaching them to make their chapel ministries more effective through the application of OD technologies. A major theological seminary develops a Doctor of Ministry program for pastors, with emphasis on "church organizational behavior." Ministers, Christian educators and church committee members become preoccupied with "process management."

When the pastor looks beyond the local parish to the denominational environment, even more organization-mindedness is encountered at regional and national levels. A presbytery engages a group of consultants to lead selected local churches in goal-setting exercises, as a pilot project to establish a model for the entire prebytery. A bishop appoints a committee to conduct a performance evaluation of his diocesan leadership, and the committee employs an evaluation consultant. Another bishop places an OD consultant on his staff.

Eight major denominations, within a period of five years, engage in organizational studies leading to the restructure of their national level mission agencies. In every case the outcome is a more centralized and unified denominational structure. Within five more years, two of these eight denominations conduct further studies to "restructure the restructure." A fund-raising company sells its services to denominations on the basis of its "systems approach" to the raising of capital funds. A major denomination initiates (and later quietly drops) a churchwide system known as PBE (Planning, Budgeting, Evaluation). PPBS (Planning, Programming, Budgeting Systems) becomes commonplace. A denomination establishes an independent Office of Review and Evaluation to evaluate the work of its mission agencies and recommend organizational changes as needed. Board and agency staff members, once known as "denominational leaders," are now referred to as "church bureaucrats."

Many such examples could be cited by any reasonably alert church member. Never in history have Christians been so organization-minded as they are in contemporary America. From local congregations to newly powerful regional judicatories to denominational headquarters to ecumenical consultations, everywhere today OD, MBO, PPBS, goal-setting and process management are the center of attention. Organizational theories and technologies are being applied by a host of consultants, experts, and managers. All are trying to help God's people do more effectively in their organizations whatever it is they want to do.

Few ministers and congregations remain untouched by this pervasive movement. A whole new vocabulary has been adopted. A cartoon on the cover of a recent issue of a national religious journal showed two collared clerics shaking hands, one saying to the other, "Welcome to a parish where we've brainstormed our problems, prioritized our goals, formalized our strategies and maximized our ineffectuality."[2] The last phrase of that cartoon character's remark is a clue to another phenomenon. The infatuation of churches with organizational matters is a love-hate relationship. Many are disturbed by what they see. Congregational goal-setting does not lead inevitably to goal-reaching. The promised results of skilled process management are not always apparent. Some do, indeed, see it as a "maximizing of ineffectuality." It is by no means clear that ministerial "managers" are turning churches into "successful organizations." And even if they are, not all church members are convinced that the Kingdom of God is well served thereby.

As pastors and congregations observe their denominational hierarchies, the same questioning attitude is apparent. Church people are sharing the nation's general hostility toward professionalized services and large bureaucracies. From the perspective of the pew, restructured denominational organizations appear to be foundering, and church members who once hoped restructure would solve a host of problems now blame restructure for a new set of problems. Increasingly, denominational agencies are being seen as bureaucracies: as impersonal, unresponsive, and self-serving as government agencies can be.

The ambivalence of church members as well as pastors is manifest. On the one hand, organizational and managerial concepts are all around us in the secular world. Contemporary America is a highly corporatized society, dominated by large, bureaucratically organized institutions. Whether the work environment of the church member is business, industry, labor, government, education or even the arts, he or she is accustomed to organizational language. OD, MBO and process management are commonplace. Even full-time homemakers, who maintain one of the few remaining non-bureaucratic segments of society, are familiar with these concepts through the news and entertainment media. Such church members are likely to be comfortable with the idea of approaching church problems through OD or MBO. Those who have been personally involved in these processes in business or institutional life and have seen the results demonstrated may even insist that the church straighten out its problems by similar methods.

But on the other hand, many church members see the church as having "spiritual" purposes. Biblical images dominate their perception of what the church ought to be like. A church that seems to be "just another secular organization" is likely to disturb them. They want the "differentness" to be apparent.

The minister of a small congregation, who participated in the 1978 General Assembly of the Presbyterian Church, U.S., reported his reaction to his presbytery:

The Assembly itself resembles a stockholders meeting of General Motors or IBM more than anything else. The style of the meeting leaves much to be desired. One wonders if the Spirit of God put such a thing together. But I guess it is possible.[3]

What is the role of the Holy Spirit amidst all the managerial techniques? Does the Holy Spirit become nothing more than the human spirit of good will, high purposes and religiosity in which all the managing takes place? Many today are frustrated, disturbed, even angry, at the organization-mindedness of the church. They see restructuring as responsible for diverting money from a much-needed emphasis on mission. They are sick of organizational jargon, fed up with "bureaucratic wheel-spinning." They want to forget organizational matters and "get on with the business of the church."

Even the establishmentarians, who run church organizations — leaders and functionaries in the bureaucracies — tend to be ambivalent about the organizational world. Clergy bureaucrats continue to regard their basic role as that of pastor. Even after twenty-five years in church agencies, the pastoral self-concept is carefully guarded. The ideal image is that of the bishop or board executive who gives up the trappings of power and returns to a modest pastoral assignment with a local congregation.

A fashionable approach to sociological investigation of the parish clergy in our time has been "role" studies. A number of these studies have shown that while pastors of congregations spend the largest share of their time in administrative duties, they are least comfortable with the administrative role. They claim to dislike it, and they downplay it in their own self-image.

Such job ambivalence indicates the complexity of the ministerial job in a managerial age. It is impossible to "get on with the business of the church" without organization and management. In today's highly corporatized American society, life tends to be dominated by large, bureaucratically-organized institutions. It may be, as some maintain, that effective mission *requires* the use of management methods and organizational techniques. But two things are clearly necessary. One is an understanding of what organization and management *cannot* do — for unless the church is far more than a human organization, it is not the church. The other is an understanding of what organization and management *can* do, in that unique human organization which the church is.

Management techniques are ill equipped to fill the role of the savior of the church. Nor are they a proper scapegoat for the church's unsolved problems. At most, they are means by which the church does things: its tools. If church people are clear about who they are and united about what they want to do, even a poor organizational structure and a haphazard management process will probably serve as the means of doing it. But if a church lacks clarity about what it is and unity as to why it exists, the best organizational techniques in the world cannot impose that clarity and unity, and no amount of goal-setting, team-building, or conflict-management can bring it about.

Dr. James Forbes of Union Theological Seminary (N.Y.), speaking at a recent denominational Consultation on Mission, used vivid imagery to point up the church's inner conflict. He described an imaginary encounter, on his way to the consultation, with a strange creature which was impossible to describe but appeared "like fire . . . like a dove . . . like wind." This creature, said Dr. Forbes, "had been invited to attend the consultation as a consultant." But "the Being was not pleased with the role that had been assigned." And he sent the consultation a message:

I cannot attend your meeting as a Consultant, because I am the *Director* of Cosmic Missions. Your programs may be in conflict with what I intend to do. Therefore I will come to the consultation only if you are willing to yield yourselves and your programs to me, so that I may place you and your programs in the larger plan I am now executing throughout the whole creation. If you accept my invitation to be a humble part of my greater operation, then I will come to your consultation and help to prepare you for the role I shall assign to you, and I shall give focus to your efforts, and will empower you for the tasks which lie ahead. And furthermore, if you will receive me as Director during the consultation, then I shall not leave you when it ends, but shall be with you and in you, as you go forth to act on that which I shall show you.[4]

This sermonic flight of fancy points to a far deeper ambivalence about organization-mindedness than just discomfort with administration or weariness with managerial jargon. It points to the possibility of conflict at the very heart of the church's identity, between human managers and the transcendent Manager.

The parish of Joe Johnson, the minister we encountered at the beginning of this chapter, is located in the vicinity of a theological seminary. After attending the Management Workshop, and following it up with an OD Seminar of the kind routinely offered to clergymen today, he happened on an occasion to be in a meeting with several seminary professors. He asked for assistance — books or other resources — in exploring the "theology of church organizations." The professors seemed somewhat aghast at the idea. There is no such thing as a theology of church organization, he was told, and from their attitude, Joe gathered that there never would be!

Not all seminary professors would agree; some consider their church organizational studies to be theologically based. But even in seminaries where both church management and ecclesiology are taught, there may be little or no discourse relating the two. Bibliographies for the respective courses are sometimes drawn from different fields, with little if any overlap.

There are understandable reasons for the dichotomy. The contemporary tendency to focus on organizational matters is quite foreign to traditional Christian ways of looking at the church. Only in a germinal sense can the New Testament church be described as having had any organization at all. In time, the church *did*, of course, organize. It had to in order to survive. The necessity for some form of human organization has always been recognized by Christians. But it has frequently been recognized with misgivings. Discussions about institutional forms have generally been theological, concerned with Biblical prototypes, relationship to God and the meaning of Christian community rather than with the achievement of organizational goals.

The organizational terminology now current in the church comes out of a different world. One source is the academic discipline of organizational sociology. Another is the widespread post-World War II phenomenon known as the human relations movement. A third is management science and the body of experience of the business world. A variety of organizational insights have been applied to churches — sometimes indiscriminately — on the basis of the undeniable proposition that churches *are* organizations. But churches are human organizations of a special kind. They are not *just* human organizations. The extent to which the concepts represented by this terminology are applicable to the church has not yet really been examined.

As a result, the pastor of the local church faces a threefold dilemma. The first is theological. How compatible with basic Christian truths and assumptions are organizational and managerial theories and all the techniques and technologies associated with them? Every minister, as congregational preacher and teacher, has an inherently theological role. When management techniques and organizational methodologies are adopted for the minister's own use, they must be interpreted to the congregation. Church members must be led in an examination of both the organizational and the Biblical views of the church, and the degree of congruence or conflict between the two.

21

The second is evaluative. What has been the effect of the organization-mindedness of the church? What are the results of the application of management techniques? In what ways are these techniques changing the church? How effective are they in doing what they set out to do?

The third is pragmatic. How can these managerial and organizational techniques be used in the local church in a way that will be both compatible with the classical Biblical view of the church and helpful in terms of results? How can they be integrated with long-tested church practices?

* * *

It will be the purpose of the remainder of this book to try to offer some practical help to the pastor who wishes to deal theologically with these issues.

The starting point will be to look at the church's own organizational heritage. It is largely a theological heritage, for the church in the past has tended to describe itself in theological rather than organizational terms. What the church has been talking about in theological language is its uniqueness — that which makes it the church.

We will then examine briefly the sources of management theory and techniques now current in the church. The terms "management" and "organization" are used in this book to refer to two aspects of what is essentially the same phenomenon. "Organization" usually refers to the systems, structures, processes and relationships between people in institutions and enterprises. "Management" refers to the control exercised over those systems, structures and processes to achieve goals. The basic phenomenon, however, is the same.

In Part II, we will seek to look analytically at what has been happening to the church in this managerial age. We will examine the church as a goal-seeking organization by looking at the basic assumptions of management science about the nature and purposes of organizations and how these apply to the church. We will look at the power of the pew, as we analyze churches as voluntary organizations. We will examine the church as a bureaucratic organization dominated by professional managers, and we will finally take a look at some of the effects of the managerial revolution on the church.

Against this background, in the third and most important

part of the book, we will turn to some practical applications for the local congregation. Thinking from both a theological and pragmatic perspective, we will examine specific techniques, and their use in the church. We will deal at some length with leadership issues, examining the managerial model for ministers; with funding issues, in terms of stewardship; and with evaluation processes and their usefulness for congregations. We will also look at goal-setting, Management by Objective, organizational restructuring, and the way the church renewal movement has used organizational techniques. Finally, we will return to the theology of the church for the church's most basic organizational technique, a very old one indeed — trust the Holy Spirit.

Chapter Two

The Organizational Heritage of the Church: Theology Mindedness

Who is a theologian? My own inclination is to say, "Not I." I am a minister, and — at present — a church bureaucrat. Yet if theological reflection were left solely to those who teach theology in seminaries, Christian thought would be poor indeed. One reason for the church's ambivalence about organization and management is the failure of ministers and bureaucrats to think theologically about what we are doing. We may not be professional theologians. But we do study the Bible — as well as the work of theologians and the classical formulations of belief such as creeds and confessional statements — for a theological purpose: to enable us to deal with our faith with clarity of mind as well as fervency of heart.

The task of the pastor when thinking theologically is to make what is *done* congruent with what is *believed*. This calls for clear religious convictions, a clear understanding of management practices, and the continual relating of the two. Only from such a down-to-earth theological perspective can pastors employ managerial techniques usefully and appropriately in that special kind of organization, the church.

Classical Ways of Looking at the Church in the Christian Tradition

It is helpful to begin with a look at the classical ways in which Christianity has viewed the church.[1] Ecclesiology, the theological expression of the nature or image of the church, has a long history. It is not our purpose here to develop, or even state, a theological definition of the church. But for the pastor who thinks about management techniques from a theological perspective, it is worthwhile to take a look at some of the things which theologians have said. It is important to note that *none* of the traditional ways of looking at the church deals with its nature as an organization. Very few take note of organizational arrangements at all. Most do not even suggest, except indirectly, that the church *is* an organization. The traditional interest of Christians in the church has simply been of another kind. Their theological emphasis has been on the transcendent *source* of the church and its *relationship* with God through Christ, rather than on the organized ways in which Christians have gone about the church's business.

New Testament Images of the Church

Our thinking about the nature of the church that Christ established has been dominated by Biblical images. Some of them were intended as descriptions of characteristics of the church. Others were simply images of the Christian life, which have been applied to church organizations by later scholars.

The standard modern treatment of the New Testament images of the church for our times is that of Paul S. Minear. He has identified ninety-three such images, figures of speech, or word pictures in the New Testament. Some thirty of these are minor images such as the salt of the earth, the building on the rock, the bride of Christ. They illuminate particular aspects of the nature of the church and thus contribute to our understanding of it.

Minear singles out four major images, which are actually

clusters of images illuminating particular themes. The church is the *People of God*. The church is God's *New Creation*. The church is the *Fellowship in Faith* of those who have been redeemed by God's act. The church is the one *Body of Christ,* with many diverse members.[2] Each of these phrases is a reference to both God and people. Each illuminates some aspect of the relationship between people and between God and people. So *relationship,* rather than organization, may be regarded as the central theme in these Biblical images. Not one of the images, in fact, could be regarded as organizational in the modern sense of that word, although some of them certainly have organizational implications.

Classical theology of the church, like the Biblical images which provide its starting point, has largely ignored organizational matters. Some aspects of ecclesiology, however, are especially significant for church managers today. Four of them will be addressed here. One is the special role of the Holy Spirit in the church. Another is the centrality of the local congregation — the New Testament *ecclesia* — in the concept of church. A third, related to the doctrine of man as well as to ecclesiology, is the emphasis on human responsibility to God within the church. A fourth is the coexistence of unity and diversity which characterizes Biblical and classical descriptions of the church. Each of these theological themes has special relevance to today's organizational issues.

The Holy Spirit and the Church

One of the striking characteristics of contemporary Christianity is the renewed awareness of the centrality of the Holy Spirit in the life of the church. This is true, not only at the popular level (where the charismatic movement and the new emphasis on personal spirituality are highly visible trends) but in scholarly theological discussions as well.

The unique mark of the church — which sets it apart from all other organizations — is the gift of the Holy Spirit. "Because of its foundation in Christ and its existence for the future of the Kingdom of God," says contemporary theologian Jurgen Möltmann, "the church is what it truly is and what it can do in the *presence and power* of the Holy Spirit."[4] The third Person of the Godhead is inseparable from the church. In the classic phrase of John Calvin, echoed both by Moltmann and by Hans

Kung, the church is the "creation of the Spirit." The power of its members is the power of the Holy Spirit moving upon them, and all activity of the church (including the way it operates as an organization) which seeks to express God's purposes must be understood in this light.

All those unique aspects of the church flowing from its transcendent dimension and setting it apart from other human organizations are mediated through the continuing presence of the Holy Spirit. The Biblical image of the Body is incomplete without Christ as the Head. But it is through the Spirit that the Head rules the Body. Christ as founder, teacher, model, Lord; God as sovereign, ruler, manager — all of this the church experiences *through the presence of the Spirit,* which is in fact the central element in its corporate life. There is indeed a sense in which our theology of the Holy Spirit grows out of the church's unique experience of sovereign God and incarnate Christ.

To take seriously the presence and the power of the Holy Spirit in the church will have a profound effect on the way the church is organized and managed. This is a central theme of this book. To take the Spirit into account when dealing with organizational matters means that it is not enough to "open with prayer." Neither is it enough to give a meeting an appropriate "scriptural theme." It is not even enough to pray (and assume) that the Spirit will work through us as *we* solve problems, set goals, and make plans. The presence and the power of the Spirit are unique organizational realities. The Spirit may be seen as the wheel within the wheel. The church has historically affirmed the special presence of the Holy Spirit within it. But the church has not always acted in its organizational life as if it understood all the implications of that affirmation.

The Importance of the Local Congregation in the Theology of the Church

It is worth noting that the Biblical images we examined above are most directly applicable to the local congregation, rather than to denominations or to the universal conception of the church. In part, this is undoubtedly a reflection of the fact that the New Testament church consisted at first of just a few congregations even though it soon multiplied rapidly into many small, local entities. Even in the latter stages of New Testament expansion, when the concept of the church was broadening, the words of the apostles were conveyed in letters commonly addressed to one particular local congregation. Many aspects of a believer's relationship to God and to fellow-believers which the Biblical images of the church depict, can *only* be experienced within the congregation. Thus Küng, in his modern classic *The Church* says:

The local church does not merely *belong* to the Church, the local Church *is* the Church. The whole Church can only be understood in terms of the local Church and its concrete actions. The local Church is not a small cell of the whole, which does not represent the whole and which has no purpose in itself. It is the real Church, to which in its own local situation everything is given and promised which it needs for the salvation of man in its own situation; the preaching of the Gospel, baptism, the Lord's Supper, different charisms and ministries.[5]

Möltmann, too, stresses the importance of the local congregation as the heart of what "church" is.

Both, of course, emphasize the reality of the wider church, the all-embracing fellowship. Certainly the Biblical images extend to the church universal. The wider dimensions of the people of God, the new creation, the fellowship, and the body, are real and can be experienced. But the basic relationships are experienced by particular Christians in the particular body of which each is a member. In a recent commencement address C. Ellis Nelson told the graduates of Princeton Theological Seminary, that

... the natural habitat of the Spirit is the congregation — not the church. The word "church" (ecclesia) is used in the New Testament to describe an organized group of believers. It is a neutral, colorless term. When the Apostle Paul wanted to describe a congregation, he used the word "koinonia," meaning "communion" or "joint participation." ... The natural habitat of the Spirit is the congregation, not the General Assembly.[6]

The concept of the congregation as the natural habitat of the Spirit is one which will be used extensively in this book. The usage should be clearly understood at the outset. There is no intent to suggest that the presence of the Spirit is *limited* to the local congregation, or even to the church as a whole. The Bible places no limit on the freedom of God in this world. In fact one task of the church, possibly understood more clearly today than in earlier times, is to discern where the Spirit is at work in the world outside of the church and align itself with that work wherever it is encountered.

The church as a corporate body has in a special sense, however, been given the Holy Spirit, symbolized by the tongues of fire which appeared to rest on those present at Pentecost (Acts 2:1-4). While the Spirit can be privately experienced by individual Christians, as evidenced by a vast body of mystical and devotional literature and by the contemporary charismatic movement; and while the Spirit does speak through prophetic voices, through church leaders, even through bureaucrats; nonetheless corporateness is a most conspicuous element in the church's experience of the Spirit.

Here again there is no intent to claim that the *corporate* experience of the Spirit is limited to the local congregation. In the "gathered" church at regional, national and ecumenical levels, the reality of God's presence is also manifestly experienced. Significantly, both Küng and Möltmann stress the coming together in corporateness as an essential element in "church" at any level. "The assembling and coming together on the basis of the jointly heard call of God is the church's fundamental act," says Möltmann. He continues, "It is the *assembled people* of God. Consequently it will present its unity through assemblies in local, regional and universal spheres."[7]

Finally, there is no claim that because the local congregation is "the natural habitat of the Spirit" congregational forms of church government are to be preferred to other forms. Each of the traditional forms has its Biblical warrant, its theological justification, and its traditional validation. (I am, indeed, committed to a connectional form and convinced that the Holy Spirit acts through church courts.) But the local congregation *is* the basic model of the church. Even more important, it *is* the place where a majority of the members of the Body of Christ most naturally and directly experience the presence of the Spirit.

For this reason the church seeking to discern the wheel within the wheel as it functions through its organizational processes and structures, must pay particular attention to the local congregation. The one Body, made up of all its members, each experiencing the reality of the Spirit in his or her own congregation, is the foundation of those organizational structures and processes. The Spirit in the local congregation is the starting point.

"Public opinion," even when it is an expression of the church members' collective perception of the will of the Spirit experienced in their congregations, may be wrong. It often is. It was clearly wrong when southern Presbyterians, at the time of the founding of my own denomination, expressed their nearly universal conviction that God supported slavery. It has been wrong when churches have supported racism or condoned antisemitism. It may have been wrong when churches with one voice have supported nationalistic wars, joined in expressions of civil religion, identified with particular economic systems, or launched crusades. One could, in fact, make a case for the claim that Christian "public opinion" is nearly *always* wrong and that the historical authenticity of Christian witness has been carried forward through the agency of lone dissenters, righteous remnants and unsung prophets.

Yet despite its fallibility at any particular moment, the church's collective experience of the Holy Spirit does have a central place in its processes. The local congregation *is* the Spirit's natural habitat, where most Christians experience God's reality. No matter how complex denominational organizations and ecclesiastical institutions become, a person studying organizational issues must turn to the local church to see the reality of the basic New Testament images. This is an extremely important concept in light of today's organizational issues.

Human Responsibility to God

While the Biblical images and the classical theological statements about the church focus primarily on God rather than on human beings, nearly all of them also have implications regarding human responsibility. By the very act of creating the church God assigned responsibility to people. People of God, Fellowship of Faith, Body of Christ — the Biblical images imply human agency as well as divine purposes. The Great Commission, the gift to the church of the Holy Spirit, the concept of discipleship — everything at the heart of a God-centered understanding of the church says that humans are expected, indeed commanded, to *act responsibly as God's agents* in the church. Human beings then, serving as God's agents, have enormous responsibility.

In the doctrine of creation, as a classical statement puts it, we see that God made human beings "after his own image, in knowledge, righteousness and holiness, having the law of God written in their hearts, and power to fulfill it, with dominion over the creatures, yet subject to the fall."[8] Though this Christian view of the human potential recognizes the destructive power of sin, it also recognizes the restorative power of grace. Those in the community of the redeemed, therefore, are not only responsible for how they act toward God. They have within them the capability of acting responsibly as God's agents, particularly within the community of faith where the power of grace is most directly operative.

Not only do human beings have this capability, they have tools available as well. The doctrine of creation also teaches us that God made the world, and all things in it for himself, "and all very good."[9] God's agents in the church, therefore, have never hesitated to call upon all the resources of the created order. Their own rational powers, their discoveries, tools, and technologies, all are used in carrying out their God-given responsibilities. Christian theology has not opposed attempts to expand human knowledge and gain a better understanding of the created order. Exploration, both in the fields of natural and behavioral science, has been encouraged rather than rejected by the church. The only insistence has been that truth be the standard, since truth can never be in conflict with God's will.

A theology of human responsibility to God must always be understood, of course, in light of the reality of human sinfulness. Any consideration of church organization and management must take that seriously. The last word on human potential in organizational matters always rests with God, who "makes foolish the wisdom of the world" (I Cor. 1:20).

Theological Thinking about Unity and Diversity in the Church

In terms of impact on organizational matters, one of the central theological issues in the church has been that of unity with diversity. How can there be such variety of human perspective, perception of God's will, response to God's grace and contribution to God's purpose in a community dedicated to one Lord, one faith, one baptism? This has puzzled Christians since the very beginning of the church.

Christian theology has never been willing to sacrifice either unity or diversity. The metaphor of the body, used by Paul so frequently as to make it a dominant New Testament image, has been the normative image allowing us to retain both. The corporate wholeness of a body made up of members as diverse

31

as an ear and a hand with each member contributing to the good of the whole has provided the best answer to this seeming contradiction. In the application of this metaphor, the Holy Spirit is the key to both the unity and the diversity. For there is "one Spirit" present in the corporate Body. But the diverse gifts found in that Body are all gifts of this one Spirit, so that diversity is not to be regarded as a handicap or an evil but rather as a conscious endowment by the Spirit of richness and variety to the Body.[10]

Historically the issue of unity with diversity is one that the church has never been able to resolve once and for all and set away neatly wrapped up on the shelf. The church has always lived in the tension between the two. Diversity of perception, understanding and response to the Spirit has usually been a centrifugal force, leading sometimes to internal tension and factionalism, sometimes to external (organizational) sectarianism and divisions. Unity in the Spirit has usually been a centripetal force, leading to internal harmony and external (organizational) quests for organic unity or expressions of conciliar oneness.

Prior to the Protestant Reformation there had been periodic ruptures in the organic unity of the church. Separation of the Copts, division between Eastern Orthodoxy and Roman Catholicism and the periodic defections of smaller groups like the Waldensians and Albigensians, all are evidences. For the most part, however, the church handled the coexistence of its unity and diversity by insisting on a formal adherence to organic unity while permitting a great deal of informal, internal diversity.

The Reformation brought a massive shift in the church's method of keeping unity and diversity in balance. The major Reformation doctrines are traditionally summarized as justification by faith, the authority of Scripture and the priesthood of all believers. All three represent a shift in the direction of the primacy of the individual believer as over against the corporate whole. This shift legitimated far greater diversity of personal response to God than had previously been permitted. The result was a new model for balancing unity and diversity. Diversity was soon experienced in a variety of organizational forms. While the ideal of full organic unity was never lost, it was replaced in practice by a quest for spiritual unity across denominational lines. There were, of course, massive social and economic forces at work within the historical developments that brought about the Reformation. But they are beyond the scope of our immediate concern. However the theological dimensions involved are of paramount interest to the church.

From the perspective of the doctrine of the church, the theological revolution of the Reformation has had organizational implications of enormous significance. It legitimated denominationalism. And perhaps even more important, it provided the theological basis for perceiving the church as a voluntary organization rather than as an inviolable mololithic institution. Justification by faith, individual access to Scripture (authoritatively interpreted by the Holy Spirit alone), and especially the priesthood of all believers — each may be regarded as a theological statement of the principle of the individual's responsibility in relation to God. Authority is removed from the church as an organization, and the individual's relationship to the organization becomes a voluntary one.

The forces in Roman Catholicism, brought into the open by Vatican II and dominating church developments since, are moving in a similar direction. This may represent the delayed ascendency in Catholicism of the same shift in balance between unity and diversity that the Reformation brought to the rest of western Christendom. Certainly the basic Reformation doctrines have received increased prominence in Catholicism. Even more evident is the applicability of the concept of the church as a voluntary organization to present day Catholicism. This, also, we shall examine later.

How Has Theology Dealt with Organizational Matters?

The basic Biblical images, as we have noted, have nothing to say about organization. Traditional theology has said little more.

Organizational structures for human institutions revolve around certain major issues, such as leadership, power, communication and goal-achievement. To form an organization is to formalize structures of leadership, power, and communication in a social grouping. But these are precisely the functions which Biblical theology assigns to God! The

33

church exists under God's leadership; Christ is its Head. The Holy Spirit is the empowering force. God is the focal point of communication, through prayer; and interpersonal communication within the community of faith is to be governed by the greatest gift of the Spirit, love. Much organizational activity revolves around achieving the purposes for which the organization exists (its goals). But in the case of the church, the purposes are God's and their achievement — the full establishment of His Kingdom — ultimately depends on God.

Most of the basic organizational processes, then, are theologically reserved for the Lord of the Church. Insofar as Biblical images and classical theology are concerned, it might be concluded that the church was created to be an organizationless movement and that the functions ordinarily performed by organizational structures were to be left entirely to God.

Another way to describe the non-organizational nature of Biblical images and classical theology of the church is to say that God is expected to be the "manager." This is, of course, a distortion of what the apostles and the theologians have meant. Managerial functions were not even considered by New Testament writers when using the Biblical images, nor by formulators of creeds and confessions. They have also been foreign to the thinking of most theologians in the past. The idea of organizational "management" is a contemporary mode of thought.

One contemporary theologian, however, when asked to reflect on organizational and managerial problems, called attention to the striking similarity of classical descriptions of several attributes of God's sovereignty, providence, power, foresight, planning, and implementation of plans and contemporary expectations of the manager in an organization.[11] The human managerial responsibility to foresee all contingencies, thus eliminating the element of surprise, may even be regarded as hostile to God's role in the church. The preservation of mystery, the bringing in of the unexpected, the element of divine surprise may be inherent in God's role, while openness to the unexpected may be inherent in that of human members.

None of this, of course, has kept the church from organizing. The very existence of the apostles, with a special measure of leadership charisma, status, authority and power, provided a rudimentary human management structure. In fact, one of the first acts of the apostolic church was an organizational one — the filling of the leadership vacancy created by the defection of Judas Iscariot (Acts 1:28). An additional organizational structure, at a greater level of complexity — the allocation of functional responsibility — was devised almost immediately. As soon as "the disciples were increasing in number," a special group was organized to take care of the widows and the poor (Acts 6:1-6). But there was no *planned* organizing or conscious management in the modern sense. Those seeking organizational clues in the New Testament record (or seeking New Testament prototypes for existing organizational structures — a more common enterprise throughout church history) have had to search for evidence in the accounts of pragmatic decisions made by the early church.

In the centuries following, little attention was given to organizational matters. One Roman Catholic writer suggests that traditional ecclesiology has been "organization blind."[12] Certainly, traditional thinking about the church has focused on a very limited range of organizational concerns. Beyond the principle of "order" ("Let all things be done decently and in order" [I Cor. 14:40] — a theological basis of sorts for church government), doctrinal reflection on these matters has classically focused on two areas: the distinguishing marks of the church, and the ministry.

The Nicene Creed, formulated for Catholic theology, identified the classical marks of the church. The church is one, holy, catholic and apostolic. Following Calvin, Protestant thought has focused on Word and Sacrament as the marks of the church. The two formulations have not generally been considered mutually exclusive, since Protestants, too, consider the church to be one, holy, catholic and apostolic.

Leadership concerns in classical thinking have focused on ministry, not management. Regarding the ministry, apostolic succession has been central in Catholic doctrinal thought. For Protestants, Word and Sacrament have been central categories in formulating a doctrine of ministry as well as a doctrine of the church. Even these quasi-organizational aspects of the church, however, have been dealt with in terms of theological reflection rather than their organizational implications.

The church, then, has always been organized. It has spent

much of its time — some would say too much — on certain organizational matters. But it has never treated organization as a theological category. Traditional treatments of the forms of church government — episcopal, presbyterian, and congregational — have been formulated quite apart from examination of what a sociologist might refer to as organizational principles. Instead, theological dimensions and Biblical precedents have been given primary consideration. There is, in short, no classical "theology of church organization." Theology has largely ignored the subject.

The Anti-Organizational Strain in Church History

One line of thought throughout the history of the church — like one theme in the New Testament images — has, in fact, been downright hostile to organization. A pure Christian community, in this way of thinking, would be "spiritual" (God-directed) rather than "worldly" (human-directed or organized). Such a community would depend entirely on God for management, for the marshalling of forces and energy, and for guidance in its activities.

Christian history has seen a long series of Spirit-filled movements that have sought to eliminate, or at least minimize, church organization. Such movements have generally emphasized the Christian's personal experience, and have therefore been individual-oriented. The experience of community is not foreign to them. Indeed, the closeness of the group, of those who have experienced the immediacy of the Spirit, is a major element. But the group must remain small and informal. Organization and routine are the enemies of ecstacy and enthusiasm. A spiritual fellowship should need no organized forms, according to this view. Yet organization and routinization inevitably follow as functions of size. As soon as the new movement grows beyond a very small group, it must organize.[13]

Sociologist Max Weber, who has contributed as much as any other single theorist to an understanding both of the nature of organizations and of the sociological nature of religious dynamics, illustrates the tension in terms of a phenomenon he labels the "routinization of charisma."[14] It is a point in Weber's thought at which his insights about organizations and religion uniquely come together. He uses the term charisma not to denote speaking in tongues, but in the sociological sense of personal magnetism having its source in an immediate experience of Divine Spirit. Social movements, he says, begin under the leadership of charismatic persons. Jesus Christ, of course, is the most obvious example. From the Christian perspective, his charisma results from the immediacy of the divine presence, from the Word made flesh.

As long as the charismatic leader of a movement is present, says Weber, people are stirred and motivated to respond. The movement is held together and propelled by the personal force of that charisma. Formal organization is not needed. But once that leader is no longer physically present the charisma — the spiritual motivation — must be institutionalized and the group organized, if the movement is to become permanent. Large numbers of people working together require rules, order and standardized procedures. Such routinization is, of course, deadening to charisma. Members of the institution inevitably become less "spirit-filled," more routinized.

One after another, charismatic movements (in Weber's sense) have arisen, in opposition to a deadening, institutionalized church. Each such charismatic renewal within the church calls members to a rebirth of commitment, enthusiasm, and immediacy of Christian experience. But each such movement, in turn, either becomes institutionalized as a new group or sub-group within the church, with the experience it celebrated routinized, or it dies. The "Jesus Movements" of the late sixties are a recent example; by now the groups they spawned are either institutionalized or long gone. The hostility toward "organized religion" and "the institutional church" which was also part of the counterculture of the late sixties and early seventies was based on an accurate perception: "organized religion" *is* always deadening to immediacy of experience and enthusiasm.

However, the charismatic movement within the churches today seems something of an exception to the traditional pattern of spirit-filled movements, since it is not overtly anti-organizational. Those participating in it, in most instances, have remained active in their own denominations, often in leadership roles. Thus it is having the effect of bringing renewal within existing church organizations, rather than starting new ones. It does manifest the traditional non-organizational dimension, however, in its crossing of denominational lines, its minimizing of the importance of organizational issues, and its sense of community which completely transcends institutions. A charismatic Presbyterian minister left his pastorate on being called to a position on the staff of a denominational agency. In the process of leaving, his presbytery severed his relationship with them in a highly formal and institutionalized manner. The actions of his ministerial colleagues were only slightly more personal. In contrast, the local charismatic group in which he and his wife had been participants (which incidentally was made up largely of Roman Catholics) provided a warm send-off. They came together for extended prayer and the laying on of hands. To the departing couple, their action was far more truly an expression of the church than was the institutionalized dismissal of the presbytery.

Because the Christian church is always *more* than an organization, because the Holy Spirit is always present in it, routinization never completely eliminates charisma. But tension between the two elements — enthusiasm which abhors organization, and routine which demands organization — is always present.

* * *

In summary, neither the Biblical images of the church nor classical theological treatment has much to say about organization or management. Even doctrines that may be seen today as having significant organizational implications, have consistently been dealt with non-organizationally. The seminary professors, referred to above, who told Joe Johnson that there is no such thing as "theology of church organization" were accurate insofar as classical theology is concerned. The church has persisted in treating theology and management as if they were unrelated matters. For the contemporary congregation and its minister, however, the fact that theology has little or nothing to say about organization does not lessen the need for organizational processes.

The church never has been, and never will be, able to dispense with organization. The need for organization is inherent in the human dimension of the church. In an analogy used by James Gustafson, the human community is an earthen vessel for the divine treasure.[15] In looking at the present organization-mindedness of the church, we recognize, on the one hand, that organization, whether good or bad, is real and it must be taken seriously. Bad organization can impede what the church is trying to do, just as good organization can facilitate its efforts. But on the other hand, any view of church organization must take seriously the presence and the power of the Holy Spirit, the wheel within the wheel. The non-organizational nature of its theological heritage must be recognized. The inherent tension between divine sovereignty and human management, between transcendent Presence and institutional organization, between charisma and routine, between unity and diversity — this is the context within which the pastor's managerial dilemma must be worked out.

CHAPTER THREE

WHERE DOES THE CHURCH GET ITS MANAGEMENT THEORY?

Clearly Joe Johnson didn't get his management-mindedness from the Apostle Paul or from John Calvin. Where did it come from? Before examining the specific sources, it may be helpful to place Joe's experience and that of all organization-minded congregations and ministers in a broader perspective. The application of organizational and managerial modes of thought to church life is not an isolated phenomenon. It is a manifestation in the religious sector of one of the most pervasive characteristics of contemporary Western culture.

James Burnham, near the end of the first half of this century, wrote a book about *The Managerial Revolution*. In that pre-World War II period he was especially concerned with totalitarian (communist and fascist) governments, which he saw as one expression of managerial ideology. He also noted that all

Western societies have been irreversibly changed. They are no longer dominated by capitalists, but by managers and bureaucrats.[1] A number of other social analysts have since commented on the same phenomenon. Jacques Ellul is a French sociologist and social philosopher widely read in the United States. In his book *The Technological Society*, he identifies Burnham's managerial age with what Arnold Toynbee calls the "age of organization." Ellul refuses to divide history into discrete stages, but he agrees with both that the triumph of managerial and organizational perspectives characterizes our times. Others have described the same technological/managerial dominance in terms of an "engineering approach" to the human condition.[2] George C. Lodge in *The New American Ideology* analyzes the values of a society now dominated by large organizations ("bureaucracies" and "technostructures"), headed by managers.[3] This is the context within which Peter Drucker, perhaps America's foremost management theoretician, writes. America, he says, has become "a society of institutions." He sees management as "the specific organ" on which society's institutions depend not only for their operations but for their survival.[4]

The managerial age has brought with it two widespread phenomena which should be examined briefly before we look in detail at the implications for the church. One is the "corporatization" of institutions in our society. The second is the "professionalization" of that society — the dominance of the "experts" in various areas of technical, organizational and managerial skill which make the technological society work.

The "Corporatization" of Society

Most institutions have succumbed to what Sociologist Ted Mills has called "creeping corporatism."[5] They have becomd huge, technologically sophisticated, bureaucratic entities. In part, this corporatization of society has been a function of sheer size. American institutions are characteristically big. They are made up of — or deal with — huge numbers of people, sums of money, quantities of goods.

Second, they are organized bureaucratically. Bureaucracy, as we shall see in more detail a little later, is not inherently evil. Bureaucratic organizations are designed to rationalize relationships, to operate efficiently, and to base internal policies

41

on merit and competence rather than capricious favoritism. But perhaps for these very reasons, bureaucratic organizations are less responsive to individuals than to internal rules and "standard operating procedures."

Advanced technology is a third characteristic of corporatized social structures. Ever larger numbers of people are bureaucratically managed, controlled or serviced, ever more efficiently, by sophisticated electronic data processing. And not only the production of goods, but a wide range of human activities and services are controlled or affected by the application of sophisticated "technologies," mediated by "experts." In an era of behaviorial science there are human technologies just as surely as there are mechanical and electronic technologies.

A fourth aspect of corporatized social structures is the loss of individual control. Corporatized structures seem to be relatively impervious to attempts to influence or change them. They appear to have taken on a life of their own, independent of the collective will of those who organized them, support them, or make up the membership. The individual American has less and less opportunity for personal initiative and for making an impact on his or her environment.

The self-evident model is government. Whether anyone or anything — a president, an administration, a political movement — can assume real control of the federal government and significantly change its inexorable course has become a hotly debated political issue. Many citizens have given up; they are resigned to a government so massive, so powerful, so self-perpetuating, that it is impervious to the will of voters, or even presidents.

But government is not the only social structure that has become corporatized. Businesses, labor unions, military services, educational institutions, professional societies, charitable organizations — even farms — have followed the same course. In the main, the most thoroughly corporatized organizations are the very large ones. But the tendency is present even in relatively small ones. Bureaucratic organizations, advanced technology, dependence on experts, and resistance to control or influence by individuals — the "corporate life" taken on by the organization itself — presently characterize a great many American social institutions, both large and small. As we shall note later, churches are no exception.

The Professionalization of Society

The managerial/technological society is marked not only by corporatized institutions, but also by the dominance of professional experts, who are the custodians and purveyors of the sophisticated human technologies that make the society work. The term "professional" rather than "technician" is used here because of its broader connotation. "Professional" is used in its basic sense of one who engages in a calling requiring specialized knowledge and often long and intensive academic preparation. The professional in American society, says sociologist Adam Yarmolinsky, is one who has "special knowledge, special skills, special resources, and special responsibility."[6]

We used to think of professionals as doctors, lawyers, ministers, teachers, and perhaps engineers. In addition to the classic professional specialties, a whole host of new ones has developed with the proliferation of human technologies: economic, governmental, educational, vocational, and a variety of specialties relating to social welfare. Managerial technology dominates and uses them all. Managers are the preeminent professionals of the times, and most other professionals — even those with technical specialties — are now, to some extent, managers.

The professional experts make up the "new elite" in a managerial/technological society. Michael Novak speaks of them as the "professional-managerial class."[7] They form a group which "understands the means to conceive, organize, direct and control," says Ellul. As such, they are widely separated from the masses, who can only execute.[8]

Ellul is prominent among a group of social analysts who provide a radical critique of the dominance of the professional-managerial class in our society. Ellul sees technology in its modern managerial/organizational form as having developed what could almost be described as a life of its own. It controls more and more. It *establishes* the conditions of life. It is not just a servant, but the *shaper* of contemporary society. It has almost assumed the kind of role society once ascribed to God.

Ivan Illich is a contemporary social analyst who has developed this theme further, in terms of the effect on society of certain highly developed technologies which provide essential services. These technologies (education and medicine are the two Illich has treated in detail) and the professional experts who practice them, have achieved a kind of dominance over the human beings who are the recipients of the services. Illich charges that this is counterproductive, and even disabling.[9] John McKnight, of Northwestern University's Institute of Urban Affairs, broadens the concept to apply to what is now an entire "service economy," dominated by professional experts, prominent among which are the managers.[10] Whether or not one accepts such sweeping indictments as those of Ellul, Illich, McKnight and others, certainly the dominance of professional managers and their technologies in contemporary American society is generally recognized.

Since its early days the church has had "professionals." But the managerial age has brought a new dimension to professionalism. The extent to which churches have been professionalized in this contemporary managerial sense is an important aspect of the task facing the theologically concerned pastor and congregation. But there are even more basic theological questions about the technological faith of a managerial age. The essence of management is control. It is the mastery of everything that is contingent or uncertain. On this central issue, Ellul quotes another French sociologist, Antoine Mas:

It means resolving *in advance* all the problems that might possibly impede the functioning of an organization. It is not a matter of leaving it to inspiration, ingenuity, nor even intelligence to find a solution at the moment some difficulty arises; it is rather in some way to anticipate both the difficulty and its resolution.[11]

The dilemma for the minister, examining manifestations of this managerial perspective in church life, may be cast into bold relief by placing, alongside the quotation from Mas, a quotation from the Westminster Confession, which might be regarded as descriptive of another perspective on management:

He is the alone fountain of all being, of whom, through whom, and to whom, are all things; and hath most sovereign dominion over them, to do by them, for them, or upon them, whatsoever himself pleaseth. In his sight all things are open and manifest; his knowledge is infinite, infallible, and independent upon the creature; so as nothing is to him contingent or uncertain.[12]

Sources of Management Techniques in the Church

An examination of the use of management and organizational techniques in the church is a specific and focused task. Against this background of an overview of a managerial/technological society, marked by corporatized institutions and professionalized leadership, we turn now to an examination of the specific sources of organizational and managerial thinking current in the church.

The validity of an insight is not necessarily determined by its source; truth may come from a variety of sources. But it is important for the pastor who thinks theologically to know the context from which a particular mode of thought comes, the theoretical assumptions that underlie it. From the religious perspective, what an idea implies theologically may ultimately be more important than the pragmatic question of whether or not it works. The following seeks only to trace in brief outline the sources of current church organizational thinking. It is intended as a summary, on the basis of which pastors and lay members may raise the appropriate theological questions in testing organizational and management techniques in the church.

The church gets its organizational theory from three major sources, all related, but nevertheless traceable as separate strains of thinking and practice. The first source is academic and theoretical — the formal discipline of *organizational sociology*. Sociologists have developed and elaborated a conceptual framework for the study of organizations. Two names stand out. The first is Max Weber, the pioneering sociologist who in the early 20th century outlined the characteristic "rational organizations" in terms of the classical organizational structure known as "bureaucracy." The second is Talcott Parsons, whose structural functional approach to the study of society taught us to look at organizations in terms of "systems."

The second strain of organizational thinking, and perhaps the most important in terms of influence on church organizational thinking, is the *Human Relations* or *Human Potential movement*. This amorphous but pervasive mid-twentieth century movement has embraced, or spawned, or expressed itself in, a bewildering variety of methodologies, therapies, even fads. It is, or has been, related to all those activities variously known as human relations training, laboratory training, sensitivity training, T-groups, encounter groups, human potential development, Growth Centers, change agentry, applied behavioral science, humanistic psychology, and currently Organization Development. Most of what is known as OD in church circles comes primarily from this strain of organizational thinking, as does the application of group dynamics known as Process Management.

The third strain comes from *business* and industrial management. It teaches us to look at organizations in terms of the management of their operations and achievement of their goals. It provides guidance in dealing with a host of concrete organizational problems — decision-making, personnel management, planning, budgeting, evaluation. Its best known current contribution to organizational thinking is Management by Objective — MBO.

Every pastor who has attended an OD Workshop or a Management Seminar knows that in practice the three strains of organizational thinking are inseparable. Whether billed as an OD Consultant or a Management Consultant, the basic bag of tools brought by one kind of resource leader to a particular workshop may be largely interchangeable with the bag of tools used by the other. Both may quote the same theoretical sources. As we shall note, the human relations movement and the management science since mid-century have developed symbiotically — they have fed on and contributed to each other. But it probably is helpful, even if somewhat artificial, to examine the three strains separately.

And it is probably also helpful, even at the risk of oversimplification, to note the specific orientation of each. Organizational sociology (at least the organizational sociology examined here) is *structure* oriented. The human relations movement is *people* oriented. And business management is *goal* oriented.

Organizational Sociology: Classical Theory

Nearly every discussion of organizations from the structural standpoint starts with Max Weber. His classic description of

46

"rational organizations" was partially derived from church sources. He based his observations on the Prussian army and the Roman Catholic church of his day.[13] Today the term "bureaucracy" which Weber used, is often understood in a negative sense as referring to red tape, depersonalization, rigidity, bumbling incompetence, safeguarded tenure, and resistance to change. These characteristics are evident in contemporary bureaucracies, and every bureaucratic organization has had a tendency to develop them. In Weber's original usage, however, the term is not pejorative. He used it as almost synonymous with the term "organization" itself. The function of bureaucracy, as he described it, is to bring rationality and order into organizational life. Every organization is in this sense bureaucratic.

There are four main characteristics of highly structured rational organizations as described by Weber.[14] One is a *hierarchical authority structure,* with each lower office under the control and supervision of a higher one and with each official accountable to his superior for his subordinates' decisions and actions as well as his own. A second essential characteristic is a clear-cut *divison of labor.* Each official is responsible for specific functions, and the incumbent has the necessary authority to carry out these functions. Third, the way official functions are carried out is bound by *rules and precedents,* recorded in writing, providing consistency and fairness and avoiding the capriciousness of individual decisions in each individual case. Fourth, incumbency of officials is based on *technical qualifications and competence,* furnishing a safeguard against arbitrary personnel actions.

So-called "non-bureaucratic models" of contemporary organizations, departing from the classical model described by Weber, have been described by contemporary organizational sociologists. "Matrix" models group together certain qualified persons for specific tasks, but may group the same persons in other ways, with a different mix of skills and chain of accountability, for other tasks. Organizations engaged in research and development, or in other such frequently changing tasks, develop highly flexible organizations in which units are formed, disbanded, and re-formed for specific projects. This is sometimes called the "industrial network" model. Another term is "coalitional model." But all non-bureaucratic organizations become to some extent bureaucratized, in the sense that they exhibit somewhat stable patterns of behavior, based on some structure of roles, specialized tasks, and accountability.[15]

Robert C. Worley, an expert on church organizations, has identified the classical hierarchical bureaucratic model with nineteenth century conditions, and sees the newer matrix or flexible task team models as being appropriate to twentieth century conditions. He sees the persistence of pyramidal models as remnants of the nineteenth century culture.[16] This is an issue, however, on which there is difference of opinion. A number of business concerns which earlier discarded pyramidal organizations in favor of newer models have since returned to a more traditional authority structure.

Sociologist Charles Perrow suggests that the degree to which organizations are characterized by hierarchies of authority, rules, and specialization (that is, are "bureaucratic") is determined by two variables. One is the "routineness of their technology," by which he means stability in the way they perform their tasks. The other is the stability of their environment, which determines the demands made upon the organizations.[17] Organizations doing relatively stable jobs in relatively stable ways tend to fall back on the classical ways of dealing with problems of accountability, competence, and order.

Systems Theory

The most significant addition to structurally-oriented organizational theory since Weber has come through the application to organizations of "systems theory," for which Talcott Parsons has been seminally responsible. Every social system is seen within its environment. It has boundaries of its own, which distinguish it from its environment, and mechanisms to maintain its boundaries and assure its continuity. But its place in its environment is emphasized.

"System" is a broader concept than "organization." Systems theory emphasizes relationships, and the effect of every part of a complex, interrelated set of components and processes on every other part. It is therefore hard to pin down with a precise definition. An organization is a social grouping for a particular purpose, with boundaries that enable one to examine it in theoretical isolation. But systems theory points insistently to the relationship of that theoretically isolated organization with its environment. It sees every system as a sub-system of a larger system. Each system, in turn, has internal sub-systems of its own.

Systems thinking has had enormous influence on the entire society. It is no longer possible, in thinking about social phenomena, to divide them into neat categories and deal with each one in isolation. With regard to organizations, the scope of concern has been broadened. It is not enough to deal with charts reflecting authority relationships and with formal rules; not only must the organization concern itself with a wider range of informal relationships and processes, but it must see itself in its environment.

Thus a systems approach to the church as an organization would see the church as a sub-system within larger systems, community, national, and worldwide. Systems theory points to the place of the church in these other systems, the way it is affected by them and its effect on them. (In treating congregational life from the organizational perspective, Worley dwells at length on the ways in which environment influences a congregation.[18]) Another current treatment of church organization from the systems perspective describes the church as an "input System from the Environment," a "Transforming Process" (consisting of the Organizational Structures, the Theological-Missional Purpose and the Intra-Interpersonal Relationships) and an "output System to the Environment."[19] A "Systems Approach" study paper prepared for a denominational task force (United Church of Christ) began with the definition, "A system is a rational ordering of input and internal components in order to achieve a given output."[20]

Perhaps the most significant adjunct (if not result) of systems thinking in the church is the current emphasis on the effect of the church on society. Social consciousness within the church is by no means so recent as systems theory. It has long characterized the liberal wing of Christianity. But a growing group of "Evangelicals for Social Concerns" is becoming increasingly influential in the conservative wing. Significant impetus has come from "Third World" evangelicals, such as C. René Padilla and Orlando E. Costas.[21] Strongly conservative in theological outlook, they have been convinced by social realities in developing nations that Christ requires Christians to seek not only private piety but social change as well. They are both widely read in the United States.

It would be an over-simplification to ascribe to systems theory any credit for this change. But certainly systems thinking has helped to create a cultural climate and provided a conceptual framework in which the interrelationships of church and world, of public life and private life, are more clearly seen than was once the case.

Theological reflection on systems theory raises certain questions. An "instrumental" view, which sees the church primarily, if not solely, in terms of its social "output," is a significant departure from classical theological thinking. Is the church a means to social ends? The radical critique of the church of the 1960's came from this perspective. The church was dismissed as "irrelevant" because it was seen as ineffective in bringing about the kind of social change desired by the critics. Their forecast of its imminent demise, because it was seen as serving only the internal purposes of its members, reflected an "instrumental" view. The issue will be examined in detail in a later chapter, in terms of the goals of the church as they relate to its inherent justification as the People of God.

Influence of the Human Relations Movement

Most of what the church knows as Organization Development has its source in the human relations movement. Process Management, the application of behavioral science to group experiences, has a smiliar source. The heart of that movement has been an emphasis on group experiences which lead to personal and social change.

The human relations movement had its beginnings in the early 1940's in the work of the social psychologist Kurt Lewin, whose interest in planned social change led to research in "group dynamics." Lewin developed a theory of "re-education," as an emotional as well as cognitive process in which old values are replaced by new ones.[22] Students and followers of Lewin further developed the process, which was labeled "laboratory training," and established an organization that became known as National Training Laboratories, or NTL. (In 1967 the name was changed to "NTL Institute for Applied Behavioral Science.") The movement to which it gave birth became extremely diverse and widespread, particularly in the 1960's when it reached fad status as the "Human Potential" movement. Various kinds of encounter groups became a national pastime. But NTL provided the continuity for the movement and a home base for its more serious, less flamboyant manifestations.

Business and industrial organizations were the earliest consumers of "laboratory training," which soon became popularly known as sensitivity training, or T-groups. Among its ablest theoreticians were professors in the graduate schools of business administration and management. Some of the most important writings in the field were published in the *Harvard Business Review,* particularly in the period before NTL began its own *Journal of Applied Behavioral Science,* and a close relationship with business management has continued throughout the life of the movement. As one method of bringing about organizational change through emphasis on the *people* in the organization, the reorientation of their values, and the facilitation of their self-fulfillment, it has been and remains a popular managerial tool.

In time, of course, a wide range of non-business organizations also became involved. In the 1960's, with the proliferation of Growth Centers and therapy groups of a bewildering variety, the emphasis of much of the movement shifted from personal change designed to bring about organizational change, toward personal change for its own sake. The wide array of continuing manifestations of the Human Potential movement in the seventies — Transactional Analysis, Gestalt Therapy, Primal Therapy, Sensory Awareness, Bioenergetics, Rolfing, Psychosynthesis, est, Arica Training, Biofeedback, Transcendental Meditation — have moved far beyond the "laboratory training" origins and melded with a variety of other movements. They focus almost exclusively on individual self-fulfillment, and have little in common with the present Organization Development movement. But the common roots are clear, and many of yesterday's Growth Center trainers are today's OD consultants.

One important clue to understanding the form of Organization Development which stems from the human relations movement is the close relationship between that movement and Humanistic Psychology. The humanistic school of psychology originated mainly with Abraham H. Maslow and Carl R. Rogers, who described their movement as a "third force" in psychology, over against behaviorism and Freudianism. Humanistic psychologists lay great emphasis on the realization of human potential, which is seen as almost limitless. It is a "psychology of being." "Humanness" is its central theme, and it emphasizes the sensory as well as cognitive awareness of the whole person. Maslow's famous "hierarchy of needs," with self-actualization at the top, is the heart of its conception of human nature.

Humanistic psychology has not been an "ivory tower" academic discipline. Its theoreticians have been its practitioners also. Maslow, Rogers, and other pioneers, such as George R. Bach and James Bugental, were actively involved in the human relations movement. They themselves functioned as "trainers" (group leaders) and more importantly, as trainers of trainers. Humanistic psychology remains an active movement in the United States. The Association for Humanistic Psychology, its professional and research organization, now has around 5000 members.[24] From its beginnings it was intricately interrelated with the human relations movement, providing the conceptual undergirding for the latter's methods and approaches.

A second important clue to understanding the human relations movement is that (to quote its most authoritative NTL-related theoreticians) it "has its roots in a *system of values* relative to mature, productive and right relationships among people" (emphasis added). Early ambivalence grew out of the belief of its "behavioral scientist" practitioners that science should be value-free, which collided with the fact that "laboratory training" was a process of value reorientation. But this ambivalence was relieved by humanistic psychology's open espousal and promotion of "human" values. A clearly identifiable value system based on faith in the human potential has been promoted by the human relations movement. While a full exposition of the value system is beyond the scope of this treatment, a brief look at those values particularly relevant to organizations may be helpful. With regard to persons within organizations, the human relations movement values self-realization, free self-expression, informality. It places little value on self-restraint, "role" behavior, formality, the subordination of the self to the organization or the job. With regard to style of operation, it values spontaneity, flexibility, openness, permissiveness. It devalues planning, control, standardization. With regard to decision-making, it values collegiality, mutuality, group activity. It devalues authority (which is, perhaps, the dirtiest word in its lexicon). With regard to the nature of organizations, it values change, process, becoming. It devalues structure, tradition, stability (understood as resistance to change). It values feelings and devalues the intellectual. It values the "here and now" and devalues history. The value system is promoted both by the assumptions of movement (the values are "givens") and by the methodologies it uses.[26]

Although the human relations movement itself has been highly people-oriented rather than structure-oriented, it has left its mark in myriad ways on the church "restructurings" of the past decade. Churches seeking to solve organizational problems by restructuring have rightly called on the best organizational skills available to them to do that job — those with training and experience in organizational matters. Since there has been virtually *no* organizational or managerial training available, academic or experiential, which has not been permeated by the human relations movement, naturally the organizational values of the restructurers have reflected the values of the movement. Consequently, most restructured church organizations have emphasized interaction, collegiality, group decision-making, and flexibility. Some plans for church restructuring have devoted more attention to descriptions of hoped-for processes, than to the organizational structures themselves. In attempts to avoid the "rigidity," authority, and particularly the hierarchical model of "rational organization" forms, they provided highly diffuse forms of accountability.

The main thrust of the movement, however, remains people rather than structure. The Center for Organization Studies of the NTL Institute has used the term Organization Development — OD — to denote its human relations oriented approach to the modification of organizational behavior. Others use the term (or its variant, "organizational development") in other ways, so that its usage is by no means as precise as those having an NTL background would have preferred. To a considerable extent, however, the NTL approach has shaped OD. Its stock in trade — the OD technologies — has included "training" (usually group experiences), team building, conflict management, data feedback (usually in a group experience), and a variety of "interventions" to meet particular organizational needs.[27] "Structural interventions" — changes in organizational structure — are not strictly in accord with OD theory (behavioral science deals with behavior), but they are justified because both structure and environment affect behavior.

Process Management is also associated with the human relations approach. It simply means the application of human relations technologies in group endeavors, to "manage the process."[28] The terms "enabler" and "facilitator," popular in church circles, come out of this context. An enabler or facilitator is a relatively uninvolved technician who understands the process by which things are accomplished, and who enables others to achieve goals.

Humanistic Values in a Theistic Church

What is the place of the humanistic values of the human relations movement in a theistic church? Certainly, they cannot be rejected out of hand. A theological rationale can readily be established for each of the particular technologies or interventions brought to the church by OD consultants. There have been relatively few attempts to bring theology and Organization Development together, but when such attempts have been made, this has generally been the approach. One such attempt, for instance, was explicitly labeled "Toward a Theology for Organization Development."[29] Its author, H. Newton Malony, went down a list of OD techniques or principles — goal-setting, emphasis on people within organizations, emphasis on the group process, emphasis on the potential of persons, conflict resolution — and found each of them to be in accord with Christianity, using Biblical quotations and references to theologians.

Clearly justification could be found within the Christian tradition for a much longer list than the foregoing. Such an approach falls far short of providing a "theology of Organization Development," however, since it lacks overall theological coherence. It only provides piecemeal justification for specific practices.

Yet there is, in the background of the human relations

movement, a highly coherent system of thought, emphasizing human goodness and potential, which does lend itself to holistic theological examination. An important clue to an understanding of the whole movement is its relationship to certain religious movements and themes of the fifties and sixties. The "secular Christianity," "radical theology," "Death of God theology," and "religionless" Christianity of that period were marked by the rejection of transcendence and a strong emphasis on "humanization values." "Becoming truly human" became the byword.

Such writers as Robert Bellah and Norman O. Brown pointed to the birth of a "new religious consciousness," quite unrelated to such traditional manifestations as churches, institutions and corporate worship. This new consciousness is non-theistic, and is devoted largely to realization of human potential.[30] Such secular or radical theologians as Harvey Cox and Sam Keen, Jewish leader Richard Rubenstein and Episcopal priest Allan Watts became actively involved in the Human Potential movement. One of its striking features was the number of ex-ministers who became trainers or who opened Growth Centers. The values of the radical theology movement were virtually identical with those of the human relations movement.[31]

While the radical theology of the sixties was itself a short-lived phenomenon, its influence was considerable. Perhaps one of the most persistent channels of its influence in the churches has been the human relations movement with which it was so closely allied. The popularity, for a period, of sensitivity and encounter groups in church circles, the large number of continuing education events for the clergy which still feature some variety of human relations training, the group therapy model adopted for Clinical Pastoral Education, the establishment of church-sponsored or religiously-oriented Growth Centers and the continuing acceptance of OD consultants, all testify to the close relationship between the human relations movement and American religious institutions. But such a theology, having no meaningful place for a personal or sovereign God, is not compatible with the theological conceptions of the majority of Christians, particularly those in or near the classical mainstream of Christian thought. It is only fair, however, to recall that it represents one strain of theological thinking which has been present in some degree in the church for centuries, and which has influenced many other strains of thought. It cannot, therefore, be totally rejected as a coherent theological system, particularly in light of today's pluralistic Protestantism.

Furthermore, the application by churches of some of the techniques and insights of Organization Development may be fully compatible with a more orthodox theological stance, even though the theological climate out of which these techniques and insights grew may be rejected by those in the mainstream of Christianity. This is particularly true of the deep concern for all human beings as persons, which strikes a responsive chord for many in the church today. That concern may have been derived, in this specific instance, from a non-theistic humanism, but for Christian thinking it is founded even more basically on the infinite love of God for every individual person. This emphasis may have been neglected in Christianity. It is in keeping with mainstream theology to recognize that God, who used Cyrus the Persian and the Athenian cynics for his own purposes, may also use a theologically questionable movement to bring the importance of a concern for every person forcefully before the church. *Some* aspects of the ideological/theological roots of this movement, however, evidenced by *some* applications of Organization Development, will be questioned by those in the mainstream Christian tradition.

The Question of Authority

One such aspect is the anti-authority strain in the human relations movement. Authority in church organizations may be examined from two perspectives. Pragmatically, it may or may not be useful in organizational situations, and it should be open to examination from this perspective. It can hardly be rejected on ideological grounds, however, since authority is basic to the relationship between God and human beings. The figure of Christ as Head of the church clearly depicts an authority relationship. The authority relationship between human beings is not explicitly developed in Scripture, but the relationship between God and humans is the church's model. The existence of authority has seldom been challenged in classical theological thinking. The emphasis rather is on the *right use* of authority.

In the human relations movement, there has been an ideological assumption that authority itself is bad. This reflects the belief that to have any other person controlling any aspects of one's life inhibits one's full freedom, autonomy, and potential for self-actualization. Such an assumption could be supported theologically only by a highly self-centered kind of belief.

The anti-authority strain in OD has left its mark on the church organizationally, through a strong emphasis on groups rather than individuals in decision-making and in organizational operations generally. It has left its mark structurally in organizations that deemphasize personal accountability, and that are, in some cases, practically leaderless. While such organizational forms might be justified pragmatically if they can be shown to be more *effective* than those stressing personal accountability, no clear evidence of this kind is yet available. There is some evidence, indeed, that church organizations have been suffering from "leaderlessness." Questions may also be raised about the amount of time spent in interminable meetings by those church bureaucrats who value the group more than the leader. Is the amount of money spent traveling to and from meetings in airport motels justified by the results?

While these are pragmatic questions, it is also possible to raise the more basic theological question as to whether a persistent and long-term devaluation of authority in organizations may not subtly encourage a devaluation of the authority relationship between God and humans. It appears that the excesses of anti-authoritarianism in the church have now largely dissipated. An address and article by sociologist Peter L. Berger, widely read and commented on in the early seventies, sounded "A Call for Authority in the Christian Community." Berger, who himself had earlier been instrumental in bringing some aspects of the human relations movement into the church, connected his call for authority with a reaffirmation of Christian belief in a transcendent God.[32] The devaluation of authority persists, however, as a continuing strain within the human relations movement which affects its approach to Organization Development.

The Question of Sin

A second fairly basic theological question might be raised concerning the optimism, regarding human abilities and potential, inherent in the human relations movement. It is reflected in OD's optimism that its consultants and technologies have the capability of solving organizational problems and perfecting organizational operations.

A symbol of this unbounded confidence in human beings may be seen in the title of Abraham H. Maslow's book on business management, *Eupsychian Management*. (The term "eupsychia" was coined by Maslow to designate "the utopian society of self-actualizing persons.")[33] The human agents commissioned by God in the church have every reason for confidence in their God-given ability to carry out the tasks assigned them. But they are aware of the difference between creature and creator. And their confidence, in the Christian context, operates with a deep awareness of the reality and ubiquity of sin. It is dependent on grace. Yet there is good reason to suspect that the church, in many instances, operates much as if it were just any organization, placing more confidence in its process management, its OD technologies, and its managerial effectiveness than a serious consideration of human sinfulness might justify.

Management Science

The current fashion of looking at those who function in church organizations as "managers" is derived primarily from the business world. We have noted earlier the symbiotic relationship between the human relations movement and the business world. Business groups were among the earliest customers of the laboratory trainers, and businesses funded and encouraged its rapid expansion. The partnership has continued, and a human relations orientation is characteristic of many managers and management theoreticians today. The numerous management seminars, workshops, and training events now available to "managers" of every kind are almost invariably based on some group experience growing out of the human relations movement.

Business management's distinctive contribution to the organizational thinking of the church, however, lies in its stress on goals. Enlightened business management in recent years has shown great interest in the people who carry on its activity. But its interest in the *outcome* of their activity — products, sales, and profits — has remained its primary focus.

The basic elements of modern organizations with which all managers deal include budgets, personnel, organizational structure, and technology. Managers in business enterprises deal with two additional elements: material (if products are manufactured) and marketing. Some managers of servicing systems, even in non-profit organizations, utilize marketing to create a need for additional services.

For such basic organizational processes as fiscal and personnel management, the church has always found its models in the business world. Recent church organizational interest has found many of its structural models there. Its technologies as well — planning procedures and a newer emphasis on evaluation — have a similar source.

While certain kinds of evaluations, often imprecise and informal, have always been used as a basis for management decisions, newer managerial models stress carefully designed and focused kinds of formal evaluation. Personnel evaluation, fairly new in churches, also comes from the business world. "Prioritizing" in church circles is another concept borrowed from business management. In essence, it refers to nothing more complicated than the process of deciding which things are most important, and then *giving* those things first claim on funds and other resources.

Systems theory has contributed ways to management science of integrating various aspects of management into one overall process. A typical model begins with planning, moves on to implementation, then evaluates, then feeds back the results of the evaluation into a revised planning, followed by modified implementation, further evaluation, more feedback into planning, etc. There are a number of variations of this "closed loop" model, so called because the cycle forms an endlessly repeated circle. The late and largely unsuccessful PBE (Planning, Budgeting, Evaluation) system of the United Presbyterian Church was such a management model. PPBS (Planning, Programming, Budgeting System) has become a name for such systemic models, now recommended even to local congregations.[34] Such systems typically provide a yearly cycle, calling for the performance of specific tasks at particular times to make the overall flow of planning, programming, budgeting and evaluation work.

Perhaps the best known and most widely emulated current

management process is that known as Management by Objective, or MBO. A term first coined by Peter F. Drucker in 1954, management by objective has become such a widely used slogan and catchword that its status approaches that of dogma in the managerial world.[35] Drucker himself calls it so basic as to be a "constitutional principle." A proliferation of books, films, training courses, seminars, tape cassettes and lecturers promote it. Variations abound, such as Drucker's own "management by objectives and self-control"[36] and "management by objective and results" (MBOR). There are even those designed specifically for church use like "Renewal by Objectives" (RBO).[37] The application of MBO now extends far beyond the business world, into every kind of organization at every level. Pastors of innumerable local churches are now, as we have seen, making use of MBO principles.

While the theological relationships and implications are not as immediately apparent here as they are in the case of the human relations movement, two characteristics of organizational understandings derived from the business world should be noted. One is a tendency to think in terms of the "product" of organizational activity. Since business is generally directed toward the creation, production, promotion, sale of some kind of "product" (the frame of reference holds, even if the "product" is a service), other organizations adopting and adapting the frame of reference tend to search for analogies in their own operations. Can mission be regarded as the church's product?

A second characteristic, even more basic, is the goal-orientation of this kind of organizational thinking. "Management by Objective" expresses this — an "objective" being nothing more than a specific and manageable chunk of a goal.[38] It is almost impossible to utilize organizational insights from business management without adopting the underlying assumption that *organizations exist to achieve goals*. We shall examine this assumption in some detail in the next chapter.

We noted earlier some striking similarities between descriptions of the manager's role — as planner, anticipator of all contingencies, coordinator of complex systems, and achiever of purposes — and the classical descriptions of the sovereignty of God. There are from the religious perspective some inherent dangers in human management. The very frequency with which managers are perceived as manipulators by people in the organizations they manage, the treatment of people as "personnel," the existence of a "managerial class," are clues to the idolatrous possibilities. From a theological perspective, one must ask whether, in light of these dangers, managing is not inherently a usurping of God's role — whether it is not the sin of Adam and Eve, who sought to "be like God."

The three strains of organizational and managerial thought we have been examining are manifestations of behavioral science, which is perhaps only another way of saying that they are *non-theological* modes of thought about human behavior. As such they are characterized by the absence of any inherent sense of the sovereignty of God and the absence of any real awareness of the sinfulness of human beings. A basic question for the pastor then is whether these modes of thought are fatally flawed by these missing dimensions, or whether they are simply theologically "neutral" and can be "redeemed" by applying them in the context of a Christian worldview which takes seriously the sovereignty of God and the sinfulness of human beings.

The purpose of what has been said throughout this chapter by way of theological reflection, has been to point up such questions about management. The questions generally have been left unanswered, except by implication. The implications, however, have often been negative, and one might be tempted to wonder whether the end point of the process would be to brand organizational sociology, the human relations movement and management science as heresies, calling for their rejection. The logical conclusion after considering some of these questions might be that modern organizational theory is incompatible with a Biblical/theological understanding of the church.

No such conclusion is intended. The perspective for theological reflection here offered is one which strongly affirms the human as well as the transcendent dimension of the tension in which the church lives. Its basis is the theological affirmation of human responsibility to God, examined in the last chapter.

Nor can technology be rejected on theological grounds. Technology itself is not the issue in this critique. A technology is nothing more than the application of knowledge, skills, and at times mechanical or electronic labor-saving devices, to the accomplishment of a particular task. Christianity does not have a quarrel with technology as such.

Similarly, the level of sophistication of a technology is not the issue. Skilled spading of the earth is no less Christian than unskilled spading; a horse-drawn plow no less Christian than a hand spade; a tractor-drawn plow no less Christian than a horse-drawn plow. The use of computers, the application of an understanding of the complexities of human dynamics, the use of highly complex forms of financial accounting systems — none of these is in any sense unchristian. The issue here is not the technology involved or the level of sophistication of the tools used.

The church has a special role in carrying out God's purposes within the created order. From the Christian perspective, it would be hard to imagine a more worthwhile application of any valid findings of behavioral science or any useful techniques than applications within the church itself. Clearly, then, there can be no *inherent* incompatibility in the application of management techniques to that unique human organization, the church. The theological issue involved must be seen in terms of the *nature* of these organizational insights and the *effect* of applying them, rather than in questions regarding the appropriateness of technology itself.

Approaching the use of management techniques from a Christian perspective however, implies several standards.

1. Biblical teachings regarding the church, together with the church's theological insights regarding those teachings, must have primacy in any real or perceived conflict between these and organizational insights. The Biblical account is always the starting point for the church. Management theory and technologies, in other words, must be measured by Biblical understandings rather than vice versa.

2. Biblical/theological and organizational insights must be integrated, rather than overlaid one on the other. Despite its transcendent dimension, the church is undeniably a human organization. But to deal with it organizationally as if it were no different from any other organization, leaving its "spiritual" nature to be dealt with by others in another way, is an unacceptable kind of compartmentalization. An integration of organizational and Biblical/theological understandings would lead to more effective organizational applications of Biblical

insights, on the one hand, and to improved (from the Christian perspective) management techniques, on the other. The church, for instance, may adopt from business management personnel policies calling for equity in the treatment of women and minorities. But Biblical standards of justice — and perhaps the church's own awareness of past injustice and its need for repentance — would give a theological dimension to such personnel policies, making them more Christian and also more effective.

3. The effect of the application of organizational understandings to the church must be evaluated holistically, rather than piecemeal. It is not enough to find a bit of Biblical/theological support for each organizational technology in proof-text fashion. The question that must be asked is whether or not the total impact is in accord with Biblical/theological understandings of the church. Various organizational techniques or managerial practices, considered individually, could possibly be found theologically justifiable. The combined effect, however, might be to make the church human-centered rather than God-centered. The result would thus be out of line with an acceptable Biblical/theological doctrine of the church.

When these standards are faithfully applied, the church's awareness of human responsibility to God compels it to take seriously all available organizational methods and managerial skills. It must make full use of techniques which are appropriate to its own unique organizational needs. Let us lay to rest once and for all any lingering suspicion that the Biblical view of the church is inherently in conflict with management science or organizational techniques. Even though its uniqueness has at times led to anti-organizational movements, the church is and will always be a human organization. Its first responsibility is to God. Yet while functioning in faithfulness to God and his purposes, it must use the best human resources available. And it must use these resources within a church that must always remain God-centered.

The God-centeredness referred to here has specific meaning. It means projecting the relationship existing between God and God's people, which is suggested by the Biblical images, into down-to-earth organizational problems. It means rejecting compartmentalization of the "spiritual church" and human church. It means an openness and expectancy to God's movement in staff and committee meetings, in the framing of work plans, the shaping of budgets, and a host of specific organizational procedures. It means a faith that things *do* happen in church organizations which are not explainable in terms of human and group dynamics. It means an awareness of human limitations: the power of the Creator over against the powerlessness of the creature and the sinfulness that taints all human organizational endeavor. It means making *trust in the Holy Spirit an organizational reality.*

* * *

We have looked at portions of the church's own organizational heritage, which is largely a theological heritage. We have examined the sources of organizational methods and managerial techniques currently being used in the church, and we have considered some of their theological implications. Against this background, we now turn, in Part Two, to an analysis of what has happened to the church in the managerial age.

PART II

THE CHURCH IN THE
MANAGERIAL AGE: AN
ANALYSIS

CHAPTER FOUR

CHURCHES AS GOAL-SEEKING ORGANIZATIONS: THE MANAGERIAL PERSPECTIVE

How has the church fared in the managerial age?

Paul M. Harrison, Professor of Religion and Society at Pennsylvania State University, is the author of one of the few sociological treatments of denominational bureaucracy. He recently wrote an article on the current state of his denomination, the American Baptist Convention, beginning it with an account of a telephone conversation with a denominational regional executive. Tongue in cheek, he preserved his friend's anonymity by identifying him (because he was "profoundly choked up over a proposal for the reorganization of the national and regional structures of the denomination") as "Deep Choke." His account of the opening of the conversation:

Paul Harrison: I'm not equipped to study the convention now. I dropped analysis of religious organizations years ago for moral reasons. I'm studying theological ethics.

Deep Choke: All the more reason. The ABC is centralizing without a center and rationalizing with insufficient rationale.

P.H.: You might need Woodward and Bernstein.

D.C.: The *Washington Post* isn't interested in the northern Baptists.

P.H.: They should be. If they could learn about Baptists, they could reveal the true secrets of Jimmy Carter.

D.C.: Let's be serious. Listen, I think the situation may be worse in the convention than 20 years ago when your book was published. At least we had some of the liberals and fundamentalists around. Today the people on the reorganization committees wouldn't acknowledge a theological idea if it were formally introduced to them.[1]

Another critic, writing in the same journal about another denomination (the United Presbyterian Church in the USA) was equally harsh: "Enchantment with business-model forms of operating resulted in a new national church organization so complex and confusing hardly anyone could understand it. (Most of the Potemkin-village aspects of this part of restructure seem to have been quietly scrapped.)"[2]

Is it that bad? We shall seek to analyze, in the second part of this book, the state of the church in the managerial age. The managerial theories and techniques drawn from the secular sources we examined in Chapter Three have been applied enthusiastically in the church. But they have been applied in a unique organization, which as we have seen in Chapter Two, previously understood itself in a completely theological and non-organizational way. And it seems clear that the two modes of thought — managerial and theological — have not yet been fully integrated.

A possible reason, already suggested and dealt with briefly, may lie in the very nature of the church as an institution. There is a real question as to how well it fits the most basic of modern organizational assumptions.

What is an organization? Says Amitai Etzioni, an eminent organizational sociologist, "Organizations are social units (or human groupings) deliberately constructed to seek specific goals."[3] Says Charles Perrow, "Organizations are established to do something; they perform work directed toward some end."[4] Peter Drucker, using the concept of "institution" to refer to the same collectivity others call "organization," says, "An institution exists for a specific purpose and mission, a specific social function."[5] This is the starting point. By definition, contemporary organizational theory assumes that *all organizations exist for goal-seeking purposes.*

It follows that the business of management is to help organizations achieve their goals. Even highly people-oriented techniques, such as OD, are promoted and justified by their practitioners as the most effective ways of reaching organizational goals. Every organizational characteristic or process — structure, leadership, communication, team building, conflict resolution, process management, planning, budgets, personnel, operations, planning — all are focused on the *goal* being sought. Management theory, as we have seen, uses the goal-seeking nature of organizations as the basic principle behind "management by objective." The goal-seeking definition of organizations is an automatic assumption as management techniques are applied in the contemporary church. How well does it fit?

Classical Understanding: The Church Exists to be the Church

It is an interesting exercise to examine the recently compiled *Book of Confessions* of the Presbyterian Church, U.S., which brings together under one cover a number of classical confessional statements accepted within the Reformed tradition (the Apostles' and the Nicene creeds, the Westminster Confession and Larger and Shorter Catechisms, the Heidelberg Confession, the Scots Confession, the Geneva Catechism), one modern confessional statement (the Barmen Declaration of the German church in 1933), and a new Declaration of Faith, which was proposed (though not adopted) as the denomination's present confessional stance. All the classical confessional statements in the book include declarations about the church. They deal with its foundation, its composition, its holiness, its catholicity, its relationship to God in the headship of Christ and the presence of the Holy Spirit, its governance, its discipline, its ministry, its sacraments, the marks of a "true church," and the communion which exists within it. But *not one* of these classical statements so much as *mentions* its *goal,* its *mission,* or its *purpose.*

The 1933 Barmen Declaration has a short article on "the church's commission," which "consists in delivering the message of the free grace of God to all people in Christ's stead, and therefore in the ministry of his own word and work through sermon and sacrament." The new Declaration of Faith, however, has a full chapter on "The Christian Mission," elaborating the purposes for which "God sends the church into the world."[6]

The change of perspective is significant. The church, according to the classical theological understanding of its nature, was *not* "deliberately constructed to seek specific goals." Traditional theological thinking has seen the church as established simply to be the church, not to achieve *any* specific goal or goals. The goal-oriented perspective of modern statements that focus on mission is relatively new.

To point out this change in the mode of thought about the church as organization is not to deny that there was purposeful activity in the church prior to the birth of modern organizational thought. Clearly, there was. The Christian obligation to discipleship, to commitment expressed in witness and mission, has never been in doubt. Modern statements of faith such as the Presbyterian Declaration quoted above, which treat the church in terms of its mission, are not departing from classical Christianity or adding a new element to it. The teachings have been there all along. Every assertion about the mission of the church in the "Declaration" is cross-indexed with references to classical confessional statements and numerous scriptural passages.[7]

But classically, purposiveness has been implicit rather than explicit. It is the description of the church *in terms of* its organizational goals which is new.

No theological statement, classical or modern, thinks of the church as deliberately constructed by human beings to carry out *human* purposes. Classical statements, however, do not even perceive it as constructed to enable human beings to carry out *God's* purposes. The goal-seeking element is simply missing. So with many traditional theologians, Karl Barth explicitly disavowed the view that the work of the church is to improve society. He saw its existence, rather, as centering in the presence of God. The work of the church, he said, is "to call men, to recall to them that God reigns and is present."[8] There has been in church history a recurring tendency to reject even the term, "institution," to insist that the church is a fellowship under

God's reign, a community, its true constituency known only to God, invisible as well as visible, universal, beyond human limitation. And there has been a strong insistence that its ultimate ends will be brought about, not by its members, but by God.

From the beginning, of course, the church has been thought of as a human organization. The church is universal and invisible, but the form in which we know it is quite specific and highly visible. Even with regard to the church as a human organization, however, classical thinking has focused on the matters dealt with in the confessions: doctrine, discipline, ministry, word and sacraments. Always the assumption has been that the church exists not to *do* something but to *be* something — a people of God, a community of faith, the body of Christ.

Implicit Goals of the Church

What difference does it make? Is it quibbling over terminology to suggest that the church may not fit the modern goal-seeking organizational definition? Christians are by no means without goals, nor have they ever been. Even if the church is seen primarily as a community of the faithful, called by God, existing only to be that community, *internal* goals are certainly implicit. At the very minimum, Grace Church in Farmington intends to pay its minister and run a Sunday School. To the members, these are goals. The nurture of the faithful, the provision of a sense of community, the ministry of word and sacrament so that the community of the faithful can remain faithful, all are taken for granted in every congregation. Clearly they can be regarded as goals. Organizational theory does not imply that the goals must be external to the organization; it recognizes that a number of organizations exist solely to provide services or satisfactions to the members.

But it is not even necessary to regard the church as an internally focused organization to apply the concept of goals. Christians have never been without purposes *external* to the church. Grace Church supports a missionary, too. The call, in the words of the Barmen Confession, "to deliver the message of the free grace of God to all people in Christ's stead" — by word and by deed, through a wide range of methods — has been recognized in the church since the beginning. The call to

71

discipleship, to show forth the love of God through acts of charity and concern, has always been incumbent on Christians. Nor can it rightly be claimed that the call to mission and discipleship has been purely an individual call to those within the church, with no claims on Christians as a community. Classical Christian thinking has generally recognized the corporateness of response to God's saving grace, as well as the individual response. Nearby every congregation has its corporate sense of outreach. Of implicit goals and purposes, internal and external, individual and collective, there are plenty.

What *is* clear, however, is that the modern organizational mode of thought, which sees goal-seeking as the central and characteristic element in organizational behavior, is an *imposed* mode of thought. It has been overlaid on a centuries-old theological mode of thought, which has looked at the church quite independently of whatever goal-seeking activity is implicit in its existence.

There is, of course, nothing inherently wrong with imposing a modern mode of thought as a new way of seeing an ancient institution. Whatever else the local church may be, it is also a human organization, made up of a group of people joined together to do something. At least to the extent that it *is* a human organization, it ought to be able to profit from the application of whatever insights are available to students of human organizations about the dynamics of "people joined together to do things." New modes of thought frequently cast light on old assumptions. Looking at long-existing diseases in light of modern knowledge about viruses and bacteria, for instance, has made it possible to control those diseases. The germs were there all along; people were just unaware of them. Similarly, applying a modern goal-seeking perspective of organizational behavior to an organization which did not originally think of itself in goal-seeking terms could bring fresh understanding of its basic nature and reveal more effective ways of doing what it has tried to do all along.

There is, however, another possibility. The new mode of thought may not be entirely applicable. At one period, the application of modern knowledge about disease-causing bacteria to diseases which, we have since learned, are not caused by bacteria at all, but by viruses, did not prove to be helpful. The assumptions of the goal-seeking paradigm are clear. It is assumed (1) that organizations exist to reach goals; (2) that the goals can be articulated, agreed on and accepted by the organization; and (3) that the resources of the organization can be focused in a coordinated way on achievement of the goals. Do they fit Grace Church? Does it *exist* to pay a minister, run a Sunday School, and support a missionary? Are there better goals? What about those members who believe the money that goes to support a missionary should be devoted to changing an archaic system of criminal justice instead? Which side is right? Which is wrong? How can its resources be focused to reach clearly articulated and agreed-on goals? Does the church have a meaning and purpose beyond even the best and most clearly articulated goals?

If the assumptions do not fit, then organizational techniques and insights derived from the goal-seeking model may need to be reexamined. The church may need to determine the extent to which these techniques *can* be effective in an organization that does not fit these assumptions. Even more basically, it may need to ask if their application could unwittingly distort, and even pervert, our understanding of the very nature of the church.

Problems in Treating the Church as a Goal-Seeking Organization

Imposing the understanding of organizations as goal-seeking entities upon the classical understandings of the church has, indeed, created a number of new problems. The first is in identifying *what* the goals are. This in itself is a problem almost unique to the church.

With most organizations, while there may be some haziness about goals, and while there may be accretions of customary activity unrelated to the goals, the intended goals are fairly self-evident. A manufacturing company exists to manufacture a product. A service organization exists to perform a service or a range of services. A governmental organization exists to provide some aspect of control and order. A charitable organization exists to provide a charity. A fraternal organization exists to provide fraternal relationships. Such organizations occasionally find it necessary to *reevaluate and clarify* their goals. In some instances it may be necessary to *identify changes* in traditional goals. In others it may be desirable to *cast off accretions of non-purposeful* activities which do not contribute toward reaching the set goals. But it has always been possible, in ordinary organizations, to be reasonably clear about what the goals are.

Not so with the church. Transcendent as well as human, invisible as well as visible, universal as well as particular, this unique organization has not readily adapted to the modern organizational need for a clear identification and specification of goals.

The Mission of the Church

The obvious way of dealing with the difficulty of identifying goals has focused on the existence within the church of the ready-made concept of "mission." The church has long used this term to describe at least part of its purposive activity.

What is the "mission of the church?" The term has had a curious evolution in church circles. If one were to look up the word in a pre-1945 dictionary, the primary definition would probably be a classically religious one, such as "the act of sending, or state of being sent with certain powers, especially to propagate religion." The term mission was inseparable from the term missionary, and it meant sending out people to propagate religion by making converts. The Great Commission, to "make disciples of all nations," was the mission text. The plural form of the word "missions," came to be the normative way of referring to the overseas mission enterprise.

Among several secondary definitions in the pre-1945 dictionary would have been the military usage of the word "mission," namely, the stated purpose for which a military organizational unit exists. The military definition probably evolved originally from the classical religious usage. A military unit had a "mission" that it was "sent out" to perform in battle. By extension, each military unit in time established for itself an ongoing defined "mission," a statement of the total task for which it existed.

In a fascinating turnabout, the military definition has now replaced the classical religious one for many church people. In the post-World War II period organization specialists took over the military meaning of the word and applied it to all manner of organizations. It became popular and useful for a division of an industrial concern, a governmental department, or a charitable foundation, to develop a clear and concise statement of its "mission." "Mission goals" came to be understood as the ends toward which an organization works in carrying out its mission. And organizational thinking has applied this usage in the church.

In 1935, the term "mission of the church" would, for 99 out of 100 church people, have conveyed a clear picture of sending out missionaries to Africa or elsewhere, to convert non-Christians to Christianity. The image is still the same today for many church people. For many others, however, the military/organizational sense of the word has replaced this image, and "mission of the church" refers to the totality of whatever the local church, the larger regional unit, or the denomination sees as its purpose. Accordingly, the Presbyterian Church, US, has a Division of Central Support Services, whose "mission," in the organizational sense, is to provide some fiscal, data processing and managerial and support services for the General Assembly bureaucracy. The classical distinction between the "sent out" mission task and the internal maintenance task of the church is erased in this usage.

The current confusion in the church may be seen by examining the subject index of the card catalog in a seminary library. One will find listed under "mission" or "mission of the church" a few books (generally 1960's or later) reflecting the new organizational usage — and generally arguing that the church does *not* exist solely to send out missionaries but for a much broader purpose. But there will be literally thousands of listings reflecting the older understanding — "missions" literature.

In the organizational sense, then, the term "mission" is being used to imply all that the church exists to do — synonymous, broadly speaking, with the term "goals." But what is the nature of the mission? The answer is not clear. The term is still used, in the traditional sense, to denote that which Christians are "sent out" to do. For many, this still means "making disciples of all nations," which connotes primarily, if not exclusively, the overseas mission enterprise. For others, the church is "sent out" to do a broader kind of witnessing than making disciples, and some would place the primary emphasis on social change. For many, the distinction between the "sent out" functions and the internal maintenance functions is hazy, if it exists at all, and may be considered undesirable. A former missionary expressed his frustration with the contemporary lack of clarity, in a letter calling for reestablishment of "the real meaning of the word *mission:*"

It has come to be identified with any and all activities of the church. We even read about "doing mission." What in the world does that mean? Mission means *sent.* One is *sent* on a mission or *accepts assignment* on a mission. A generation ago the meaning of the word *mission* underwent a subtle change and transformation because of a commendable attempt to have every member of the church realize that followers of Jesus Christ were *in mission.* One could not delegate that responsibility to a few paid professionals or missionaries. But that idea simply has not worked. When a nebulous idea of mission is undertaken by a group of individuals without a distinct sense of call or vocation, the word loses its meaning.[9]

Parties or Factions in the Church

Differing views of what mission is tend to be identified with different "factions" or "parties" in the church. The existence of these parties is a second major factor in the church's difficulties with the goal-seeking organizational paradigm. Much has been said and written, over the years, about the divisions within Christianity. In addition to the denominationalism which has divided it organizationally, ideological divisions are frequent *within* denominations, and even within local congregations. A writer on the present state of the Episcopal church described his denomination largely in terms of "the various groups:" schismatics and loyalists, Anglo-Catholics, traditionalists, humanists, evangelicals, charismatics, liberals, radicals, "high Church," "low church" — and "the WASP establishment!" Some of the terminology might be different, but the list could be matched in almost any mainline denomination.

There are two major factions cutting across denominational lines. "Modernist" and "fundamentalist" were the terms used to describe them in an earlier period. "Liberal" and "conservative" labels have been used for some years. More recently, terms describing competing concepts of the basic goals of Christian mission, social action and evangelism, have reflected contemporary goal orientation.

John R.W. Stott has spoken of "Evangelical Christians and Ecumenical Christians." These terms come out of a context which identifies the ecumenical movement with social change goals (seen by evangelicals as characteristic of the World Council of Churches). They tend to be resented by ecumenical Christians, some of whom are unwilling to have the term evangelical co-opted by the opposition, and some of whom are unwilling to have ecumenism identified solely with an orientation toward social change. Nevertheless, the terms have gained wide currency, particularly outside the United States. Early in 1977, on a tour aimed at learning about overseas churches and mission programs in Latin America, I found them widely used, in all the countries I visited, to identify two antithetical manifestations of Christianity that seemed almost completely out of communication with each other.

Dean R. Hoge, in an extremely helpful book on the present status of Protestantism, *Division in the Protestant House,* does much to illuminate the present state of mainline denominations.[12] He points to the presence of two basic theological "parties." Building on the work of Martin E. Marty[13] and David O. Moberg[14] he calls these "Public Protestants" and "Private Protestants," adding an additional insight that the striking characteristic of the contemporary situation is the "collapse of the middle" — the absence of a large group of moderates to bridge the two extremes.

Supporting theory with empirical analysis, Hoge shows that the two parties differ strikingly in their mission priorities. The Public Protestants — theologically liberal, socially optimistic, and reflecting the scientific humanistic world view of the contemporary university — place the highest priority on issues of national social reform, injustice, and local social problems. They are least interested in personal evangelism — locally in the United States or overseas. The priorities of Private Protestants — theologically conservative, pessimistic about the possibilities for social change, and reflecting the classical evangelical Christian world view — are exactly opposite. They are most concerned with evangelism, least concerned for social action.[15]

Pluralistic and Consensus Churches

A key sociological distinction may be more important than ideological labels in understanding the effect of these parties, or of their difference of perspective, on churches as organizations. This is the distinction between *pluralistic churches,* in which various ideological factions coexist, and *consensus churches*, which are ideologically homogeneous.

From the sociological perspective churches are, of course, voluntary organizations. This is a characteristic which will be examined in considerable detail in the next chapter. Lon L. Fuller, in an insightful analysis of voluntary organizations, has shown that two basic principles hold such organizations together: shared commitment, and a legal principle (a constitution, by-laws, established existence). Both principles, says Fuller, are present in almost all voluntary organizations. Such organizations tend to move from the first principle to the second. (We have noted this tendency in the church earlier, in terms of Weber's analysis of the "routinization of charisma.") Organizations dominated by the first principle — shared commitment — cannot tolerate internal groupings, says Fuller. But when dominated by the legal principle, voluntary organizations not only can tolerate but in fact *need* internal groupings based on deeply shared commitment.[16]

In religious denominations, widely shared commitment means a high level of internal consensus and common goals. The more conservative denominations tend to operate with such a high level of internal consensus. Dean M. Kelley, in his perceptive analysis, *Why Conservative Churches Are Growing*, ascribes the relatively prosperous state of these denominations to their focus on an historically indispensable function of religion, that of giving meaning to life. He also credits the strength of their commitment and discipline, and their strictness.[17] But a key point is that they do what they do in a relatively unified way.

The "mainline" denominations are sometimes described as liberal, but they are not so much liberal as pluralistic. All of them include within their membership a wide range of social, ethical and theological perspectives — some of them mutually contradictory. (The acceptance of pluralism may in itself, of course, be a "liberal" attitude.)

The difference between consensus denominations and pluralistic denominations is illustrated by two recent schisms in American Protestantism. In 1973 a group of congregations left the Presbyterian Church, U.S., to form the Presbyterian Church in America. The schism had been resisted for years by the pluralistic Southern Presbyterians, with a series of compromises, study groups and movements aimed at reconciliation. The 1976 schism in the Lutheran Church-Missouri Synod grew out of the opposite dynamic. It was in effect initiated by the denomination's hierarchy through disciplinary steps and the application of sanctions, in an effort to *resist* pluralism and to maintain the Missouri Synod's historic high level of consensus.

Pluralistic denominations have, of course, a reservoir of shared commitment. But in terms of Fuller's analysis, they are held together primarily by the legal principle. The internal consensus groupings needed by such pluralistic denominations are often provided by local congregations, which tend to be relatively homogeneous. The voluntary-association principle is strongly at work as persons choose a congregation with which to affiliate; they usually select a group that thinks the same way they do. While some diversity is present in every congregation, knowledgeable church people in any city can identify particular local churches as "liberal" or "conservative," "missionary-minded" or "social activist." Newcomers "shop around."

In a homogeneous congregation, a broadly-supported consensus regarding its particular goals (which might be different from the goals of another congregation of the denomination, and recognized as such) can be achieved fairly readily. So much is this the case that the contemporary "Church Growth Movement," based on principles developed at Fuller Theological Seminary in Pasadena, California, utilizes, sometimes implicitly and sometimes explicitly, a "homogeneous unit" theory. According to this theory, churches work best if they are relatively homogeneous. Otherwise, too much effort is wasted trying to work out internal problems and divergent views. Said Melvin F. Schell, president of a "Growth Ministries Incorporated" organization in a major metropolitan area, "The more unlike we are, the more communications problems the church has. If a church is too heterogeneous, it tends to expend too much energy internally and doesn't have energy left to grow."[18] Advocates of such a theory are careful to maintain that the church is always open to everyone, and that church growth strategies aimed at homogeneous congregations are not intended to be racist or exclusivist. The effect of adopting this strategy, however, is to seek local congregations which are consensus groups, whether or not the denomination is homogeneous.

When consensus exists that a particular task should be undertaken, any religious group, large or small, will have little difficulty doing it. When that consensus does not exist, the whole goal-seeking model for understanding church organization tends to break down. Theological diversity, diversity of faith responses, diversity of perceptions regarding relative priorities — all make it extraordinarily hard to agree on organizational goals. And we can certainly agree that it is impossible to pin down common goals for the church universal. To the extent that we see each congregation as a local embodiment of the church universal (as Küng suggested it should be), there is little hope for agreement as to what are the *inherent* goals shared by the whole church. And it is even difficult within a pluralistic congregation to experience a commonality of goals.

Goal-setting Techniques

Lack of clarity about the nature of mission, and the presence of actions or parties that do not agree on mission, have not, however, prevented the application of goal-setting modes of thought. Modern managers have developed techniques to assist organizations in identifying and clarifying their goals, and nowhere have these goal-setting exercises been applied more earnestly than in churches. Goal-setting is perhaps the most widely used of all organizational techniques in the church. Rare is the congregation which has not engaged in some form of it.

Technically, the goal-setting exercises are often skillfully designed and conducted. Their utilization of the dynamics of small group interaction is such that it is often possible for even heterogeneous groups to hammer out agreements on goal statements. Groups create a group culture — a world of their own — and the intensity of the group experience is often such as to create at the time a considerable measure of acceptance ("ownership" in the managerial jargon) of the goal statements, even on the part of participants who are in basic disagreement.

Long-range and wide-scale commitment to goals so established, however, is considerably harder to achieve. Participants in the process often have second thoughts once the group culture developed during the exercise is dissipated. And commitment from dissident members who were not part of the goal-setting group is hardly ever achieved.

The success of goal-setting techniques is probably directly related to the level of consensus already existing within the particular congregation to which they are applied. In local churches where a high level of consensus exists (as it often does, even in pluralistic denominations) these exercises have been useful. They help congregations specify their goals and examine their activities in terms of whether or not they are contributing to these goals. But in congregations with a good bit of diversity, they have little long-range effect, at best. At worst, they have sometimes become battlegrounds between factions with competing goals. They have even in some instances led (or perhaps clarified other dynamics already leading) to a congregational split.

At regional and national denominational levels, the picture is similar. Consensus denominations, with little internal diversity and therefore little disagreement about goals, have seldom felt the need for goal-setting techniques. Among the pluralistic denominations goal-setting attempts have not been notably successful, and local churches have suffered from the failures. Representatives of various groups with competing goals have sometimes hammered out compromises and devised ambiguous wordings on which all could agree. But such "goals" tend to be so general and inclusive that they are meaningless. In other instances, winning factions in parliamentary battles have "set goals" for the whole group which have been ignored by the losing factions. Goal-setting as a way of imposing the goal-seeking organizational paradigm on denominations has not been notably successful.

A Case History in Denominational Goal-Setting

A classic case history is a "Consultation on the Mission of the Church" conducted by my own denomination, the Presbyterian Church, U.S., in 1978. I was directly involved in both the inception and implementation of the consultation. It came about as a by-product of an Organizational Modification study, conducted by the Office of Review and Evaluation, to deal with problems in the recently restructured General Assembly agencies. (I had also been involved in that, as a member of the restructuring committee!) It had become clear by this time that many of these problems were not of an organizational nature and could not be solved by structural tinkering. This was particularly true with regard to the church's mission overseas which had become the focal point of much controversy. The report of the Office of Review and Evaluation, following its study, proposed in orthodox managerial fashion, that the problems be solved by denominational goal-setting! It recommended a consultation, broadly representative of the denomination's constituency. Although the purpose was not clearly stated, the intent was clear — to enable the denomination to "agree" on its "mission."

The jockeying for position began with the naming of a task force to plan the Consultation. The denomination's General Assembly Mission Board — divided, like the rest of the denomination, but dominated by those with a Public/Ecumenical orientation — selected a task force heavily weighted in the same direction. So clearly was this the case that one of the three "conservatives" named (out of fifteen) made an issue of it on the floor of a Mission Board meeting, refusing to serve. But a substitute conservative was found, the public rupture was papered over, and the task force set about its task.

The task force members were extraordinarily competent and dedicated Christians. They made every possible effort to be fair to all viewpoints. They listened attentively to everything the conservative minority had to say, and in most cases did what the conservatives asked. They made the consultation more representative than any previous such gathering (with one delegate from each Presbytery rather than the predominance of mission agency bureaucrats which had marked previous consultations). They invited some conservative speakers.

Yet the direction was clear from the beginning. The majority of the Task Force was strongly committed to an ecumenical, social activist faith. This was particularly true of key members, who made up the inner circle. The official position of the denomination, reaffirmed by majority vote in Assembly after Assembly, had been strongly ecumenical and social activist. So in designing a consultation in which one-third of the members came from other denominations and ecumenical agencies, both U.S. and overseas, they were not only responding to the divine imperative as they experienced it, but to the official position of the denomination. Early on, the selection of the consultation theme, "One Mission under God," ruled out a conscious pluralism and prepared for a win-lose kind of unified goal-setting. This, too, was fully in accord not only with the intent of the consultation but also with the General Assembly's repeated affirmations of a "one mission" approach. Had the task force done other than what it did, it would have been untrue to denominational policies as well as to the members' own experience of God's love and will for the church.

And so the stage was set. The sixty Presbytery representatives, selected in most instances by the Presbytery's managerial group, were for the most part "one-mission" managerial types — many of them regional church bureaucrats. The overseas delegates were predominantly from ecumenical agencies rather than the overseas denominations (some of them quite conservative) with which the PCUS works. People from the pew were very sparsely represented, and the only cohesive group with a Private/Evangelical outlook was a contingent of missionaries (not all the missionaries present, but a majority), whose major commitment was to the preservation of a strong, and preferably evangelical, overseas program.

The Consultation met in an isolated setting, and the eight-day experience was an intensive one. The assignment was so huge as to be almost impossible. The process designed to make it possible was extremely complex, with persons and agenda moving continually from small group to small group. The process management was skillful. Remarkably, the consultation produced a document of some thirty-seven typed pages, in two parts: one entitled "God's Claims" and the other "Mission Proposals." Strongly ecumenical and public policy oriented, it has been widely hailed by Christians of that persuasion as the most "forward looking" document yet to be produced by a major denomination. If adopted and genuinely implemented, it would clearly set a new direction for denominational mission. Such were the dynamics of the group experience that the Private/Evangelical minority, which had struggled throughout, first to try to shape, and then to influence the outcome, did feel on the last day some measure of "ownership." The final communion service, marking the end of what had been a unique group culture, was a moving experience. The brotherly and sisterly love felt on that occasion between partisans of opposite positions was beautiful to observe.

Yet even on that final morning, the evaluation instrument filled out by participants before their departure revealed the failure of the group to agree on "one mission." What had resulted was majority rule, not consensus. The instrument revealed that while the document produced had the approval of a substantial majority of the non-PCUS overseas participants, and the support of about two-thirds of the domestic PCUS participants, it was supported by only a minority of the PCUS missionary participants. Even before the report went to the General Assembly, a campaign to defeat or modify it was underway within the denomination's evangelical wing.[20] The denominational "goal-setting" exercise had become one more "majority party" victory, to be fought against, supported lukewarmly, or sabotaged from the pocketbook, by the losing minority.[21]

Organizational Activity Motivated by Faith

Whether one uses organizational terminology of "goals" or the church's traditional terminology of "mission," or "mission" in the modern organizational sense, there is one further reason for the confusion and ambiguity about attempts to fit the church into a goal-seeking organizational mode of thought. *Motivation* for purposive behavior within the church is a key issue. We noted in an earlier chapter the church's traditional theological assumption that it is governed by God's purposes. "God sets the goals" would be the contemporary organizational way to put it.

This means that at the human level, reasons for engaging in particular kinds of activity in the church tend to be *ideological* (growing out of faith in God) rather than *pragmatic* (intended to bring about a particular result). Reasons for doing things are focused on the *source* of the dynamic which sets the action in motion, rather than the anticipated outcome. Churches undertake particular forms of activity "because it is God's will," or "because it is right," or "because we are moved by the Spirit," or even, in the jargon of church bureaucrats, "because it is God's agenda," rather than "because it achieves certain results."

No motives are unmixed, and anticipated results are undoubtedly part of the motivation, in most cases. But to the extent that the motivation *is* ideological (a response to God's grace), the outcome can be regarded, from the classical

Christian perspective, as almost irrelevant. "I planted, Apollos watered, but God gave the growth," said Paul. "So neither he who plants nor he who waters is anything, but only God, who gives the growth" (I Cor. 3:6-7). Following this Biblical pattern, activity has been undertaken because it is God's will. Responsibility for results is God's business, and the Christian ought not to worry about it.

The classic wording of countless thousands of church pronouncements expresses this principle: "We are called to . . ." Church people do particular things because they feel themselves to be *called* by God to do them. Generally, they are certainly not uninterested in the outcome. But to the extent that the classical pattern is followed, the input (from God) rather than the outcome (to the world) is the real point.

Clearly, activities that "we are called to" engage in can be labeled goals, and they frequently are. But the "response" orientation which brings them into being is worlds away from the "product" orientation of the contemporary goal-seeking organization.

Such an ideological source of "organizational goals" is quite foreign to modern managerial thinking. Indeed, it is almost unique to the church. There are many ideological organizations. Political parties are major ones, and there are other focused activist organizations, highly committed to particular tasks for ideological reasons. But they must justify their ideology in terms of *results*. They claim no transcendent source of motivation for their activity. Traditional Republicans act out of a strong commitment to conservative economic, political and social policies, but only because of a conviction that such policies *bring beneficial results*. Their behavior, though ideological, is still goal-oriented.

Churches alone focus on the other end of the equation: the *beginning* point rather than the *end* point: the source of behavior rather than the outcome. The organizational implications are far-reaching. A whole range of managerial assumptions are brought into question. We shall examine the implications in some detail in a later chapter, in terms of the doctrine of stewardship.

For immediate purposes it should be noted that if the ideological motivation is eliminated, or even played down, one is led in the direction of an "instrumental" view of the church. If it is the outcome that matters, the church is *valued* in terms of the results of its activities. It becomes a means to an end, a tool for reaching human goals — even if it is believed that the human goals were established by God. As we have noted earlier, systems theory, with its emphasis on the relationship of the organization to its total environment — the place of each sub-system in larger social systems — also has a tendency toward such an instrumental view of the church. The focus is on the place of the church in its total society, and the temptation sometimes becomes irresistible to value the church in terms of its effect on that society. The church becomes a means to social ends, not intentionally but as a by-product of organizational and managerial modes of thought.

* * *

Are churches then goal-seeking organizations? Can the modern managerial definition, "organizations are social units deliberately constructed to seek specific goals," be applied to them? Classical Christian thinking has not so regarded the church. It has been seen as existing to *be* rather than to *do*. Certainly churches carry out purposeful activity, and they always have. In this sense, goal-seeking modes of organizational thought can be applied.

But churches are unique organizations, and there are serious limitations in the application of the goal-seeking model. The Christian concept of "mission" has not proved completely adaptable to use in the organizational sense. Various parties within the church have different concepts of mission and of mission priorities. Goal-setting has not eliminated the differences.

The common thread in all the difficulties in applying the goal-seeking model to churches is a *pluralism of responses*. The fact that purposive activity on the part of Christians is classically regarded as motivated by faith in God, rather than by anticipation of desired results, that the *response* rather than the *goal* is what counts, may be a significant clue.

Modern managers assume that an organization deliberately constructed to seek specific goals can agree on those goals. They assume that all its energies and resources can be mobilized and coordinated to reach them. Churches, constructed by God to *be* the church and to respond to God's grace in faith, respond in multiple ways. Further understanding of the dilemma may be reached through examination of churches as voluntary organizations.

CHAPTER FIVE

CHURCHES AS VOLUNTARY ORGANIZATIONS: THE POWER OF THE PEW

Churches began as small groups of believers in a hostile society. New Testament churches were the People of God, called together by God's creative action into a community of faith. Religiously, the initiative was God's. But sociologically, churches were voluntary groups, separated from the rest of society by their own choice.

A radical change in this pattern came with the conversion of the Roman Emperor Constantine, in the year A.D. 312. Whole armies were baptized by imperial decree. Rome and subsequently all of Western Europe became officially Christian. During this period the church *ceased to be a voluntary organization*. People were born into it, and one's place in it was, for the most part, accepted unquestioningly. The church was a basic structure of society, like the family or the nation. Its worldview was so universal that its authority — even coercive power — was very real indeed. To some extent this pattern has continued as a cultural reality in the Roman Catholic church until fairly recent times.

The Protestant Reformation, however, brought a re-voluntarizing of the church. Some elements of the old pattern continued for a time in those countries that adopted Protestant state churches, but Protestantism was basically voluntary. Central Protestant doctrines undercut the non-voluntary status of the medieval universal church. Justification by faith made the faith of the individual a key element in membership. Biblical authority replaced ecclesiastical (organizational) authority and elevated the role of the individual as interpreter. The priesthood of all believers was in a basic sense an organizational principle.

Traditional sociological analysis of religious organizations has been in terms of the "church-sect" typology, first suggested by Max Weber in the early twentieth century, and later developed further by Ernst Troelsch.[1] This analysis distinguishes between the two types primarily in terms of the sect as a voluntary association of adults over against the inclusiveness of the church into which one is born. (There are other characteristics, but none so basic sociologically as this.)

However accurate that may have been at one time, there is no such thing as a "church-type" (non-voluntary) religious organization in the United States at the present time. Sociologist Andrew Greeley, himself a Roman Catholic, finds the concept of denomination more useful. A denomination, he says, is not some sort of halfway house between sect and church but the kind of "religious organization which emerges in a society which has no established church (official or unofficial) but permits and encourages the practice of religion by the various organized religious communities."[2]

The new tides which have swept American Roman Catholicism in the wake of the Second Vatican Council have, in a sense, brought a "Protestantizing" (voluntarizing) of the Catholic Church. This is particularly true with regard to attitudes and thought forms of members, which are important from the organizational perspective. Attitudes formerly regarded as "Protestant," relating to the right of the individual member to make his or her own choices, are now general among

Catholics. In the contemporary United States the Roman Catholic church is just as surely a voluntary organization as are the Protestant denominations, as several other Catholic writers besides Greeley have recognized.[3]

To say that the church is a voluntary organization is a sociological observation. Interestingly, however, the concept is given considerable attention by one influential contemporary theologian, Jurgen Möltmann, who sees the future of the church not in the traditional forms but in a new "voluntary association of members in Christian fellowship." He is not, of course, speaking organizationally. He does not expect traditional church-type forms to disappear, nor is he calling for reorganization, but for a "double strategy" to deal with the "crisis of ecclesiastical institutions." Reform from above in the established institutions must begin with the church's ministries. But the hope for the future is, with new life appearing through "grass roots communities," voluntary associations of committed believers. Möltmann thus provides contemporary theological affirmation of the voluntary organizational principle.[4]

What is the significance of the voluntary nature of the church as an organization? In particular, what are the effects of voluntary membership and activity on the dynamics of an organization and on the applicability of managerial methods and organizational techniques?

Organizational Theory and Voluntary Organizations

The problem with regard to organizational and managerial matters is not that the church is unaware of its voluntary nature. Theological concern for the Divine initiative may lead some to reject the concept of the voluntary church, but most Christians have little difficulty reconciling theological and sociological modes of thought. Ask any church member, "Is your congregation a voluntary organization?" and the answer is likely to be, "Yes."

The problem is, however, that the managerial techniques adopted by the church have nearly all been developed in *non-voluntary* organizations, and little thought has been given to the fit. Nearly all the insights about the nature, structure and dynamics of organizations which we have discussed so far have come either from the business world or from government.

Management theoreticians have long noted that there are

differences between profit-making and non-profit organizations. In the latter category have been included governmental agencies, public service organizations (such as hospitals, educational institutions and welfare agencies) and sometimes churches. Officials of such agencies have for the most part been happy to adopt the label "manager," and managerial principles and technologies have been seen as equally applicable to the non-profit organization.

But little if any distinction has been made between voluntary and non-voluntary organizations *within* the non-profit category. A recent book on *MBO for non-Profit Organizations* notes in a brief one-page treatment of volunteer organizations that "volunteer organizations are considered among the more difficult when applying MBO," but suggests that it can be done. A *Harvard Business Review* article on "Better Performance from 'Nonprofits' " states at the outset that "the unique characteristics of voluntary organizations should be sources of strength, not weakness." But after a thoughtful identification of these differences it proposes solutions for the "nonprofits" which are derived from the experience of the business world. Throughout it fails to distinguish between "nonprofit" and "voluntary."[6]

The general assumption of management science, then, has been that most major differences in organizational dynamics are accounted for by the presence or absence of the profit motive. And certainly there are some important differences of this kind. The assumption, however, can be challenged. It is a supportable hypothesis that insofar as the *applicability of managerial principles and techniques* is concerned there is little difference between profit-making organizations and most non-voluntary non-profit (such as governmental) organizations. The major differences, from the management standpoint, are between voluntary and non-voluntary organizations. It is the element of voluntarism that brings in radically different dynamics in funding, in participation by those who carry out the organizational purposes and hence in management itself.

Several organizational typologies note differences between voluntary and non-voluntary organizations for the sake of classification.[7] Etzioni, however, sees no essential differences except in the methods used to insure compliance, which in voluntary organizations must be persuasion rather than coercion or remuneration.[8] Much of the existing research tends to focus on the kinds of persons who join such associations and the ways in which they are funded. There appears to be an assumption, as with Etzioni, that organizational dynamics are largely the same whether participation is voluntary or not. No doubt this is the case in many aspects of organizational life. However, some important differences can be identified.

Characteristics of Voluntary Organizations

De Tocqueville, in one of his most widely quoted passages, commented on the proclivity of Americans for forming voluntary associations for all kinds of purposes:

Americans of all ages, all stations in life, and all types of disposition are forever forming associations. There are not only commercial and industrial associations in which all take part, but others of a thousand different types — religious, moral, serious, futile, very general and very limited, immensely large and very minute. Americans combine to give fetes, found seminaries, build churches, distribute books and send missionaries to the antipodes. Hospitals, prisons and schools take shape that way. Finally, if they want to proclaim a truth or propagate some feeling by the encouragement of a great example, they form an association. In every case, at the head of any new undertaking, where in France you would find the government or in England some territorial magnate, in the United States you are sure to find an association.[9]

Attention to "the voluntary sector" of society has been renewed in recent years by public interest groups. Their perspective, however, is not managerial. Remarkably little writing or research has been done on the structure or functioning of voluntary organizations from the management perspective compared with the vast amount available on non-voluntary organizations.

The Prototype: Small Local Association

The prototype of the voluntary organization (and perhaps, orginally, of all organizations) is the small, local association made up of a group of like-minded persons who get together for an agreed-on purpose. It is characterized by the possibility of face-to-face contact between the members and of personal member participation. It is homogeneous, at least in the limited area of life with which the organization is concerned. There is mutuality of purpose, generally with democratic leadership and policy making.

When such an association is examined in terms of the four organizational elements usually regarded as the tools of management in goal-achievement — budget, personnel, technology and structure — it becomes readily apparent that this is *not* the kind of organization on which such a theory is based.

Budget: Funds for the small voluntary organization have their source in contributions from the members themselves. This may be in the form of a mutually-determined assessment (dues), voluntary contributions of no set amount, or a combination of the two. Dues most often cover basic maintenance functions, while additional contributions or funds raised by members from the public are used for special projects. Funds raised by members from other sources generally involve contribution of time or work by members and remain therefore in the category of voluntary funding from members.

Personnel: Generally there are no "personnel" (employees) in the small voluntary organization. The members themselves are the participants, on a volunteer basis. Churches are among the few local voluntary organizations with paid staff. Clergy, however, are employed for specialized ministerial functions and leadership. Volunteer members are still the "personnel" who perform the organizational tasks.

Technology: Although particular technologies may be used by members in their tasks, the concept is almost irrelevant to the small voluntary organization. People, rather than technology, are central in the purposes and activities of such organizations.

Structure: Structures of small, local voluntary organizations are democratic and participatory. They are usually governmental rather than operational; that is, they are designed to enable the organization to make decisions and run itself rather than produce something. They are generally controlled by the membership itself and are not subject to managerial manipulation.

Such a managerial analysis points toward a conclusion that the concept of "management" is not readily applicable to the small, local prototype voluntary organization. Even when professional leadership is employed, the tools of management are not available to such a manager.

Authority and Power in Voluntary Organizations

A key to understanding the difference between voluntary and non-voluntary organizations is the *power* issue. We have noted earlier the paucity of literature on voluntary organizations. Some of the scarce theoretical work has centered around issues of power and authority though no clear model for applying these concepts to voluntary organizations has yet emerged.

Max Weber has provided a classic analysis of authority and power in organizations. He draws a careful distinction between the two. Power, which implies coercion, is seldom a factor in voluntary organizations. Authority, in Weber's usage, requires the consent of those over whom it is exercised; it presumes voluntary compliance. Weber identified three types: traditional authority, which grows out of widely-held cultural beliefs; legal authority, which is legitimated by belief in the supremacy of law; and charismatic authority, embodied in a leader, originally understood as divine authority but now generally as personal force or magnetism.[10]

We are concerned with issues of power and authority here only for the purpose of distinguishing between non-voluntary and voluntary organizations and between various types of voluntary organizations. The presence or absence of coercion in accordance with Weber's distinction is a simple test for immediate purposes.

The key element in authority, as distinct from power, is voluntary compliance. Weber has therefore been the starting point for most analysts of the authority-power issue in voluntary associations.[11] There are, of course, many complixities in voluntary and non-voluntary compliance; there are undoubtedly subtle ways in which voluntary compliance can be coerced. Wherever there are employees, power exists, since remuneration is the most widespread form of coercion in modern society. But the distinction is nevertheless sufficiently valid — and sufficiently important in voluntary associations — to be used as a starting point.

With voluntary organizations generally, authority is a highly relevant consideration but power is not. In the case of small, local prototype voluntary organizations, even authority is not a major issue. They operate largely in terms of mutuality and cooperation. Some authority is vested in leaders on the basis of both legal and charismatic principles, but members themselves retain most of the authority and exercise it collectively.

When the concept of management is introduced, however, not just authority, but power becomes an issue. For managers need power. Authority may be regarded as the right to make decisions, but power provides the ability to carry them out. In the small voluntary organization, where decisions are carried out collectively and voluntarily, such power is not necessary. But when decisions are carried out by managers, power is essential. The fact that managers have such power over supervised staff employees, but not over volunteer members, is the watershed principle.

It ought to be noted that there are treatments of power from other perspectives, and one which is especially relevant should be mentioned in passing. Robert C. Worley finds the chief distinction between voluntary and non-voluntary types of organizations in the *diffusion* of power which characterizes the former. Power (by which he means control over the resources through which goals are achieved) is lodged in every member or subgroup within the voluntary organization.[12]

Much of Worley's analysis of organizational characteristics of a congregation is in terms of form of power. In structure, in political activity, in polity, and in control of resources he contrasts traditional centralization of power with what he considers a more appropriate modern diffusion of power. We have noted earlier his contrast between "nineteenth century" pyramidal organizations and newer matrix or task-oriented models. In political activity, he contrasts traditional "structuralist" control by small groups with newer "pluralist" political activity characterized by openness, coalition groups and caucuses, and multiple decision-making processes. In polity, he contrasts "traditional" (written constitutions and stability) and "new" ("goals, rules and procedures legitimated through public goal-setting, planning and evaluation") emphases. In control of resources there is a contrast between older set procedures and newer flexibility.[13] Whether or not one accepts Worley's preference for certain types of organizational structure and political and polity processes, certainly his emphasis on the diffusion of power is congruent with the sharing of authority by all members, suggested here as characteristic of the small local voluntary organization.

Large, Long-established Voluntary Organizations

As small prototype voluntary organizations become long established, and as they increase in size, they tend to spread geographically. Affiliated local units are formed in other areas. The typical pattern of American voluntary organizations, particularly in the 18th and 19th centuries, has been the expansion, first statewide and ultimately nationally, of small local voluntary associations.[14]

Authority issues become considerably more complex in large and long-established voluntary organizations. Direct, personal authority based on "charismatic" presence is harder to establish. Elaborate authority structures are developed, calling heavily on traditional and legal legitimation.

Such organizations are less directly responsive to members and their activities are more routinized than is the case in small, local organizations. William McBride points out that participation in voluntary associations always involves acceptance of institutional structures and rules of the social whole. In large, well-established organizations, such acceptance becomes increasingly necessary. Members are less likely to resign immediately from large voluntary associations whose activities run counter in certain ways to their own individual desires than would be the case if the group were small and personal.[15] A considerable measure of cultural continuity is established: accumulated funds, an established place in the community or social order, a network of dependencies and interrelationships, vested interests.

Such large and established voluntary organizations, however, as long as they remain voluntary, still exhibit certain basic characteristics. One is consensual goals, representing general agreement on the part of the constituency. Another is voluntary participation in goal achievement and voluntary financial support in the form of mutually levied assessments or voluntary contributions. A third is the absence of coercion with dependence on mutual agreement, persuasion and legitimated authority.

Federation-type Voluntary Organizations

David L. Sills identifies two basic types of larger voluntary organizations, the federation type and the corporate type.[16]

Using his concepts and terminology, the kind of large voluntary organization we have been discussing, which retains all basic characteristics of volunteerism, is the federation type. Such an organization has a number of local units and usually a central office coordinating such joint activities as are supported by members. Nearly all large voluntary organizations begin as the federated type.

Funding in such organizations may be by contributions, but is often by dues. Units tend to be reasonably autonomous, and national activities are generally limited to coordination of local units and whatever agreed-upon national goals exist. National conventions or assemblies, made up of representatives from local units, generally set national policy. Elected leaders may function as full-time executives (in which case they become paid staff) or as part-time leaders with largely ceremonial and figurehead functions.

A professional staff may be employed, but it is not dominant. In federation type organizations, professionals are likely to be few in number, and their sphere of activity limited to such specialized functions as coordinating activities performed by local units, operating pension funds or insurance programs, or influencing legislation (lobbying) in behalf of the members. If local units retain a large measure of autonomy, if national goals are restricted to those matters in which local groups have a shared interest, and if professional staff employees are few in number and limited in their responsibilities, problems are kept to a minimum.

When national goals begin to extend beyond the direct interests of local groups, however, when they are directed toward a desired impact on the entire society, when technologically sophisticated means of achieving the goals are employed, and when the employed staff becomes a pool of expertise large enough to become a power center in its own right, problems arise.

Authority is a central problem area. The authority issue for elected leaders is quite different from that with employed staff. Leaders elected by membership at large are strengthened in their authority by a mandate from the electorate. However, they are likely to be volunteers themselves elected to largely figurehead positions with limited responsibility. For employed staff persons who are given operational leadership the authority issue is especially intense. They do not have a mandate from the membership, are seldom selected on the basis of personal charisma, and are often relatively unknown by the membership.

A second problem area for such large voluntary organizations, therefore, is disagreement, even conflict, between professional staff and volunteer members. Professionals are employed for their expertise. They tend to feel that they are better equipped to make wise decisions and set policy directions than the amateurs who make up the membership. But members, feeling that they have voluntarily and jointly undertaken to organize for a particular purpose, feel that decisions should be made and policy set by them. Professionals are often seen by volunteers as manipulating and seeking to control members. Volunteer members are often seen by professionals as interfering in matters in which they have no competence.

A third and related problem area has to do with organizational goals. Volunteer goals and professional goals are sometimes divergent. Goals are especially likely to be a problem area for the constituency of an organization characterized by a wide range of diversity.

Finally, conflict between national headquarters and local units also becomes common. It may also be an aspect of the professional-volunteer conflict since the local unit is more likely to be under the control of volunteers.

In all these problem areas the intensity of the problem varies directly with the level of interest and participation of the volunteer membership. If the members are relatively uninterested and uninvolved in what happens, professionals will be relatively free to do whatever they choose. But the catch is that the level of financial support and activity by volunteer members also varies directly with their level of interest and participation.

Corporate-type Organizations

Partly in response to these pressures but also partly in response to conditions of modern life and the corporatization of society itself, a new type of organization corresponding to Sills' corporate type has evolved. Generally speaking, it is the national voluntary organizations with a strong goal orientation

— and particularly those that exist to perform services or achieve goals *external* to the organization itself — that have become corporatized. Affecting the society in a significant way requires not just interested volunteers but expertise, sophisticated technology and, most of all, *power* to focus the organization's personnel and resources.

These organizations — and the category includes most of the national health, welfare and public interest agencies — are classified by Sills as voluntary. Most of them originated as voluntary associations and have been through the classical evolution from local to large federated type voluntary organizations. In the process of corporatization, however, *they have lost most of the characteristics of voluntary organizations* and strictly speaking should no longer be so classified. Rather they have evolved into a new type of *non-profit, public interest corporation*.

The corporate organizations of this type are run at the national or top level by professionals, supervised (sometimes perfunctorily since membership is often honorific) by boards representing the public. Their paid employees are organized bureaucratically to carry out the tasks of the organization and are subject to the same controls and forms of coercion (primarily remunerative) as the employees of any profit-making or governmental organization. Local chapters may utilize small corps of highly dedicated volunteers who believe in the cause. Volunteer activity is, however, generally limited to specific, non-policy determining areas and is carried out under the direction of professionals. Control is in the hands of the professionals. Funds come not from volunteer members (unless every contributor is automatically labeled a "member") but from public appeals with large numbers of givers contributing small amounts out of generalized good will, some feeling for support for the particular cause, or social/employer pressure. Often such support is through a United Fund campaign in which contributors do not even know the name of many of the organizations supported. Such supporters "contribute to" but do not "participate in" the organization. The difference is significant. The organizations operate under some constraints of public opinion but are essentially *private corporations* run by professional *staffs*. They may "use" volunteers to perform particular tasks in local areas but they are no longer "voluntary organizations" in the original sense of reaching consensual goals through voluntary participation, and it is important that this change in their character be identified and recognized.

Considerable attention is given in the literature on large national voluntary organizations to the tendency of professional bureaucratic leaders to become alienated from the rank and file and to the struggles which follow such alienation;[17] to manipulation and control of members by executives;[18] to the difficulty of "using volunteers" who are both expensive and ineffective;[19] and to voluntary organizations (such as the YMCA, certain national health organizations, and to some extent the American Red Cross) that consciously change their goals to meet changing social needs.[20] These problems, however, are seen from a different perspective if one recognizes that the organizations concerned are no longer in reality voluntary organizations. They are non-profit public service or public interest corporations run by professional managers, operating largely through employed bureaucracies and supported by funds raised from the general public. They *use* but do not *consist of* volunteers. The ultimate test is where the authority lies. In these public interest corporations, it lies in the managers, shared to some extent with whatever board of directors or governors exists. But by no stretch of the imagination does it lie with volunteer members.

The identification of this type of organization, still generally but probably incorrectly referred to as voluntary, is important for our purposes. The denominational mission bureaucracies, regional and national, tend to follow this corporatized model rather than the federation-type model of voluntary organization which church governing structures still follow. The distinction is a significant one when pastors and church members seek to understand contemporary problems of church bureaucracies.

Differences Between Voluntary and Non-voluntary Organizations

It is possible at this point to identify some basic differences between voluntary and non-voluntary organizations, the characteristics of non-voluntary organizations from this perspective being fairly consistent whether the particular organization concerned is a profit-making enterprise, a government agency or public interest corporation.

Authority in voluntary organizations is in the hands of the members. It is delegated to leaders who have popular support through authority structures that are often loose and flexible. Such authority has legal legitimation but it remains heavily dependent on the tradition of the organization and the leader's personal charisma. In non-voluntary organizations authority is in the hands of employed managers, who have not only authority in Weber's sense but *coercive power* as well. They must ultimately retain the support of the employing body (usually a board at the top level), but professional expertise is the key factor in retention of power. They are not directly dependent on the support of members.

Goal-seeking in voluntary organizations is participatory, and dependent on consensus of the members. In non-voluntary organizations it is centralized, focused, and under structured managerial control. Orders (although the term itself may be avoided) are given and obeyed.

Compliance in voluntary organizations is voluntary, dependent on persuasion on the part of leaders and acceptance on the part of members. Compliance in most non-voluntary organizations is based on remuneration, which is a form of coercive power. (Other forms of coercion are applied in certain types of non-voluntary organizations, but in today's society remuneration is the normative form.)

Use of professional experts in voluntary organizations is limited to particular areas in which there is consensus among the members that particular tasks can best be performed by professional expertise. Such professionals are subject to direct control by members. In non-voluntary organizations professional experts are dominant. They must maintain support of the source of remuneration, but they are in operational control and often set policy as well. Expertise is the basic principle, and they are likely to employ sophisticated technologies.

The organizational structure of voluntary organizations is democratic and focused on issues of representation for purposes of decision-making. There may be bureaucratic organization of professionals in limited areas but always under the control of members. Non-voluntary organizations are bureaucratically organized — not necessarily according to the classical hierarchical model but in terms of structured roles, specialized tasks, and fixed accountability.

Not all organizations, of course, fall entirely into one category or the other. There are voluntary organizations with some non-voluntary characteristics and vice versa. Particularly in the case of the private public interest corporations discussed above, which have evolved from voluntary organizations but have lost most of the elements of voluntarism, some voluntary aspects remain.

Church Organizations

With church organizations the transcendent dimension, which is neither voluntary nor non-voluntary in the human organizational sense, is an ever-present element. This makes it impossible to apply *any* organizational principle directly and simply without constant awareness of the difference made by the unique presence of the Holy Spirit. Generally speaking, however, these characteristics of voluntary and non-voluntary organizations are reasonably consistent and they provide a convenient test of the kind of organization with which one is dealing.

The claim is not made here that churches should be voluntary organizations. There is no suggestion that any type of organization, voluntary or non-voluntary, is more Biblical, more traditional, more holy or more in keeping with God's will than any other. The purpose is simply to identify, from the sociological perspective, the characteristics of existing church organizations. Managerial thought-forms and assumptions as well as particular managerial techniques, in our corporatized society, have been developed in non-voluntary organizations. This identification, therefore, is an important element in understanding what has happened to the church in this managerial age.

Local Congregations

Local congregations exhibit most of the characteristics of small, local voluntary organizations. Where parish boundaries are determined geographically, housing and ethnic patterns and local cultural traditions provide a large measure of homogeneity within the congregation. Today even Roman Catholics, when they find themselves out of step with the parish in whose geographic limits they live, do not hesitate to look elsewhere for a more congenial group with which to associate. Though priest or minister may be assigned by a bishop, control of organizational activity (as distinguished from control of sacraments and liturgy) is largely congregationally determined. There is generally consensual agreement regarding activities undertaken and a high degree of member involvement in whatever is done.

Local churches are among the few voluntary organizations with employed staff at the local unit level. A large staff may be bureaucratically organized. These staff members, however, are either directly responsive to member control (effectively true in most instances) or dependent on voluntary compliance from members to carry out organizational tasks (even in Catholic parishes), so that the voluntary pattern remains normative except in sacramental, liturgical or doctrinal matters.

Denominations as Federation Type Voluntary Organizations

At the denominational level the effect of the voluntary nature of the church is considerably more complex. In their governmental structures most denominations have continued to follow the federation-type pattern of large voluntary organizations. There are extremely important variations from this pattern, the most significant of which are related to the transcendent dimension of the church. It is impossible to isolate the behavior of denominations as federation-type voluntary organizations from the overwhelmingly important role of transcendent authority, whether mediated through Scripture, tradition, a hierarchy or the immediacy of the Holy Spirit.

To the extent, however, that purely organizational functions *can* be separated from transcendently-determined functions, denominations do exhibit many of the characteristics of federation type voluntary organizations. Even Roman Catholicism in the United States is characterized by increasing numbers of organized assemblages including representatives of the laity as well as priests, and the hierarchy is increasingly responsive to their actions and demands. In 1976 the U.S. Roman Catholic hierarchy invited more than 1300 lay and clergy delegates to an unprecedented national conference in

Detroit. The purpose was to set priorities on social issues for a five-year period. Roman Catholics are participating increasingly in ecumenical assemblages and thus indirectly affecting policies of their own church.

Among Protestants representative organizational structures are nearly universal. In the so-called hierarchical denominations effective church government is largely in the hands of representative bodies. Such representative bodies may include an "upper house" of bishops. But the governmental role of bishops is limited to specified areas having to do largely with the ministry of word and sacrament.

Theological Perspective on the Church as a Voluntary Organization

To speak sociologically of the voluntary nature of the church may correspond to speaking theologically of free will in the faith response to God's grace. From the human perspective, churches are indisputably voluntary in their composition. This is nothing more than a corollary of the fact that humans can resist or reject God's call. The non-voluntary nature of Roman Catholicism in Western Europe and of Orthodoxy in the East, in an earlier period, was never a theological necessity. It was rather a social phenomenon growing out of political, economic and cultural conditions in a particular period in particular parts of the world. It is now irretrievably lost even in those denominations and those parts of the world. We have noted earlier how the basic doctrines of the Protestant Reformation — all of which emphasized the role of the individual rather than the organization (church) in the faith response to God's grace — provided a theological rationale for the voluntary organization.

But even for the most individualistic Protestants the voluntary nature of the church is basically a sociological observation about the church as a human organization. The voluntary action of human beings remains in tension with the Lordship of Christ. The basic initiative is God's. Church members voluntarily give up their autonomy when they submit themselves in the church to the rule of Christ. The expression of the rule of Christ through the decisions and action of voluntary participants is the work of the Holy Spirit.

The Holy Spirit speaks to the church through prophetic leaders. But the church has had its share of false prophets and true prophecy through individual prophets can only be identified with assurance in retrospect. The Holy Spirit speaks also through the decisions of church governments. But church governments, too, have proved to be apostate (though less frequently, probably, than individuals), and no particular act of a church court or bishop can at the time be identified, with any degree of assurance, with the will of Christ. The voluntary nature of the church, in action as well as in composition, is expressed in the freedom of the individual Christian to disagree in conscience with both the prophets and actions of church governments.

* * *

For reasons growing out of its transcendent dimension, then, as well as for pragmatic reasons, the church as organization must take seriously its voluntary nature. It is safeguarded against excesses of voluntarism — a "Gallup poll" decision-making — by the Lordship of Christ. And it is safeguarded against human autocracy in the name of the Lordship of Christ by its voluntary nature. Only by taking seriously processes derived from its transcendence, as well as processes derived from its human organizational character, can the balance be preserved.

The most important exception to generalizations about the voluntary nature of church organizations is to be found in church bureaucracies. Denominational mission structures, regional and national, exhibit quite different characteristics. They are often closer to the corporate type organization than the federated voluntary type, and many of their current problems may be associated with this anomaly. In the next chapter we shall look at greater length at corporatized organizations and at the effect of corporatization on organizational and managerial dynamics in church organizations.

CHAPTER SIX

CHURCHES AS BUREAUCRATIC ORGANIZATIONS: UNIFIED MISSION AND EXPERTS

Can the Holy Spirit work through a bureaucracy? This is an important question in view of the fact that denominations today are largely run by bureaucrats.

While examining the church from an organizational perspective earlier in this book, we noted two pervasive twentieth century trends which were closely related. One is the "corporatization" of institutions in our society. The other is the "professionalization" of that society, with the growing dominance of experts in the various areas of technical and managerial skill. Both of these trends have affected churches at every level. They are particularly apparent in the larger regional and denominational organizations.

We have seen that the basic images of the church are most directly applicable to local churches, where the community of faith is directly experienced by believers. As noted in the last chapter, these local churches are voluntary organizations. Every local congregation exists, however, as part of a larger church system, and is significantly affected by that larger system. It seems clear that part of the current organizational malaise of churches is the growing dissonance between local congregations and larger denominational systems. The local congregation itself may be relatively free of internal bureaucracy and professionalism. The changes wrought in larger denominational systems by these trends, however, have become major factors in the life of every congregation and pastor.

Since the term "bureaucratic" conveys a clearer meaning to most people than the jargon term "corporatized," it will be used for most of this discussion. Its meaning, however, is broader than the traditional one which refers only to a particular kind of hierarchical organizational structure. As used here it also refers to the employment of sophisticated human technologies; to the tendency of a bureaucratic organization to develop a "life of its own," impervious to control by members; to the dominance of professional experts in such an organization. It is intended to convey in shorthand form the presence in church organizations of all those aspects of modern institutions which have led social philosophers to dub this the managerial age, the age of organization, or the technological society.

Distinction Between "the Church" and Mission Agencies

The bureaucratic trend in church organizations has been widely marked by a number of writers and commentators and, of course, has been crystal clear to the person in the pew. It has been noted and described primarily in terms of denominational organizations, rather than in terms of the local church. James Gustafson, for instance, described the bureaucratization of the churches in the early sixties. He called it a shift of power from the "grass roots" to executives, and noted that it is a process common to many voluntary organizations. The change takes place as a function of growth in size, in geographical scope, in complexity of decisions, and in the need for concentration of social power to be effective in a bureaucratic society.[1]

Paul M. Harrison's *Authority and Power in the Free Church Tradition* is by far the most searching and sophisticated analysis of Protestant denominational organization thus far produced. He examines the bureaucratization of the American Baptist Convention (now called American Baptist Churches in the USA) and the kinds of authority and power exercised by its board executives. In so doing he identifies a new kind of authority (in addition to Weber's classic charismatic, traditional and legal categories) operative in such a large voluntary organization. He calls it "rational-pragmatic authority." It is based on technical qualification and competence in performance, together with mastery of an informal system of power within the denomination's voluntary membership. Harrison sees denominations, in their modern bureaucratic organizational form, as similar to all other modern bureaucratic institutions. Baptists, he says, despite their traditional insistence on the freedom and autonomy of the local congregation, "have formed an impressive denominational organization . . . which in important ways bears a striking resemblance to the large social structures found in the spheres of government and business."[2]

Andrew M. Greeley discusses bureaucratization of the churches as a necessary aspect of institutionalization in today's society; it is part of the rationalization, formalization and bureaucratization of all human life. He then focuses on the survival in the churches of human concern and religious enthusiasm in spite of this bureaucratic institutionalization.[3]

Hugh F. Halverstadt, in a doctoral dissertation which adds significantly to the sparse literature on church organization, not only notes the corporatization of the churches, but suggests that the process be consciously carried further. In a corporatized society, he says, giant organizations "run the ship." The church must become such a giant organization in order to help steer the ship — that is, to help make social policy in the nation.[4]

The trend is clear and widely recognized. Yet one element is missing in the conventional analysis. These writers and many others, pointing to the bureaucratization of "the church," have regarded mission agencies which carry out denominational goals as "the church." They have failed to distinguish between the *mission agencies* of the denominations, which have indeed become as bureaucratic as they suggest, and the *governmental structures* of the denominations.

There is ample reason for identifying mission agencies as

"the church." In our culture we have come to think that all organizations exist to achieve goals. One automatically assumes that the church system engaged in doing things, achieving goals, carrying out "mission," *is* the church. The identification of bureaucratic mission agencies as "the church" is widespread among church members themselves. No one made the identification more confidently than the various denominational restructuring committees of the late sixties and early seventies, who designed the present organizational structures. Lyle E. Schaller's summary of the organizational restructuring between 1965 and 1974 of ten denominations and the National Council of Churches is perhaps the most comprehensive overview of denominational restructuring available. He points to the difference between agencies (which were restructured) and governmental structures (which, for the most part, were not). But even Schaller treats the movement as a restructuring of "the churches."[5]

Clarity, however, is important. The pastor and local congregation are baffled by the gulf between "the church" as experienced in that congregation and "the church" as represented by the denominational agencies. The bureaucratic mission agency system is *not* the denomination. If the mission structure were suddenly to disappear, the network of local congregations and regional and national jurisdictions would remain intact. The basic denominational governmental structures would be untouched. Most of the constitutional documents scarcely mention the mission agencies.

This is not to suggest that the mission agencies are not important; they are certainly the central business of many church governmental structures. But it is useful to remember that *it is not "the church" which has become a large bureaucratic organization, but its mission agency system* — something quite distinct from the church itself.

Historic Patterns

An historical perspective is helpful at this point. In Chapter Four we noted that goal-seeking activity (mission), has always been implicit in the concept of the church. It has *not*, however, been thought of as the direct purpose of the church. Classical organizational concerns have focused instead on governance, discipline and ministry. For most of its history the church has handled this difference between government and mission in a very simple way. It developed *two different kinds of organizational structures* for the two kinds of activity.

Official church organizational structures have focused on those concerns dealt with in classical theologies and confessional statements: order, discipline, ministry, word and sacrament. As noted in the last chapter, they tend to follow the pattern of federated voluntary organizations.

Denominational mission structures are a relatively late arrival on the church scene. For most of Christian history mission activity has been voluntary and has taken place *outside* the formal church governmental structures. Voluntary mission activity has always depended on activists who do the work and money-givers who support it. The historic pattern has been one in which the activists, with the approval of church authorities, have gone directly to the members to arouse enthusiasm, enlist support and collect funds.

The Roman Catholic Church developed admirable structures for carrying out these mission activities in the various lay and priestly religious orders. They have been permitted to be self-governing internally. Teaching orders, missionary orders, charitable and serving orders have been permitted to focus on their own particular mission interests, and they have had free access to church members to develop support and collect funds.[6]

The Protestant equivalent of the Roman Catholic order, as a structure for mission activity, has been the voluntary association. We noted in an earlier chapter the importance of shared commitment in organizational dynamics. These voluntary mission associations in Protestant history have been consensus groups, formed around commitment to a particular kind of mission activity. Most early mission associations were not formally related to churches and their support was interdenominational. The shared commitment around which the consensus was formed grew out of Christian experience. It was Christian response. But it was not seen as related to *organizational* Christianity.

William G. McLoughlin, in tracing the history of Protestant philanthropy, notes that in the early years the American population was so overwhelmingly Protestant and the climate of social thought so pervaded by a religious tone that it is impossible to separate public from Protestant philanthropic efforts. They were one and the same. At the earliest stage the multitude of charitable societies had no nationwide pattern. "Virtually all were local in origin and function, and a large percentage of them were denominational in origin and backing," says McLoughlin.[7]

The nineteenth century brought the gradual development of statewide and national societies, in keeping with the classical pattern of voluntary organizations. They continued to be interdenominational. Although many had been founded by the clergy, they came to be dominated by laity. Even the most "churchly" forms of mission — religious education and the spreading of the gospel at home and abroad — developed under nonchurch auspices. The history of the nondenominational Sunday school societies and foreign mission societies in this period is well known.

In the latter half of the nineteenth century, denominationally related committees and boards began to replace the independent societies, to provide channels for publication and education, foreign and domestic mission. However, they remained separate from church governmental structures, even though under the control of those structures. They were largely autonomous consensus groups within the denominations, cultivating their own constituencies, raising their own funds with denominational cooperation, and carrying out their various kinds of mission.

Whether or not such denominational mission structures should be independent of denominational governing structures was often a contested issue. My own Presbyterian Church, U.S., was formed in the Confederate States at the time of the Civil War. One of the most hotly debated questions at the first General Assembly was whether or not there should be denominational mission boards. Dr. James H. Thornwell of South Carolina believed that there should be no such agencies. He maintained that the Assembly itself should do the work of the church through its Standing Committees. He had been a moderator of the undivided Presbyterian General Assembly before secession and had lost the battle there. When the Southern Church was formed, however, he won — at least verbally. The new denomination agreed that the General Assembly should be its own missionary society and educational

111

society. But to assist the Assembly it established "Executive Committees" — which very quickly assumed the role of Boards, and became the agents of consensus groups within the denomination to carry out mission. Thornwell really lost. (In 1972, however, the denomination's Plan of Restructure set out so thoroughly and deliberately to put mission responsibility in the hands of the official governing body itself — the General Assembly — rather than autonomous boards that the action might be called "Thornwell's triumph"!)

With the development of denominational mission agencies, which were essentially denomination-wide voluntary associations, Protestant church people came to think of "mission" in denominational terms. Local outreach was not neglected, however. Although it was not always labeled "mission," work expressing Christian charity and concern, and support for denominational mission, were provided through voluntary associations in local congregations: Ladies' Aids, Women's Missionary Societies, "Circles," Men's and Youth organizations, all knit together in denominational networks.

While such local organizations operated with the consent and under the supervision of official church governing structures — vestries, sessions, councils and boards of deacons — they were traditionally allowed a large measure of autonomy. By common consent "mission," locally, was left largely to them and to other voluntary agencies (not necessarily related to the church) which were meeting local needs. There have been local and federated organizations formed to deal with responses of the Christian conscience to particular social problems, sometimes church-related and sometimes not: pre-Civil War abolitionist societies, the Women's Christian Temperance Union, the Fellowship of Reconciliation and more recently a wide range of "coalitions" — often ecumenical — of church people working for social change. Official governing bodies of the congregations meanwhile have concerned themselves primarily with those matters which, as we noted earlier, have been dealt with in traditional "theology of the church:" word and sacrament, discipline, worship, the spiritual health and growth of the fellowship of believers and the provision and maintenance of facilities and staff.

The same informal division of responsibility between the "governing" functions of the official bodies and the "mission" functions of the voluntary associations under their supervision has been observed at other church levels — regional and national jurisdictions. The classic distinction is still embedded in the official governing documents — Disciplines and Books of Order — of denominations. These governing documents say little or nothing about mission responsibilities of church governing bodies at any level.

"Sodalities" and "Modalities"

One of the clearest descriptions of the traditional difference between government structures and mission structures in church history has come from Ralph D. Winter, Director of the United States Center for World Mission. In several articles, Dr. Winter has used the terms "sodalities" and "modalities" for a perceptive analysis of this aspect of church organizational history. "Sodality," which grows out of the Latin term for "brotherhood," has been used within the Roman Catholic Church to refer to voluntary associations of likeminded groups of Christians. The word also has a similar sociological usage for voluntary groupings within tribes. Dr. Winter uses it to refer to all the voluntary mission associations within and across denominational lines. He uses the coined term "modality" to refer to the official governing structures of churches and denominations and he points to the existence throughout Christian history of both types of organizations. The classic form of sodality is the Roman Catholic order, which has for centuries existed in Catholicism under the supervision and with the approval of the hierarchy (the modality). Winter's main thesis is that Protestants have suffered from not officially providing for a Protestant equivalent of the Roman Catholic mission and serving orders.[8]

There is a sense in which the local church itself, which as we have seen is often a consensus group within a pluralistic denomination, may be called a "sodality." Within local churches internal organizations for particular purposes (especially mission purposes) are widely accepted and, indeed, almost universal. But Protestants have tended to be somewhat uncomfortable with larger sodalities within denominations. The United Presbyterian Church has a provision in its *Book of Order* for the supervision of such groups by the General Assembly. These organizations are given official recognition (as

"Chapter 28 organizations") and oversight. In my own denomination, the Presbyterian Church, U.S., however, no such provision exists. The accountability of local sodality groups to the session is provided for in the *Book of Church Order* but sodality groups at the denominational level are viewed with extreme discomfort.

Their presence within denominations, however, has been a consistent historical pattern. In fact, a number of denominations began as sodalities (voluntary consensus groups) within parent denominations. They became modalities because the original modalities (denominational governments) would not accept their legitimacy. The Conservative Baptist Association of America grew out of the Conservative Baptist Missionary Society which was originally a mission group of likeminded persons within the American Baptist churches. The Christian and Missionary Alliance, originally a voluntary missionary-sending organization, also became a denomination. The Salvation Army, long a mission and service agency outside the regular denominational structures, for many years had officers but refused to enlist "troops." It, too, has recently begun to accept regular members and has become a denomination.

It is useful to recognize the historic interplay of these two kinds of organizations which have always been present in Christianity. Denominations themselves are from a sociological perspective voluntary organizations (of the federated type, as we noted in the last chapter). In addition there are and have always been voluntary associations for particular purposes *within* denominations, and *across* denominational lines within the church universal. Protestantism, with its pattern of mutually recognized denominations, has always affirmed the legitimacy of a pluralism of modalities. Curiously, though, it has been much more ambivalent about the legitimacy of a pluralism of sodalities — which Catholicism has classically affirmed.

Official approval, however, is beside the point. With or without it, the sodalities as well as the modalities have generally been present. This *is* the way Christians have always expressed themselves organizationally. When sodalities are co-opted into the official governing structures, or when they cease to express the will of members who support them, new voluntary mission groups tend to be formed. Campus Crusade for Christ

International, World Vision International, Wycliffe Bible Translators, and the Navigators Inc., are non-denominational voluntary mission groups. Each, incidentally, has an overseas mission budget larger than that of several mainline denominations. A good case could be made for the claim that they came into being, at least in part, because mainline denominational world mission agencies *stopped* being internal denominational sodalities — voluntary groups of likeminded people. Clearly the money supporting non-denominational sodality budgets is coming from church people within denominations.

An article on the evangelical resurgence which has been a striking religious development of the late seventies comments on the tendency:

Most evangelicals are very church-oriented in that they attend regularly and are active in a particular congregation, but cooperative programs of outreach and ministry are often carried out through agencies that are structurally independent. These para-church groups, usually quite specialized in their purposes, are more flexible than denominations and able to respond much more readily to needs and opportunities. They also have a more personal touch in their programs.[9]

In other words, they reflect the voluntary principle! The article goes on to suggest that contemporary evangelical leaders today are coming from the sodality groups, rather than from the denominations as was the historic pattern.

The voluntary principle asserts itself insistently. Mission Board professionals in my denomination, the Presbyterian Church, U.S., scheduled a denominational Student Conference for PCUS college students during the 1977 Christmas holiday period. The response to advance publicity was poor, and the conference had to be cancelled for lack of interest. But during the same period, student members of the Davidson Christian Fellowship at PCUS-affiliated Davidson College, on their own initiative, planned a student conference on their campus during the 1977 Christmas holidays. They extended invitations to students at other PCUS colleges, met a good response and had such a successful conference that they laid plans to repeat it on an annual basis!

While the groups and activities mentioned here have for the most part been conservatively oriented, there have been many liberal sodalities, too — a number of the ecumenical groups and movements and issue-oriented coalitions. One of the most successful currently is an ecumenical network of Christians seeking to alleviate world hunger. Others have focused on abortion rights, criminal justice and feminist issues. Overall, the pattern appears to have been reasonably consistent through much of church history. To a considerable extent goal-achievement in mission outreach has taken place through voluntary groups of likeminded Christians (consensus groups).

Denominational Mission and the Managerial Revolution

We have seen that beginning in the latter half of the nineteenth century, denominational boards and agencies replaced the earlier non-denominational societies as major channels of Christian outreach for most Protestants. These were in effect internal denominational consensus groups. Separate agencies were developed for each form of activity — overseas mission, domestic mission and Christian education being the most prominent such "causes." They were usually semiautonomous, having their own support constituencies and organizational structures, receiving funds directly from local churches and individual members and carrying out their own programs. Supervision by denominational governing bodies was often loose and superficial.

As the denominational agencies grew, and as the managerial revolution transformed American modes of organizational thought, they took on some of the characteristics of bureaucracies, particularly in the organizational structures of their rapidly increasing staffs. They adopted modern technologies for handling funds and personnel. Basically, however, they remained voluntary organizations generously supported by large consensus groups within their respective denominations and carrying out policies consensually supported by their constituencies.

In essence (in the unique cross-hatch of "modality" and "sodality" which has characterized so much of Christian history) local congregations were the constituent units of denominational governing organizations. Less officially, and more selectively, they were constituent units of the mission agencies. This pattern remained fairly constant in most denominations through the first half of the present century.

The second half of this century has brought the managerial

age into full flower. Concurrently came the development of organizational sociology and management science which deal with organizations "deliberately constructed to seek specific goals." In this climate a significant change has taken place in mainline Protestantism. The "mission of the church" has come increasingly to be viewed as the responsibility of official governing bodies, at every church level, rather than of voluntary associations.

Corporatization of denominational mission structures did not begin in earnest until after World War II. The change has been gradual. In the postwar period denominational governing structures have gradually assumed more and more control over the former autonomous and voluntarily supported denominational mission agencies. Various activities have been drawn together as the concept of "one mission" has been stressed. Unified budgets have been instituted. Agencies have been discouraged or prevented from going directly to the people to raise money for particular causes. Managers have been given control of the allocation and spending of funds. The denominational restructurings of the sixties and seventies in many cases simply formalized and legitimated a process already long underway.

Bureaucratic mission organization has paralleled the flowering of the ecumenical movement. Unified budgets have included substantial support for ecumenical agencies. These agencies in turn have developed their own bureaucracies. The corporatized mission of mainline Protestant churches is probably best symbolized by its skyscraper monument in New York City, the Interchurch Center at 475 Riverside Drive.

The denominational and ecumenical mission agencies now exhibit all the characteristics of other corporatized social structures: centralization of activity to focus resources on unified goals; large bureaucracies; sophisticated technologies (human as well as electronic); and "experts" to manage them. On the negative side they have developed a perceived corporate life of their own while persons in the pew feel powerless to affect or control them.

The results have many positive aspects. Bureaucratic denominational mission structures have promoted an integrated "mission of the church" and have brought unified goals, trained specialists, and overall coordination by skilled managers. At its best this approach to mission has been impressive indeed. It has achieved a breadth of planning, a level of efficiency, a utilization of specialized expertise and a concentration of efforts unequaled in previous church history.

The movement has focused the attention of church people on mission as never before. When the church — locally and at denominational levels — is seen as existing to carry out mission, it is no longer possible for church members to limit their Christian response to "going to church" with an easy conscience.

Further, corporatized church agencies have made the weight of church organizations felt in a corporatized society. If one searches historical records for evidences of Christian influence on national and local policy, such evidences abound. The abolition of slavery, prohibition, labor laws, educational policy — a whole host of illustrations can be found. But the influence in the past was always mediated through a pervasive national consensus of religious people, not through church organizations. Records of congressional hearings, for instance, show an abundance of testimony by religious leaders, but always as interested persons, not as representatives of their denominations. A study I conducted of the relationship between the military chaplaincy and the churches shows that denominations as organizations did not become involved at all in the provision of their own clergy to serve as chaplains before this century, and not with any significant official attention until the Second World War.[10] Only in the postwar period have churches made their influence felt in the larger society through corporatized organizational structures.

"Corporate" or "Corporatized"?

On the face of it there would appear to be a natural affinity between organizational corporatization and the corporateness of the church. Both terms have the same root and the same thrust toward unity. Corporateness is a central Biblical theme. The very word "corporate" expresses literally the Biblical image of the "Body of Christ," which we have examined in an earlier chapter as one of the most important images of the church. Despite the diversity of its members, the church is one. The ear, the arm and the foot are all different but they make up a single body. There are many gifts but one Spirit. In light of this

118

Biblical theme of corporateness and its prominence among the images of the church, it would appear on the surface that the "corporatization" process could be regarded as an expression of Christian unity. The emphasis on "one mission," on central planning, on a unified budget and the discouraging of uncoordinated appeals for various "causes," all would appear to be suitable expressions of the corporateness of the church.

But the assumption requires careful examination. Christian corporateness implies that the individual person is very much a part of the whole, influencing and being influenced by the whole body. The fact that the body would not be complete without the participation of the ear is just as important as the fact that the ear would not be functional without the body. The ear counts, and the ear senses its contribution to and importance in the whole body.

"Corporatization," as experienced by institutions in the age of the managerial revolution, often has just the opposite effect. It is characterized by sophisticated technology rather than amateur efforts of members, elitism rather than broad participation, centralized professional planning rather than a collection of highly personal responses to a variety of spiritual gifts. Professional "managers of the body" have replaced the instinctive corporateness of an ear, an eye and a hand working together. There is a sense that the individual does not count in a bureaucratic institution, that persons are unable to have a meaningful effect on what is done, that the institution has taken on a life of its own, impervious to the will or the direction of the members who make it up. This is the typical reaction to corporatized organizations. And *corporatized churches have not been exceptions.*

The term "corporate" has a different meaning for Christians. We have noted earlier the suggestion of C. Ellis Nelson that the local congregation is the "natural habitat of the Spirit," where the sense of joint participation is present. This joint participation in the presence of the Spirit is the Christian's most basic experience of the "corporateness" of the church. The Spirit, as Dr. Nelson also suggested, works in other parts of the church. Certainly a sense of belonging to a larger corporate whole — a denomination or an ecumenical grouping — is part of the experience of believers. This is especially true when they take part in gatherings of representatives of that larger whole.

But it is utterly dependent on the believer's sense of participation. The individual person must identify with, support, and feel involved with the larger church unit in whatever it is doing. To the extent that this is true the believer is an eye *in a corporate body;* to the extent that it is not true the believer is an outsider *to a corporatized organization.*

Blurring of the Line Between Church Government and Mission Structures

The blurring of the traditional line between governmental structures (modalities) and voluntary mission structures (sodalities) has been an important element in the whole movement toward corporatized denominational organizations. Restructuring committees reflected contemporary organizational thinking in that they saw goal-achievement (mission) as the basic purpose of the organization itself (the denomination), and thus the primary business of its governing structures. The previous relative autonomy of mission agencies and voluntary groups was seen as an organizational anomaly, a fault to be corrected. As a result, regional and national governing bodies of denominations (Presbyteries, Annual Conferences, Synods, Conventions, General Conferences, General Assemblies) have become far more directly concerned with mission than was once the case, dealing with a wide range of matters once left to subordinate agencies or internal voluntary groups. Even in those denominations where this integration between governmental and mission structures has not been achieved many have seen it as a goal. In a meeting regarding possible merger between the United Church of Christ and the Christian Church (Disciples of Christ) the point was made by a UCC leader. Dr. Walter A. Bruggemann, Dean of Eden Theological Seminary, was quoted as saying that the United Church "has not integrated its major boards into the church structure, and this is a deep sickness."[12]

In part the trend toward integrating governmental and mission structures undoubtedly reflects disenchantment with control by elite groups in the old autonomous church agencies. It represents a desire to give control of mission programs to elected representatives of the church membership. At a deeper level, however, it reflects assumptions about the goal-seeking nature of the whole organization. It represents an assumption that the kind of consensus can be achieved which is required for a large volunteer organization to agree on its goals.

The basic governing structures of denominations have not been greatly changed. It is helpful to remember that the corporatization of denominational mission agencies has not significantly affected what was historically seen as the church. Interestingly enough, the constitutional documents controlling church governmental structures have remained largely untouched. Forms of church government have remained relatively constant. Bishops, presbyteries and associations have carried on their traditional roles as guardians of faith and order. Conflicts have been adjudicated. The clergy have been called, ordained and disciplined. Theological standards have been debated.

Corporatized mission agencies, however, have increasingly occupied the attention of governing structures as denominations have come to be seen as organizations existing to carry out mission. The General Assembly of the Presbyterian Church, U.S., for instance, now has separate Standing Committees (which carry the bulk of the work of an Assembly) assigned exclusively to deal in detail with Mission Board organization, Mission Board administration, Mission Board program, and Mission Board budget. It has been known to use sizeable chunks of plenary time debating the merits of one $18,000-a-year staff position!

Corporatization of American church organizations has been most obvious in the large denominational superstructures and ecumenical agencies. The tendency, however, has been present at every level of church life. One current phenomenon, noted by many observers, has been the growing influence and power of regional church organizations — presbyteries, state associations, regional Conferences, dioceses — as over against national level denominational headquarters. In part this decentralization may have been in reaction to the corporatization of central denominational organizations and their relative imperviousness to influence by individual church members. Smaller agencies closer to home are perceived as more responsive to control by the membership. However, these newly powerful regional judicatories are themselves increasingly corporatized: bureaucratically organized, technologically sophisticated and dependent on the expertise of growing professional staffs.

The definition of mission, as we have seen, has in the corporatization process been broadened to include a comprehensive catalog of all the church intends to do. With this change, one of the most striking contemporary developments has been the greatly increased emphasis on local mission, carried out by the local congregation. Rare is the session, vestry, or board of stewards which has not been reorganized into "mission units," with responsibility for coordinating the work of larger committees from the whole congregation.

Generally speaking, and for obvious reasons, the process of bureaucratization has not gone as far in local churches as in denominational organizations. Few if any congregations as yet have their own computers. But shared computer time is by no means unheard of. Experiments with credit card offerings and automatic computerized pledge payments from bank accounts have not been notably successful but they have been made. Clergy managers are mastering more and more human technologies. Staffs are increasingly professionalized with division of labor between staff experts in increasing numbers of fields. (We shall examine this phenomenon in detail in the following section.) But certainly few local congregations are as yet regarded as having taken on a life of their own, impervious to the will of the members.

Professionalization of the Churches

If the church is not entirely in the hands of bureaucrats certainly it is in the hands of the professionals. We have noted earlier that the corporatizing tendency in our society has been accompanied by professionalization of services. There are, as we have seen, several characteristics of corporatized organizations, but none is more important than the dominance of professionals who are "experts" in the required technologies.

Professionals, of course, are not new to the church. The basic concept originated in the church, with the professional clergy. Academic training for the other learned professions — medicine, teaching, law — developed in the Middle Ages under church auspices. Theology at that time was the "queen of the sciences" and the clergy, trained in theology, remained until relatively recently the only church professionals.

The clerical profession began to develop shortly after apostolic times. For most of church history, the distinctive marks of the professional clergy have been administration of the sacraments (qualification for which belongs to the transcendent dimension of the church) and the teaching/preaching function, which has traditionally required rigorous academic training. Catholicism has emphasized the sacramental role of clergy professionals. Protestantism has emphasized the preaching/teaching scholarly role. Indeed, in the Reformed tradition of Protestantism ministers are known as "teaching elders."

The rigor of the required academic training, and accordingly the degree of professionalization, has been subject to variation. The sect type of religious organization, characterized by a high degree of associational voluntarism, has tended traditionally to deemphasize professional preparation. Lay preachers with relatively little academic training have been used. This is still the case with new sects in the early stages of their development, and particularly those that stress the experiential rather than the confessional tradition in Christianity. Institutionalization, however, has generally brought increased emphasis on training and professionalization. It is fair to say that the normative pattern in Christianity has been that of a professional clergy.

The professionalization with which we are now concerned is of a different kind. Essentially a twentieth century phenomenon, it has accompanied the growing organizational understanding of the church and the corporatization of church institutions. This new professionalization has four aspects: a broadening of the kinds of professional expertise expected of the clergy; increasing clergy specialization; increasing numbers of non-clergy church professionals; and growing numbers of secular professionals in the service of the church.

First, the basic parish ministers who make up the backbone of the clerical profession have been expected to have a broader range of professional expertise than the traditional liturgical and theological disciplines. "Role" studies, the most popular form of sociological analysis of the clergy, have identified a number of roles other than teacher, preacher and priest.

Greatest attention has gone to the pastoral role, which has required training in pastoral counseling, and the administrative role, which requires training in organizational studies and church management. Almost every minister today is expected to have some measure of professional expertise as a counselor and a manager.

A second manifestation of professionalization is the growth of specialization within the clerical profession. Some ministers specialize in preaching, with other clergy on the parish staff employed to handle other pastoral duties. Some are fulltime pastoral counselors, either on church staffs or in specialized counseling agencies. Some are Christian educators, either as ministers of education in parishes or in church educational systems. Some are chaplains in the armed forces, hospitals, or other institutions. And some specialize in administration and management, either as senior pastors or in the proliferating church bureaucracies at regional and denominational levels. The church has yet to fully make its peace with clergy specialization. The generalist model for the pastor is still zealously guarded by many. But such specialization is clearly an important factor in the contemporary church.[13]

Third, there has been a rapid increase in the use of non-clergy professionals in the church. Church musicians have a long ecclesiastical history, but their ranks were joined early in this century by non-clergy Christian educators, and more recently by increasing numbers of non-clergy church administrators. Military chaplaincies are developing para-professional assistants (known in the Air Force as Chapel Managers and in the Navy as Religious Program Specialists). There are church finance officers, and professional church secretaries (who are forming their own professional organizations). Nearly every denomination has recently enlarged its traditional ministerial pension operation to cover other full-time church employees who are experts in their respective fields. The term "religious professionals" is increasingly used as a generic term to cover these as well as the clergy. Even the Presbyterian Ministers' Fund, the oldest life insurance company in America, now describes itself on its letterhead as "An Interfaith Life Insurance Company for Religious Professionals."

Finally, the churches, with their expanded definitions of

mission, have been using an increasingly wide range of non-church professionals in their mission programs and activities. While physicians, nurses and teachers have been used in missionary service since the early nineteenth century, the vocational range of today's overseas missionaries is far wider: agricultural specialists, engineers, airplane pilots, heavy equipment operators, mechanics. On the domestic scene, local churches, regional or ecumenical coalitions and denominations engage other specialists: sociologists, child care professionals, social workers, journalists — even lobbyists in Washington offices — for an extremely broad range of mission activities. And these, too, are frequently brought under church pension systems and included in the overall category of "church professionals." The professionalization of the church, then, covers a wide range of skills, expertise and specializations. The trend was satirized by Martin Marty in a *Context* newsletter:

"Skills-skills-skills-skills-skills — we have skills until they are coming out of our ears." So observes a friend in a phase of theological education that takes him off into the fields where "skills" are obsessively treated . . . Some day somewhere someone is going to go up to a leader and say, "You've helped me acquire every skill known for counseling, administering, preaching, and the like. I am the complete automatized technocrat of 'how to.' But I cannot find anyone who cares, because they are interested in me only as a minister of the Gospel, a theologian of sorts, and the Gospel and theology are a bit out of my range." It'll take a while until we hear such language, because today's seminarians seem to converge on skills-curricula and today's ministers, more often than we'd like, congregate at retreats where skills are the whole show. But the day will come.[14]

For our immediate purposes, in this study of management technique in the service of the church, we are primarily concerned with one aspect of clergy professionalization. Organizational/managerial professionals are the new elites of the church. Paul M. Harrison's concept of "rational-pragmatic" authority, which he saw as the kind of authority exercised by agency executives in denominational systems, is precisely this managerial professionalism.[15] The manager is the professional with mastery of the technologies required to run organizations. Managerial professionalization, however, is not limited to the denominational mission bureaucracies. Far from it. It permeates the churches at every level from local parish to denominational headquarters. Most seminaries today offer some form of church administration and managerial training to every candidate for the basic Master of Divinity degree. As we noted earlier, it has been one of the most popular forms of continuing education for the clergy in recent years. Corporatized church organizations, locally, regionally and nationally, are generally in the hands of highly skilled managers and organizational technicians. The term "professional" is being used here to refer to the *application of organizational technologies by persons skilled in their use, at every church level.*

* * *

Thus far in Part II of this book we have been examining three aspects of the church's adaptation to an age of organization. First we examined the church as a goal-seeking organization. We looked at ways in which the most basic managerial assumption about organizations has been applied to churches. Next we looked at the church as a voluntary organization, examining some seldom-noted differences between voluntary and non-voluntary organizations and their managerial implications. Finally we looked at the church as a bureaucratic organization, tracing the trends toward corporatization and professionalization.

Throughout we have noted difficulties with current applications of the managerial model in church organizations. There are serious questions as to how well the church fits management's definition of organizations as social units deliberately constructed to seek specific goals. There are serious questions as to how well the managerial model derived from business and government fits *voluntary* organizations. And there are serious questions as to how well corporatized mission bureaucracies fit in voluntary organizations with pluralistic memberships.

These questions will be best answered by a down-to-earth look at the results. How has the church fared in the managerial age? The final chapter of Part II will address this question.

Chapter Seven

How Has the Church Fared in the Managerial Age?

Signs are everywhere that church bureaucracies are in trouble. Indeed, corporatized mission in mainline denominations began to collapse even before it was fully developed. The first signals appeared in the sixties. Funds began to dry up before corporate headquarters buildings were paid for, and bureaucracies began to shrink even as "priority strategies" proliferated.

Nearly every mainline denomination has in recent years radically reduced the size of its headquarters staff. The Episcopal Church has done so twice. The organizational restructures which brought corporatization to full flower, have been foundering. A 1977 book by two Duke University researchers on the restructuring process in mainline Protestantism was vividly subtitled "The Agony of Church Restructure."[1]

What are the reasons? They are undoubtedly complex, but some clues may be found in the nature and dynamics of voluntary organizations in today's society, and the anomalies experienced by *corporatized* agencies of *voluntary* organizations.

Sociologist Ted Mills, who has been quoted earlier in connection with the creeping corporatism which is characteristic of contemporary American society, points to one possible reason in another characteristic of American society.[2] Mills points out that alongside the creeping corporatism — and at least partially in response to it — a countervailing trend has developed. Americans are looking ever more insistently for personal satisfaction. Sociologist Daniel Bell has referred to a "revolution of rising entitlements," characterized by a search for personal control, a loss of respect for authority and an insistent egalitarianism. The capturing of this mood may have been the most important clue to the winning of the U.S. Presidency in 1976 by a relatively unknown governor of a southern state.

The focal point of the revolution of rising entitlements is the self. It has been called the "new narcissism" and clearly has been related to the Human Potential Movement, backed by Humanistic Psychology and humanistic values, which we examined as part of the background of Organization Development. Cults and therapies for the self-centered, devoted to self-development, self-fulfillment and self-actualization, have popped up like mushrooms, finding fertile ground even in churches. Varieties of formalized "assertiveness training" have surfaced. Numbers of community political groups have recaptured local schools from educational bureaucracies. Priests' organizations have issued challenges to Roman Catholic bishops. "Rightsmanship" is practiced by minorities and other groups who have felt themselves to be oppressed: women, blacks, Chicanos, Indians, homosexuals, various ethnic groups. Separatist movements grab headlines, win elections or launch revolutions. The traditional American order is reversed as "smallness" becomes more treasured than "bigness." A century-old population trend is reversed as people leave cities and rural areas become the growth centers. Urbanologists call for planned shrinkage. A taxpayer revolt sends legislators scurrying to shrink or scuttle massive social programs.

It is in the context of a society dominated by these two movements — huge bureaucratic organizations in collision with a mood of personal assertiveness — that what is happening to the churches must be seen. Mainline Protestant mission agencies have become as corporatized as any other major social structure. National-level bureaucracies have suffered forced attrition in the past few years, but regional bureaucracies have been growing, and the bureaucratic spirit extends even to the staffs and the elaborate new organizational structures of local congregations.

Corporatized organizations are by nature unresponsive to the individual's search for control over his or her environment. They often devote a great deal of bureaucratic attention to responsiveness, but their programmed attempts to be personal — computer-printed solicitations addressed to Mr. Board O. Education and mechanically typed form letters automatically signed with "Warm personal regards" — come across as phony, and are as likely to enrage as to placate the frustrated recipients. And voluntary organizations are highly vulnerable targets for rage and frustration.

Most corporate structures are implacable. Despite the revolt, most taxes are as inevitable as death. One can only sigh and submit when the last appeal procedure confirms the original ruling by an officious GS-6 that one is ineligible for a benefit, or when the insurance company insists that the fine print excludes one's own kind of accident. It is easier to pay the bill, even if it is incorrect, after the twelfth computer-printed threatening note. But there is one exception to the helplessness of persons facing corporate giants. In *voluntary organizations* individuals can make their impact felt. "Proposition 13" came to the churches long before it came to California.

We shall look briefly now at three areas in which this tension is being experienced in the church. Readily apparent is the widespread current dissonance between the bureaucracy and the pew. Increasingly apparent, and even more convincing, is the financial crisis of mainline denominational bureaucracies. And while less evident at first glance, perhaps even more insidious in the long run is the disabling effect of professionalization. In these areas the church in the managerial age is hurting.

Mills saw a rising mood of personal assertiveness throughout American society, in collision with corporatized social structures. In church circles, the member in the pew is on a collision course with denominational bureaucrats.

It is a contemporary truism, accepted even by secular observers of the church, that denominational leadership is out of touch with the pew. Solid data can be found to support the widespread belief. A report of a Special Committee on Church Membership to the 1976 General Assembly of the United Presbyterian Church contained the following paragraph, which was quoted on the cover of a religious journal under the title, "Is Leadership Out of Touch?"

Perhaps the feeling about the national level of the church came out the clearest when the question was asked: "Is the national leadership of the United Presbyterian Church out of touch with members?" The answer was "Yes" by 53 percent of the respondents in declining congregations; 56 percent of those in typical ones, and 57 percent of those in growing congregations. There will always be those unsatisfied with any leadership, whatever its nature, but we believe that this opinion from 4,000 leaders in over 600 congregations needs to be heard and an appropriate response made. Undoubtedly most congregations have no accurate perception of how much they do in fact depend upon the higher judicatories and the extent of the service they receive. Yet, if over half of the leaders of the local congregations feel that the national leadership is out of touch, it is time for serious attention.[3]

One key to the problem is the fact that in today's bureaucratic denominational organizations *leaders* have been replaced by *managers*. Social critics have noted that this is characteristic of many institutions of our society. The dominance of managers and dearth of leaders may, in fact, be one of the most prominent characteristics of the "managerial revolution." Even a winning candidate for the Presidency of the United States — Jimmy Carter — emphasized his managerial skills as a qualification for that high office, and some have claimed that his troubles early in his administration stemmed from his managerial rather than charismatic style. It is a thesis of Robert Nisbet's book, *Twilight of Authority,* that the kind of social authority on which leadership is based has been disintegrating.

The dominance of bureaucracy has a prominent place in his analysis. Visbet sees this as preparing the way for dictatorships

and authoritarian military regimes, to fill the leadership void.[4]
What the effect will be in lesser institutions has yet to be seen.

The paucity of charismatic and widely revered leaders on the American religious scene in this generation has been frequently noted, and the fact that this has accompanied the corporatization of the American churches may be no coincidence. Certainly the managerial assumptions of the Human Relations movement, which governed the organizational restructures of the sixties and seventies, with the emphasis on collective leadership and group processes, left little room for leaders to emerge. The organizational modifications adopted by my own Presbyterian Church, U.S., in 1976 (known by some disparagingly as the "restructure of the restructure") sought to undo this inhibition of leadership by eliminating the collective management structure, and encouraging executives to travel in the church, speak, and adopt a stance of greater visibility. Results, however, have not been immediately apparent.

If the perceived gap between leader and pew is to be closed, it is probable that the churches must look to places other than the bureaucracies for leadership. The managerial role is quite different from the leadership role. In any event, the leadership function cannot be "structured" into bureaucracy. Leaders must emerge; they cannot be "hired." They may emerge in either the structures of the church at large — its pews and its organs of government — or its bureaucratic system, but it is probably far safer for the church to find its leaders in the former system than the latter. A bureaucracy exists to carry out the tasks assigned to it, not to establish the tasks. As such, it is the natural habitat of managers, but not of leaders.

The dissonance between bureaucrat and pew is most likely to be perceived when bureaucrats engage in activities at odds with the wishes of the majority of members. A widely-publicized instance was the Angela Davis incident in the United Presbyterian Church, when funds for the legal defense of Miss Davis were given through the denominational bureaucracy, when national agency employees went to jail after refusing to testify about alleged church involvement with radical activists of a racial minority. Funding by the national bureaucracy of the United Church of Christ of legal expenses of the "Wilmington Ten" was opposed by church members in the region concerned.

131

Grants by the World Council of Churches to African liberation and guerilla movements have also received widespread publicity in denominations supporting that ecumenical agency.

Prophets in the Bureaucracy

These activities, and others which may be less controversial, are often referred to as "the cutting edge." The bureaucrats who engage in such unpopular forms of mission, not supported by the membership at large, often label their activities "prophetic." The alternative — basing mission policy on the will of church members at large rather than seeking "the cutting edge" — is dismissed scornfully as "Gallup Poll" Christianity.

Since such forms of "prophecy" generally involve attempts to bring about social change, in one form or another, they are identified with the public or social activist wing of Christianity. In the era of the flowering of corporatized denominational mission organizations in the late fifties and early sixties, when large budgets and responsibility for mission planning were in the hands of denominational agencies, religiously motivated social activists were naturally attracted to church bureaucracies as seats of power of social change. Many of the present managers come out of this generation. To the extent that sizeable budgets and significant policy decisions remain with the denominational bureaucracies, they still exercise considerable influence. As a result, those of the private or evangelical wings of denominations sometimes perceive the bureaucracies as captive to the social action wing of the church.

The identification of the unpopular, the cutting edge, the change-oriented with the function of "prophecy" in church bureaucracies has become widespread. So much has this been the case that at the time of the organizational restructure of the boards and agencies of the Presbyterian Church, U.S. a basic organizational principle adopted by the restructurers (I was one of them) was "to lodge the function of prophecy somewhere in the structure."[5]

Such an organizational principle, and the practice of "prophecy" by social activists in the denominational bureaucracies, represents a fascinating twentieth century reversal of the traditional place of the prophecy in the church. Biblical prophets were never part of the establishment except, perhaps, in the case of Micaiah, the only one of the 100 "house prophets" who was willing to challenge the king of Israel (I Kings 22). Prophets were always "over against" the establishment, whether religious or governmental. While the Holy Spirit has been perceived as speaking through councils and courts of the organizational church, the prophets have been the lone persons whose voices challenged councils and courts. The role of prophecy in the church has historically been recognized in proclamation (by word and deed), in persuasion and charisma, rather than in manipulation of budgets, staffs, and foundation grants.

The valid prophetic voices have been most clearly recognized by the church in retrospect. They frequently *were* unpopular, out of touch with the constituency at large, and on the cutting edge of their times. But lessons of history as well as scripture would indicate that the prophets are likely to be found in the pulpits, the publications — even the pews — rather than on corporatized staffs. The bureaucracy is not their natural habitat. Those of us who sought, in the optimistic sixties, to "lodge them in the structure" may have been pursuing an impossible dream. People who achieve their ends through management of budgets, goals and staffs — whether their ends are popular or unpopular — may appropriately be labeled change agents. But the label prophet is highly questionable.

Financial Crisis of Denominational Bureaucracies

Leaders are expected to be out in front of followers. Differences between denominational bureaucrats and the people in the pew can be explained in terms of the greater knowledge and expertise of the managers, as over against the "least common denominator" dimension of any generalized attitude ascribed to the pew. There is undoubtedly a large measure of truth in such explanations. More pressing evidence of trouble with the managerial model for corporatized mission agencies, however, is found in continually declining budgets. In voluntary organizations, the ultimate power of the pew over unresponsive bureaucracy is the power of the purse string. More and more this power is being felt.

A 1975 study of philanthropic giving in the U.S. found that giving to churches has been declining steadily for years. An overall drop in philanthropic giving — both in proportion to the gross national product and absolutely in constant, uninflated dollars — is accounted for almost entirely by decreased giving to religious organizations. Between the years 1964 and 1974, religious contributions dropped from 49.4 percent to 43.1 percent of the total.[6]

A 1975 study conducted by the Office of Review and Evaluation of the Presbyterian Church, U.S., showed that within that denomination, when three factors are combined — the effect of inflation, the larger share kept by the local church, and the larger share sent to regional units (presbyteries) — the real income of national church agencies is *less than half* of what it was ten years ago. Further studies, however, revealed that the budgets of local congregations not only had kept up with inflation, but had steadily increased. The overall decrease in church giving is *entirely accounted for* by declining support for the new corporatized denominational mission organizations.[7] Continuing Presbyterian U.S. studies by the denomination's Office of Review and Evaluation, as reported to the 1978 and 1979 General Assemblies, show no change in the pattern. Despite recurring bureaucratic optimism, there is no evidence that the funding trends, now well established, are being reversed.

Results have been felt in radical reduction of program on the part of the denominational mission agencies. Says an analyst of contemporary Episcopalianism:

... more and more money stays in the parish. Less is available for diocesan or other extraparochial ministries — still less for national programs or overseas mission. Church institutions other than the parish can anticipate lean years, however effective they may be.[8]

The Presbyterian Church, U.S., now has, on all its national agencies, fewer than half as many staff employees as in the mid-sixties agencies. "National mission," for some denominations, has been reduced to little more than denominational maintenance functions.

But nowhere has the decline been more apparent than in the overseas mission enterprise. Nearly every mainline denomination has significantly reduced its number of overseas missionaries. The total in six major denominations dropped from 4,548 to 3,160 between 1958 and 1971.[9] There is evidence, however, that the funds once sent to national agencies to support denominational programs are going to overseas mission through other channels. In that same period, the number of missionaries sent out by independent (generally evangelical) groups has increased substantially. In a number of instances, missionaries dropped from the rolls of mainline denominations have simply shifted to independent sponsorship and continued to work in the same country. The total number of American missionaries in overseas areas has not dropped at all — in fact, it has increased. But the pattern appears to be shifting to one of non-denominational voluntarism.

Reasons for the radical decline in giving to denominational bureaucracies are certainly partly found in the regionalism trend. A far larger proportion of mission money is now being spent in local congregations and regional jurisdictions. But if the analysis in Part II of this book is correct, more basic reasons are to be found in the whole movement under examination — the corporatization of mission agencies, the managerial perspective that dominates these agencies, and their failure to understand, in their search for unified denominational mission, the voluntary nature of church organizations.

The Southern Baptists, a large denomination, can for two reasons maintain massive denominational mission activities without the kind of financial backlash experienced by other mainline churches. First, a remarkably high level of consensus exists, for a denomination with few controls or sanctions. There is generally a high level of strictness and internal discipline in the local congregation, but very little at other church levels. Nevertheless, the rapid growth of the denomination in a period when other mainline churches are declining has added members who share a similar theological and social perspective, and the system is held together by this consensus. Second, the mission activities are supported directly by congregations which back particular enterprises, with no attempt by a denominational structure to exercise central control over a congregation's allocation of funds. The Foreign Mission Board is supported directly by those who believe in and contribute to foreign missions. It is the classic Protestant pattern of a voluntary association, with denominational "sodality" organizations provided to carry out particular kinds of mission activity voluntarily supported.

If this analysis is correct, the now well-established trend in funding, however, is sure to continue. Three things seem clear:

1. In the society at large, the collision between the

corporatization of social structures and the revolution of rising entitlements will not soon be resolved. Voluntary organizations with corporatized mission structure are caught in the middle. Frustrated people cannot affect significantly what is done with their taxes, but they *can and will affect what is done with their financial contributions.*

2. The classic Christian pattern of voluntary mission activity, through relatively independent agencies, is a long-standing one, and one that has never been repudiated by much of Christendom. It has remained the basic pattern in the Roman Catholic Church, and in much of Protestantism, to the present. Only mainline Protestant denominations have fully corporatized their mission activities.

3. Corporatized mission structures present special problems for inclusive pluralistic churches. Such denominations tend to be held together by the legal principle rather than by shared commitment to particular activities. They may be forced toward a more thoroughgoing mission pluralism.

In light of these factors, it is probably not possible for church bureaucracies to continue to view their deteriorating financial situation as a temporary one, sure to be reversed as soon as economic conditions change, when "trust is restored," when the efficiency of their frequently restructured organizations has time to take effect, or when they can "get their message to the people." Nor, in pluralistic denominations, are consultations on the mission of the church, study groups, or more effective goal-setting processes likely to bring about the kind of shared commitment on which a single approach can be based.

Churches enjoy an enormous advantage over other voluntary organizations in that they are not *just* voluntary organizations. Through their transcendent dimension, they are beneficiaries of a huge reservoir of commitment *to the church* — not because of its agreed-upon goals, not because it is a well-run organization, not because it meets its members' needs, but because it *is* the church, divinely established, the body of Christ on earth.

Many Christians will continue to give simply to "the church" — whether or not they agree with denominational priorities — out of a generalized sense of loyalty and commitment to the transcendent Lord of the church. But in light of the overall budgetary decline, the heyday of corporatized denominational mission agencies seems clearly past.

The third indicator of serious trouble — perhaps the most serious of all in its implications — has to do with the professionalization which has accompanied the development of corporatized church organizations.

Arthur J. Moore, editor of *New World Outlook* published for United Methodists and United Presbyterians, raises the issue sharply:

It is interesting that critics like Ivan Illich who have analyzed the mythology of professionalism in such fields as education and medicine have not as yet done such an analysis on the church. . . . The decline in funds, the rising costs of operations, the point of view that what churches in other lands want is technical assistance which they cannot provide themselves — these and other developments support the need to professionalize operations. Nevertheless, the questions keep arising. Is this professionalizing one reason that church members feel less involved in mission today? In other countries, will we wake up some day to discover that as in the past we unwittingly exported imperialism, today we export a bureaucratic model of the church? This model is independent of theology and is practiced both by conservative evangelicals and followers of liberation theology. The longer it remains unexamined, the more powerful it becomes.[10]

One disturbing contemporary critique of professional managerial techniques may have much to say if applied to the church. John McKnight, Professor of Communication Studies and Urban Affairs at Northwestern University, has provided a thoughtful analysis of "Professionalized Service and Disabling Help" in American society.[11] He begins with the widely recognized fact that in advanced modern societies more people are engaged in providing services than in production of goods. Such nations, he says, now have service economies rather than industrial economies. They are peopled by service producers ("professionals") and service consumers ("clients"). The politics of such nations focuses on choices between various governmentally-provided services, only a limited number of which can be covered by strained budgets: medical care vs. educational services vs. military protection, etc.

Servicers meet needs. A growing service economy, coupled with growing numbers of service professionals who must earn a living, requires a growing number of needs in order to rationalize the system, says McKnight. So new needs are continually identified. Ivan Illich pointed to the proliferation of medical needs — and runaway costs — as have others.[12] Lyle Schaller, commenting on the sharp rise in litigation in the churches, finds one reason in the sharp increase in the number of lawyers. The number of law school graduates doubled between 1955 and 1969, he said, and will double again by 1980.[13] McKnight points to the promotion of a "Judicare" system, corresponding to Medicare, creating a need "to insure the rights of all people to legal services."

But troublesome questions arise. Are things really getting better as all the newly created needs are met? McKnight asks why we are putting so much resource into medicine while our health is not improving. Why are we putting so much resource into education and our children seem to learn less? Why are we putting so much more resource into criminal justice systems and the society seems less just and less secure? Why are we putting so much more resource into mental health systems and we seem to have more mental illness?

Some critics are suggesting that we may be getting just the opposite of what the servicing systems are designed to provide: *more* sickness from more medicine; *more* injustice and crime with more lawyers and police; *more* ignorance with more teachers and schools; *more* family collapse with more social workers. Ivan Illich makes this claim with regard to educational as well as medical systems.[14] "U.S. Aged Aid Plans Seen Hurting Clients," said a *Washington Post* headline, reporting testimony before a House Committee.[15] Such questioning is having a growing influence on political decisions. Says one commentator:

An ever-expanding body of research and literature (not to mention simple observations and experience) indicates that there is every reason to proceed with caution so far as Washington's domestic interventions are concerned. In housing, welfare, tax, health and job programs, candid officials will readily admit that many of Washington's initiatives have had unpredictable and unfortunate effects on precisely those citizens they were supposed to serve.[16]

McKnight's treatment gives special attention to management professionals, who, he says, are called on by other professional servicers to deal with the counterproductivity of their own servicing systems. The managers are expected to fix the systems.

Managers, as we have seen, must work with four elements in

servicing systems: budgets, personnel, organizational structure, and technology. By manipulating these elements, they seek to make servicing systems more effective. The most progressive managers, McKnight suggests, have used their skills to develop a fifth form of manipulation, marketing, which often translates into the manufacturing of new needs. People must be persuaded that they have needs (defined as deficiencies) which fit the available services. Professionals are thus providing society with *both the problems and the solutions.*

Professionals safeguard their right to define the need, and then to fill it, by "coding" both the problem and the solution into languages the ordinary citizen does not understand. Only the professionals, who do understand, can be regarded as "competent" either to identify the need or to provide the answer.

Professionals also define the outcome of the servicing process, in terms of their own satisfaction with the results. A school system, for instance, is not evaluated in terms of the learning of the children, but as to whether or not it meets the professional standards set by the professionals who run the system.

Professionals, in short, tell us we have problems we didn't know we had. They tell us what we "need" to solve them. They fill the needs. Then they tell us whether or not the "solution" has worked — according to their own professional standards. Sometimes it is impossible to be sure we are any better off than we would have been without the services (or with lesser services), and it may even be that we are worse off!

McKnight's analysis is overdrawn in some respects. At points it approaches satire. Yet in its main outline, it appears to have considerable validity, and to be supported by a number of other social critics.[17] He is not suggesting that the society should do away with professional services, which would be obviously impossible, or even that professional services should be reformed so as to remove the disabling effects. Rather, he suggests that disabling effects be recognized as intrinsic in a service economy. The solution is to select services which provide benefits that outweigh the disabling effect.

Application of the Model to Church Organizational Services

Direct consumer services — medical, dental, educational,

legal, governmental, mechanical or sartorial — may, and probably do, in part fill needs which they themselves created. There are clearly iatrogenic (medically created) diseases, and comparable ill effects from other services. Some mechanics disable the automobiles they are paid to repair. The fashion industry exists to create needs. Yet most consumer services also fill *real* needs, of which the client is aware, and from the filling of which he derives real and measurable satisfactions.

The need for organizational and managerial services, which tend to be one step removed from the consumer in that they provide services to other servicers, is not nearly so demonstrable, nor are the outcomes so measurable. It may be that these are more likely to provide unnecessary services with disabling results than direct consumer services.

Identification of Needs

A testing of McKnight's hypotheses in church systems provides an interesting exercise. McKnight suggests, for instance, that in many cases the *same* professionals are identifying the needs and providing the services that fill them. Is this the case with church organizational technologies? The need for MBO in a local parish generally surfaces only after the minister has attended a seminar or workshop in which he learned what MBO is and how to practice it. The need for "process observers" in meetings of church folk is nearly always pointed out by professionals convinced of the usefulness of such a device, and frequently by those qualified to fill the need.

In a regional jurisdiction of one Protestant denomination, a staff executive completed a Doctor of Ministry degree program in church organizational studies. Concurrently, he came to the conclusion that a group of local churches, all of which were experiencing difficulties, needed a new "organizational consultation" program to solve their problems. The program was developed and funded, and consultants were employed for each of the ailing congregations (which were pressured to participate "voluntarily" in the program through their dependence on the regional organization for financial solvency).

The point being made here is not that the minister's congregation did not need MBO, nor that the meetings did not need process observers, nor that the local churches did not need an organizational consultation program. The point is that the need was diagnosed by the same professionals who provided the answers, once the professional skills became available.

It is a well-known phenomenon in church circles that "mandates" from denominational governing bodies to mission agencies frequently originate in recommendations from those same agencies. They are defended before church conventions by experts from the same agencies and sometimes adopted as a result of political maneuvering in which the agencies were instrumental. The process is not secret; it is open, aboveboard, and well recognized. When the fact that agencies are carrying out "mandates" which they themselves originated is questioned, it is defended (by non-professionals and professionals alike) on the grounds that the agencies have the "experts" who are paid to know what the needs are and to bring them to the attention of the governing body.

The Office of Review and Evaluation of the Presbyterian Church, U.S., of which I am chairman, has a responsibility to present to each annual meeting of the General Assembly a "function review," through which various mission activities of the denomination are examined closely on a rotating basis to determine periodically whether they should be continued, discontinued or modified. It is a commendable process. Its origin, however, can be traced back to a study by that same Office of Review and Evaluation of funding trends in the denomination, which pointed out that there was not enough money to cover all the ongoing mission activities and that the denomination had a "need" for a process by which functions could be reviewed for possible discontinuation.

The point is not that the process is a bad one; I am convinced that it is a good one, and that it *is* urgently needed (although whether or not it will work has yet to be demonstrated). But like most organizational technologies in the church, the need was discovered, and the process designed, by the same professionals who provide the service.

The identical procedure is commonplace with outside consultant firms employed by church organizations to conduct "feasibility studies." The fund-raising firm employed to make a feasibility study of a capital funds drive will predictably bring a report that such a drive is feasible — under conditions which can best be met by employing the same firm to conduct the drive! Reflection on organizational technologies employed at every level of church life will reveal that this is almost always the case. The same professionals *identify the need* and then *fill the need*.

Processes and Outcomes

It is characteristic of church professionals with organizational expertise that they tend to be stronger on *process* than on *outcomes*. The technologies they promote *are* processes, and the Human Relations ideological climate out of which they come is one in which it is a compliment to be regarded as "process oriented" rather than "task oriented."

In business and industry, the management climate of an earlier period focused almost exclusively on getting the job done. Little attention was paid to the human costs involved. Against such a background, the emphasis of the human relations movement on people was a considerable gain. Out of their humanization values, human relations experts asserted that what happens to the people *is* important — that the process by which the job is done matters, and indeed, since people who are personally fulfilled are the most productive, that attention to the process (understood in human terms) can result in getting the job done more effectively.

Out of this context, organizational professionals are experts on process. Their battery of weapons includes processes for identifying the problems or clarifying the goals, and for designing the structures and procedures to deal with them. But then they tend to bow out. In theory, once the goal is established and the process for reaching it is designed, the outcome should take care of itself. Further intervention from the organizational professional should be unnecessary. In the business world, where profit is always the bottom line and there is no shortage of hard-nosed experts on outcomes, this is probably a safe assumption. But in church organizations, where the "bottom line" is much harder to identify, and where hard noses are not highly regarded, there has been a tendency to substitute process for outcome.

A team of organizational specialists within a denominational headquarters organization was horrified to discover that none of the denominational agencies had clear statements of goals and objectives. After three years of effort within the organization, employment of an external consultant to design a "common format" for use of all the agencies and development of a "management plan," the "deficiency" was corrected. Each organizational unit now has goal statements, and each year it develops statements of its objectives for the year. The collective product fills perhaps a hundred single-spaced pages of typescript.

Yet there is no real evidence that the *outcome* is very different. As far as the team of organizational professionals that initiated the whole business is concerned, its goal has been achieved, and its attention has been turned elsewhere. Common sense would point to some benefits, in terms of clarification for people inside the organization and availability of information to people outside. But the *process* of writing goals and objectives was what mattered to the professionals. For many overworked staffers the additional load of paperwork is simply an annual chore. No one knows whether or not better mission performance is an outcome, and there is even a possibility that it is worse since time devoted to the process could conceivably have taken away needed time from other endeavors.

Management by Objective, of course, focuses on the outcome. In the business world this may balance the tendency of human relations technologies to concentrate on process and ignore outcomes. But one would be hard pressed in most church circles to demonstrate that MBO brings an emphasis on results. "Are you using MBO?" is more likely to be the question than "Are you reaching your objectives?" And even when the emphasis is on the objectives themselves, the process can become a mechanical one. The call for "measurable objectives" in a sphere of life in which the most important outcomes are by nature immeasurable is likely to reduce ministry to the number of meetings held, pastoral calls made, workshops conducted or events sponsored. MBO itself becomes a *process,* the carrying out of which is more important to the professional than the outcome.

Evaluation

McKnight suggests also that *professionals control the assessment of the results of being serviced.* In school systems, for instance, "the client is evaluated in terms of his ability to satisfy the professional. The explicit outcome of the system is professional approval of behavior and performance." While this is more transparent in schools than in other systems, it is present elsewhere. What about organizational technologies in the church? How are outcomes evaluated?

The effectiveness of organizational technologies in bringing about organizational change is difficult to demonstrate. Behavioral scientists have engaged in a vast amount of research in the attempt to test such technologies under scientific conditions. There are any number of studies which demonstrate that persons who have participated in the various group experiences which make up the bulk of "OD" technologies perceive themselves to be changed following the experience. Such measured changes are generally in the direction of the values of the human relations movement; following the group experience persons feel themselves to be more open, freer to express themselves, more sensitive to others, more spontaneous, more open to further change.

Beyond these self-perceived changes on the part of participants in group experiences, results are more difficult to demonstrate. Studies designed to test the long-term persistence of such change have been more equivocal in their findings, although a number have found such change to persist. Studies to test changes in observed behavior, as distinct from self-perceived feelings, have also been somewhat indeterminate, although some behavioral change as observed by others has certainly been demonstrated. Hardest of all to demonstrate is sustained improvement in the organization itself, in terms of organizational outcomes (the "product" of the organization), as a result of whatever changes may have taken place in the persons who make up the organization. There are no clear data, for instance, to show that profit-making organizations which have employed OD technologies or even MBO make more profit than those which have not.

In church organizations, there is not agreement as to what the "product" of church organizational activity ought to be — number of converts, impact on society, number of missionaries sent overseas, social change, number of persons helped, "spiritual growth" or needs of members met. Furthermore there are no data to demonstrate "scientifically" that *any one* of these possible outcomes has been enhanced by the use of organizational technologies.

There is, however, widespread evaluation by the *professionals* engaged in using these technologies, in terms of their own professional assumptions. In 1977 one ecumenical agency (working in the field of higher education) conducted a formal evaluation of its effectiveness. This organization has a staff, members of which are provided by the participating denominations. It is supervised by a policy board, made up of representatives of those denominations. A Review and Evaluation team was formed, made up of members of the staff and policy board. The team engaged the services of a consultant, who had formerly served on the staff. Data were gathered from four "publics," the policy board, the staff, liaison staff persons representing the denominations in dealing with the ecumenical agency, and denominational executives having responsibility for work in higher education.

The findings, not surprisingly, confirmed the existing approach and style of the agency, faulting those policies and denominations (one denomination in particular) that were out of step. The report called for the assumption of liaison responsibilities by the agency itself rather than the several denominations, and for collective accountability by staff persons to each other. Such an internal evaluation by the persons concerned, focusing on the strengthening of the basic assumptions under which they work, can be a useful process. It is far preferable to the more common pattern of no evaluation of church organizations at all. It was carefully and thoughtfully done, and its conclusions will undoubtedly be helpful to the agency concerned. Yet it is, nevertheless, a striking example of an evaluation conducted *by* professionals, of their *own* professional services, in terms of their *own* professional standards and assumptions, which had the effect of passing judgment on *others* who are not supporting those professional standards and assumptions.

The process is repeated endlessly among those who apply organizational technologies in church circles. Work goals are set by professionals, according to their professional judgment as to how mission can best be carried out, and then measured in terms of their own estimate as to how well the goals were achieved.

The process consultant at a committee meeting evaluates the process in terms of his or her own professional definition of what constitutes "good" and "bad" process. In the Presbyterian Church, U.S. Office of Review and Evaluation, statistical surveys are used to learn for evaluative purposes the opinion of people in the pew regarding mission programs. But this has met with widespread suspicion and concern on the part of agency staff members. They charge that the general constituency does not have enough information or understanding to provide valid evaluative opinions. Such judgments, they say, should be the responsibility of those professionals who do have the information and understanding.

Opinion surveys are, of course, the stock in trade of the professional evaluation technologies which have become commonplace in church organizations. But evaluators probably do more surveying of the professionals themselves than of the church public. And even when opinions from the pew are sought, professional evaluators reserve the right to interpret the data, including the right to make judgments as to when "professional" data outweigh data from the consumers. The outcome of professional services in church organizations is quite generally judged by the same professionals who provide the services.

Solutions Which Produce New Problems

A final potentially disabling effect of the application of organizational technologies in churches is to be found in possible parallels to iatrogenic diseases in the medical field. A few years ago a Presbyterian congregation, faced with problems of divided authority, overlapping responsibility, and unhealthy rivalry between its governing Session, its budget-raising Deacons, and its title-holding Trustees, initiated an organizational study. As a result, it adopted the unicameral pattern which has become popular in Presbyterian congregations in recent years, combining all the functions in a single Session. After five years, however, an over-worked Session, seeing itself as spread too thin, dealt with the problem by establishing a new study group. The recommended solution was to divide the load — by electing a separate board of Deacons!

As mentioned earlier, I served from 1969 to 1972 as a member of a special Ad Interim Committee, appointed by the General Assembly of the Presbyterian Church, U.S., to restructure the denomination's boards and agencies. The organizational problems leading to restructure included five independent Boards, each making its own policy and presenting the church with competing claims; poor coordination between them; long-entrenched Board executives regarded as autocratically running their own "domains;" and diminishing budgets. The restructure solved the problems by adopting a "one mission" concept, creating one large Board, with several divisions, and establishing a "Management Team" made up of low profile division heads, to exercise collective executive authority. Three years after the adoption of the new structure, a new set of organizational problems came to be regarded as critical, The one Board was so large as to be unwieldly, and its meetings tended to become interminable debates over minutiae. The collective executive was paralyzed by the necessity of achieving unanimity from five division heads on decisions affecting each division. The low profile of division directors was perceived by the church as leaderlessness, and the collaborative style throughout the staff made it wellnigh impossible to pinpoint responsibility. Accordingly, the General Assembly charged its Office of Review and Evaluation (which by this time I headed) with responsibility for studying the organization and proposing changes. The report of the office was adopted in 1976, and the problems were "solved" by reducing the size of the Board; discarding the concept of collective Management and disbanding the Management Team; giving greater responsibility to the several divisions. Now (three years later), the new problems arising include a Board that is too small to provide enough people for each of the newly empowered divisions, a perceived tendency toward "divisionalism" at the expense of the "one mission" concept, and poor coordination between the divisions!

At each stage in this process, the church called on persons with professional training, experience, and skill in organizational technologies. At each stage, those to whom the responsibility was assigned engaged in extensive data-gathering, employed consultants, and called on a wide range of "experts." And at each stage, serious organizational problems were, indeed, dealt with. But *each set of solutions brought on a new set of problems.* Who is to say with any certainty that the denomination is any better off with its old problems solved and

147

its new problems before it, than it was with the old problems themselves?

It is important, in raising these questions about professionalized managerial services, that the baby not be thrown out with the bath water. Much has been accomplished by managers and professionals. No one would claim that the existence of iatrogenic diseases would justify getting rid of doctors. The fact that solutions to old problems often create new problems does not, in itself, mean that problems should not be solved. But because church professionals who employ organizational technologies often deal with other professionals providing services which may be several steps removed from the church members who are the ultimate clients, and who thus cannot make the kind of practical judgment that a patient does as to whether or not he is being helped by the doctor, caution is in order.

When professionals define the organizational needs of the churches, provide the answers to those needs, evaluate the results on the basis of their own professional standards — sometimes coding the whole process in professional jargon — and when their solutions tend to generate new problems which may or may not be less severe than the problems they have solved, the church is entitled to ask questions.

How Has the Church Fared in the Managerial Age?

What we have been pointing out in Part II of this book is no startling discovery. It is the fairly obvious conclusion that in the managerial age, the same changes have taken place in the church as in all other major social institutions. Churches have come to be seen as goal-seeking organizations, valued in terms of what they *do* rather than what they *are*. Organizational modes of thought, aimed at managing personnel and resources to reach goals, have been adopted. There has been little attention to the fact that churches are voluntary organizations of a unique kind, quite different from the organizations in which the managerial modes of thought were developed. Denomination agencies have become corporatized, developing their own bureaucracies and their own bureaucratic problems. They have become professionalized in the modern managerial sense of the word, depending on a host of "experts" in the vari

organizational and human technologies turning.

Much has been achieved in the process. It is managerial revolution would not have won so our society if it had not brought enormous shudders at the thought of modern technology — scientific, cybernetic or human — turned loose in without being "managed." Full credit must be given to achieved by the church in the managerial age. Many of taken so much for granted that it does not occur to question them. In a technological society, a call for the chu return to the horse and buggy age would be foolish unproductive. But the results are by no means unmixed. The are plenty of warnings, danger signs, and question marks.

What is required of the pastor engaged in theological reflection is a careful and down-to-earth examination of managerial principles and techniques, *in light of the church's own unique characteristics*. Out of such a process can come an affirmation of those techniques that are clearly appropriate to the church and give promise of usefulness, and rejection of those that do not meet these tests.

Much of what has been said in Part II applies primarily to denominations and regional church judicatories, where corporatization has been most apparent and bureaucrats reign supreme. But certainly every congregation and every pastor is affected by these bureaucracies. How to relate to them — which means how to bring them under control — is a major problem for congregations and pastors.

It is the use of management techniques and organizational insights *in the local congregation,* however, which has remains the central focus of this book. Understanding what happened to the whole church in the managerial age is important primarily as necessary background. We will be examining from a theological perspective organizational issues and management techniques as they throughout the church, but particularly in the local congregation.

148

PART III

THE HOLY SPIRIT AND MANAGEMENT TECHNIQUES: SOME PRACTICAL APPLICATIONS

CHAPTER EIGHT

THE HOLY SPIRIT AS THE WHEEL WITHIN THE WHEEL

Grace Church in Farmington, after Pastor Joe Johnson received his managerial training, decided to break out of the doldrums through goal-setting. A special team of congregational leaders was organized, and the entire membership (at least the group which attended a special church supper) was involved in the process. The whole thing was a splendid success. Down-to-earth, measurable goals were set. It was decided that over a one-year period the membership would be increased from a stagnant 280 to a thriving 325. Sunday School enrollment would grow from 193 to 250. A revitalized youth group would provide a constructive alternative for teenagers, who had begun to congregate in the High School parking lot to smoke marijuana on Sunday nights. And a new outreach group would begin a regular program of visiting and befriending prisoners in the nearby state correctional facility. Joe and the goal-setting committee were excited and enthusiastic.

At the end of the year, church membership had staggered forward to a total of 284. But Sunday School enrollment had dropped to 185 (the David family, with all eight children, had moved out of town). No suitable adult advisors for the youth group had ever been found. And the prison visitation had fizzled out after two visits, when no one showed up for the third.

What happened?

A quick evaluation and a "process intervention" to correct the mistakes next time would not be difficult. But a deeper problem has to do with the basic stance of the church as it employs management techniques and organizational methodologies. The problem is not one of whether the church should use management techniques or not. From a theological perspective questions have been raised about them all through the first two sections of this book. But the suggested answer has never been to throw them out. A theology of human responsibility to God *requires* Christians to act responsibly as God's agents, using the best available tools in God's service. It also requires Christians to live *in* the world, not to turn their backs on it. The managerial revolution in our society is an accomplished fact. Organization-mindedness is inherent in our culture. Corporatized organizations dominate the society. Bureaucracies are here to stay. Professionalism is not a passing fad.

Furthermore, the managerial revolution has brought identifiable gains. The values of corporatized organizations in efficiency, concentration of effort, and achievement of large goals are real. So are the values of bureaucratic organization. It brings rationality, justice, accountability into organizational life. If churches did not have some form of bureaucracy — which means rational organization — they would have to invent it. (As a matter of fact, they did: remember that the organization of the Roman Catholic church was one of Weber's models for his original description of bureaucracy.) Professionalization, also, was invented by the church. The values of modern professionalization — specialization, expertise, mastery of sophisticated and complex technologies — are unquestioned.

154

Management techniques are God-given tools, available for the church's use.

But far more basic are the God-given characteristics of the church itself — its unique nature as the people of God and its unique gift, the Holy Spirit. The fatal error for the church is to employ management techniques as if it were just another human organization in pursuit of human goals. The fatal error is to focus on oiling the organizational wheel, without attention to the wheel *within* the wheel which is the basic power source.

The task of the minister, confronting specific organizational issues and management techniques, is threefold:

1. To examine these issues and techniques *theologically* — that is, from the perspective of the church's "givens."

2. To use them *selectively* — that is, to employ those methods and approaches that are congruent with the church's "givens," and to reject those that reflect or promote assumptions which are at odds with those of the church.

3. To use them in conjunction with, and as subsidiary to, the *church's own unique gifts* — that is, to use them as servants of, rather than as substitutes for, the Holy Spirit.

These three principles establish the framework for Part III. We shall look in some detail at leadership issues, funding techniques, and evaluation procedures, and at a variety of specific techniques. Throughout, the basic assumption is that the wheel within the wheel — the active, moving Spirit of God within the church — is the key to organizational effectiveness.

Preliminary Limitations

There are some general limitations, more pragmatic than theological, which establish a preliminary part of the context within which management techniques should be used by the church:

1. In sheer quantity, the amount of Christian energy which has been expended in recent years in goal-setting, process design, process management, structural tinkering, program coordination, conflict management, evaluation, organizational maintenance, OD, MBO, PPBS — and meetings, meetings, meetings — may indicate that quantitative as well as theological discrimination is in order. Lyle Schaller has referred to the decade from 1965 through 1974 as "that period in American

155

church history when interest in several of the long-established 'mainline' denominations gradually shifted from evangelism, social action, and outreach to an unprecedented concern with overhauling the ecclesiastical machinery."[1] And Schaller had reference only to the structural tinkering aspect of this cluster of managerial concerns! The plaintive cry from the pew is heard with increasing frequency, "When are we going to stop concentrating on structure and process, and get on with the work of the church?"

There is danger in a simplistic call for "mission, not management," since mission cannot be carried out without some form of management, or without structure and organization. But it may well be time to ask, along with the theological questions as to appropriateness, practical questions regarding the sheer volume of the church's involvement in managerial/organizational concerns. Enough is enough!

2. Even more compelling are the questions regarding the payoff from the extensive involvement of churches in managerial/organizational techniques and concerns. As to whether the results justify the efforts and expenditures, the answer thus far is that we just do not know. A vast amount of research on the application of management and organizational techniques has come out of the academic and business world, with somewhat indeterminate results.

There are practically *no* research data on the results of the applications of these techniques in church organizations. One major exception is a study by two Duke University researchers of the widespread denominational restructuring that took place in the late sixties and early seventies. Although exception could be taken in some respects (particularly the anecdotal style and paucity of hard data), the study was an extensive one, and its conclusions about the restructuring movement were largely negative.[2]

A paper presented at the 1977 annual meeting of the Society for the Scientific Study of Religion and the Religious Research Association reported on research by Dr. Cary D. Habegger on organizational effectiveness in the church. It used a Survey of Organizations (a standardized questionnaire developed for measurement of organizational functioning in industry), applying it to a random sample of members of twelve Los Angeles area churches. The instrument, which is based on

Human Relations organizational assumptions, measures Leadership, Organizational Climate, Group Process, and Member Satisfaction. Dr. Habegger found modest positive correlation between these organizational factors and certain "measures of church effectiveness:" average annual percentage gain in church membership, average annual donation per church member, similarity of religious interests of clergy and members, "committed religion" and "consensual religion." Habegger noted in reporting his results that there has been very little empirical study of church organizational effectiveness.[3]

National church bureaucracies, where research studies are most likely to be carried on, have, as we have noted repeatedly, suffered massive losses of funding; and in the resulting financial pinch, research has been one of the first "non-essential" functions to go.

Even if extensive research had been carried on, however, it is doubtful if any conclusive answers would have been reached, for reasons we noted in the chapter on goals of church organizations and the nature of the "mission" of the church. By what criteria does one judge the success or failure of management techniques, or any other way of doing things, in the church? Increase in membership? By this criterion, whatever "techniques" have been used in the mainline denominations as a whole in the past decade must be judged a failure, since nearly all have been declining in membership. (The United Methodist and United Presbyterian Churches declined 10 percent in membership between 1967 and 1977; the Episcopal Church, 15%.) Many, of course, would not accept numbers as a criterion of measurement. Then what? Money contributed? Here, too, the data are negative, although even fewer would accept money as a criterion. Then what? Reception of God's grace? Love shown forth? Witness borne? Impact on the society? Spiritual vitality? How can any of these factors be measured?

The process of evaluation in churches, which will be examined later as one of the managerial techniques having potential for use in the church, is in the early stages of development. It is able to produce small-scale evaluations of particular forms of activity, on the basis of specified criteria. But more generic evaluations, which offer answers to the question being raised here regarding the overall effectiveness of managerial techniques, are difficult to produce. In general, one must say that research data on the use of these techniques in the church are not available.

There are many, both clergy and laity, who are convinced on the basis of their own experience that organizational and managerial technologies have been applied effectively in their own congregations or areas of responsibility. Many others feel, on the basis of theoretical knowledge or knowledge of applications in other fields, that they *should* bring good results in church organizations. But conclusive evidence one way or another, remains lacking.

3. A third practical caution with regard to the use of managerial techniques in the church grows out of the professionalization of American society. Professionals *need* to practice their professions because they need to earn a living. Beyond this, in most instances, they believe in what they are doing. They are genuinely and conscientiously convinced that the practice of the profession is good for their clients or the recipients of their services. We have seen how this leads to a situation in which the same experts define the need, provide the program or service that fills the need, and judge the results. We have seen how in some instances the services provided by well-intentioned professionals can be disabling rather than helpful. And we have seen instances in churches and church organizations of needs defined, answers designed, and results evaluated, all by the same professional experts.

In view of this phenomenon, caution is in order. There has been an enormous increase in the availability of managerial expertise. Not only are staffs of regional and national denominational organizations ready to consult with or design programs for local churches, but increasing numbers of pastors themselves have the requisite skills. Managerial and organizational needs — for reorganization, for elaborate process designs, for the application of particular technologies — should arise ideally from the membership at large, rather than from the professionals. When needs are discovered by the same managerial experts who propose the answers, such needs should be tested carefully with the congregation or the membership at large before a proposal is "bought."

Finally, and most important, the church, in dealing with its organizational problems, must be true to its own nature. While the church may, and indeed at times should, adopt managerial techniques growing out of the disciplines and assumptions of the behavioral sciences, the church has its own set of assumptions, reflecting its transcendent as well as its human dimensions. Its transcendent assumptions may be far more central to its organizational nature than are those based on observation of human organizations in general.

"Spiritual Management Techniques"

It may be useful to spell out in a preliminary way some specifics reflecting these assumptions. The church has a set of "techniques" of its own, based on its transcendent realities. They have organizational implications just as real as those imported from management and OD. The church needs to take a fresh look at the *managerial* and *organizational* uses of these "transcendent technologies" as it deals with its organizational problems and managerial needs.

To call some of the church's traditional and biblically-rooted practices "transcendent technologies" or "spiritual management techniques" may smack of banality. Yet translating them into organizational and managerial terminology serves to emphasize the fact that they have practical applications in dealing with the *same managerial problems* with which the OD, MBO, and PPBS technologies are designed to deal.

The human relations approach to Organizational Development is a way of changing organizations by changing the people in them (through the application of "OD technologies"). The principle of changing organizations through changing the people in them is a valid one. But the changing of people in church organizations through the "spiritual techniques" of prayer, worship and service, has a far longer history, and probably a far higher level of demonstrated effectiveness, than the OD technologies. There is fully as much organizational rationale for the assumption that people redeemed by God, utilizing spiritual techniques, can make the church work, as for the assumption that people "freed up" through human relations techniques can make any organization work.

Are the classical forms of relationship between God and Christians debased by treating them thus as "techniques," to be used in meeting particular organizational needs? The answer is probably yes, from one perspective. Any use of God's gifts for human purposes may be regarded as debasing them. But we are saved by a theology of human responsibility to God, by the knowledge that the gifts are intended for human purposes, and by the effort to bring human purposes — particularly human organizational purposes in the church — into accord with God's purposes.

Before my first class as a visiting instructor in a theological seminary, I was advised (somewhat apologetically) that this particular seminary had a requirement that each class session be opened with prayer — a holdover from earlier days. I must admit (somewhat apologetically!) that out of my own academic experience it would probably not have occurred to me to open each class with prayer. Yet such a requirement (not an option) makes sense. It is the organizational equivalent of the practice in the high school attended by my daughter, where all the students gather in home rooms daily to hear announcements from the principal. It is an institutionalization of a form of organizational communication.

Some denominational Canons, Books of Order and Discipline make official meetings of church governing bodies invalid unless opened with prayer. Empty formality? Not at all. To so regard it is to fail to take seriously the reality of God's presence and power in the organization. It constitutes a sound "managerial technology."

The point is that if the New Testament images have any meaning, if the sovereignty of God, the Lordship of Christ, and the empowering presence of the Holy Spirit are present realities within the human church, then they clearly have organizational implications. To isolate these characteristics of the church in a "spiritual" realm, separate from organizational realities, to confine them to the area of Sunday morning services and private devotions, is an unacceptable form of dualism. Their organizational use rests on assumptions regarding the "managerial" role of God. We have noted that in the Biblical images of the church, certain managerial functions with regard to the church as an organization are explicitly reserved for God. Under the embarrassingly prosaic rubric of "management techniques," then, let us look briefly at the organizational implications of some traditional practices within the church.

Prayer. In organizational terms, prayer may be regarded, in one of its aspects, as a form of communication between the organization and "Management." It has internal organizational applications as well. It is a form of empowerment, which may be brought to bear on any specific organizational problem. It is a technology which has a direct motivating effect on the persons employing it. To the extent that the organization's goals are determined by the will and the purposes of God, it provides a means of clarifying those goals. It provides a means of expressing the unity of the organization, of experiencing the reality of its corporateness, through the action of the Holy Spirit.

Confession and forgiveness. The experience of confession and forgiveness provides an organizational adaptation to the reality of sin, and the fallibility both of the persons who make up the organization and of the organization itself. It provides an "organizational technique" for correcting mistakes, both in relationships between organization and "Management," and in interpersonal relationships within the organization, where the confession/forgiveness model has clear and direct human applications.

Worship. In organizational terms, worship is a recognition of the authority relationship on which the organization is based. It is the formal channel for organizational guidance, through the corporate experience of the effect of the Holy Spirit on the organization. It is a source of continuing organizational renewal for the local church, and a way of maintaining organizational health. It is a primary way of developing, expressing and experiencing the unity of the organization in its achievement of its purposes and pursuit of its goals.

Use of Scripture. In organizational terms, the use of scripture, like prayer, may be experienced as a communication process, as God speaks to the church through the written word. It is a documentary source of organizational guidance, as well as an official record of early stages of the organization's development. Even without being interpreted legalistically, it provides a written source of the "legal authority," which in Weber's usage legitimates the exercise of leadership.

Sacraments. Sacraments, too, in organizational terms, may be regarded as a form of communication. They are organizational ceremonials with high symbolic significance for the members. They incorporate deep organizational meanings. They are a form of "participation" by members in the Lord of the church. They offer a corporate experience of the Holy Spirit, a binding together, and a source of organizational empowerment.

There are others. *Preaching* serves an extremely important internal communication and motivating function. The *vocational calling* of Christians plays a significant role in selection and legitimation of internal organizational leadership, which we shall examine in more detail in the next chapter. *Stewardship* provides a basic organizational function, to which a whole chapter will be devoted. The point is that these unique gifts to the church, derived from its transcendent dimension, are fully as applicable to the church's *organizational* needs and processes, as are those derived solely from the dynamics of its human dimension. To look at their organizational implications is not to debase them or the spiritual dimension of the church. It is, rather, to bring the organizational dimension into congruence with the spiritual dimension of the church.

On one occasion, before serving as consultant to a local congregation in a goal-setting process, I attended the Sunday morning worship service. When the goal-setting began on Monday evening, the context and environment were totally different. It was as if the two were unrelated. The goal-setters were asked to reflect on the difference. If the church believes that its basic goals are set by God, then goal-setting apart from worship may turn out to be a singularly unproductive experience. The wheel *within* the wheel is the church's organizational key.

Against the background of these preliminary considerations, we turn now to an examination of specific organizational issues and management techniques.

CHAPTER NINE

LEADERSHIP: THE MINISTER AS MANAGER

An organization without leaders must develop them or die. Leadership — or management — is an indispensable organizational function. It is probable that more research and study have been devoted to leadership styles, methods, and tools than to any other organizational technique.

For the church, the active presence of the Holy Spirit is the focus of organizational uniqueness. The role of the Holy Spirit is therefore the central issue as the church deals with leader/manager problems.

We have noted earlier that in the managerial age, *leaders* seem to have been replaced by *managers* throughout society. This phenomenon is not widely understood. The failure to distinguish between the leadership role and the managerial role has been a real stumbling block for attempts to deal with the problems of professional leadership in the contemporary church. And even the best scholars have been slow to make the distinction. James Gustafson, dealing with bureaucratization and specialization of function, dicussed the rapidly growing role of "executive secretary," which he saw in congregational and presbyterian systems as comparable (administratively) to that of bishop in episcopal systems.[1] It is a comparison much loved by executive secretaries, but seldom espoused by ministers of congregations! Paul M. Harrison, in identifying the "rational-pragmatic" authority of church agency executives as part of his study of church bureaucracy, sought to integrate this into Weber's categories of leadership authority.[2] Both saw church leadership and agency management as essentially the same.

We noted earlier that a clear distinction between mission agencies (which have certainly become corporatized but are *not* the church), and the church itself (made up of networks of local congregations and governmental structures) is helpful in understanding what has happened organizationally. A distinction between *leadership,* which is a function of the relationship between persons in authority and the voluntary organization as a whole, and *management,* which is based on technological qualification and goal-achievement skills, is equally helpful in the present context.

The question, in this technological age and professionalized society, is not whether pastors should accept or reject managerial *techniques.* The question is one of basic role model. Whether or not the local church is bureaucratically organized, and regardless of how much sophisticated technology it employs, a certain amount of managerial professionalization is inevitable. But "manager" as the dominant leadership image for the minister of a congregation requires careful examination.

Ministers as Managers

In raising questions about the management model for congregational leadership we are not addressing the traditional ministerial roles. The priestly/pastoral calling of all clergy, and the performance of such functions, are taken for granted. But beyond these unique professional services, the task of leadership of the voluntary members of the congregation, of enabling them to achieve their corporate purposes, is the point at which management science touches ministry.

Even in the field of management science itself, questions are being asked about the difference between management and leadership. Dr. Abraham Zaleznik, Professor of Social Psychology of Management at Harvard Business School, has raised these questions sharply. In an article in the *Harvard Business Review* entitled "Managers and Leaders: Are they Different?" he suggests that managers and leaders are indeed "very different kinds of people."[3] He outlines four areas of difference:

1. *Attitudes toward goals:* Managers, says Zaleznik, "tend to adopt impersonal, if not passive, attitudes towards goals." The goals of the organization are simply accepted. Leaders, on the other hand "are active instead of reactive, shaping ideas instead of responding to them." A leader's influence, he says, ought to *change* the way people think about what is desirable and possible within the organization.

2. *Conceptions of work.* "Managers tend to view work as an enabling process involving some combination of people and ideas interacting to establish strategies and make decisions," says Zaleznik. They help the process along by using their managerial skills. They negotiate and bargain, and they use rewards, punishments, and other forms of coercion, when necessary. Machiavelli wrote for managers, not leaders, says Zaleznik. Leaders work in the opposite direction. They develop fresh approaches to long-standing problems rather than limiting choices as managers do, he says. They project ideas into images that excite people. They create excitement in work.

3. *Relations with others.* "Managers relate to people according to the role they play in a sequence of events or in a decision-making *process,* while leaders, who are concerned with ideas, relate in more intuitive and empathetic ways," Zaleznik claims. A manager devotes attention to *how* things get done; a leader concentrates on *what* the events and decisions mean to participants. "One often hears subordinates characterize managers as inscrutable, detached and manipulative . . . In contrast, one often hears leaders referred to in adjectives rich in emotional content. Leaders attract strong feelings of identity and difference, or of love and hate."

4. *Sense of self.* Managers see themselves as conservers and regulators of an existing order, with which they identify and from which they gain rewards. Leaders, says Zaleznik, may work in organizations but they never belong to them. Their sense of who they are does not depend upon membership, or work roles. Their sense of self is not shaped by, but rather it helps to shape, the organization.[4]

Zaleznik's treatment of leadership is within the context of business organizations. He thinks in terms of the additional contribution an innovative leader makes to an organization, as over against the manager. His purpose is to encourage businesses to deliberately facilitate the development of leaders, rather than managers only, within their ranks. His analysis may have a far broader application in the managerial age, however, than to business organizations alone.

It is the third of Zaleznik's points, the relationship of the leader to the led, which looms largest in a generalized concept of leadership. The heart of leadership is relating to others. For the pastor of the church, this is clearly the key element.

Managerial and Leadership Models of Relating to People

The manager deals extensively with one group of people — those who are employed *within* the organization. "Personnel" make up one of the elements which may be "managed" in achieving goals. They form one of the manager's tools. This does not mean that they are treated inhumanely, or even impersonally. The whole "human relations" approach to management is intended to bring just the opposite effect. But organizations exist to achieve goals, and in the last analysis personnel remain one element to be manipulated in so doing.

Managers do their managing *in behalf of* someone else. They are experts, technicians, professionals, hired by someone else to achieve someone else's goals. Who that "someone else" is, is relatively unimportant. The manager relates to them — usually through a board of some sort — only to the extent necessary to achieve the goal. The emphasis is on the goals and their achievement. It is precisely because he or she is more expert and better qualified to achieve the goals than the "someone else" that the manager is employed. The less interference there is from owners, stockholders, members, or constituency, the more efficiently the management process operates.

varieties of gifts" from "the same Spirit" (I Cor. 12:4) and variations in such gifts are certainly expected. Generally, however, acquired skills in preaching, teaching, and pastoral ministries are expected to be complemented by spiritual gifts of prayer, discernment, and pastoral caring (love). The development of, or failure to develop, the gifts required to perform ministry, would be interpreted as a testing of the call. (4) The church, once again led by the Spirit, confirms the person's sense of call, and sets the called person apart to special work by endowment with a special status, ordination. Ministerial calling, therefore, is not just a personal experience. It is a formal recognition of the work of the Holy Spirit, not only in the individual but also in the community. The very word "ordain" conveys the original and still inherent meaning that the act is the work of God, not of human beings. Ordination is considered to be a permanent status, identified with the reality of the ministerial calling, unless revoked for cause by the community, or demitted on the initiative of the ordained person.

The doctrine of the ministerial call has always operated in the context of a church made up of sinful human beings, subject to error and failure. It has always been worked out through human agents and agencies. It has nevertheless, been the traditional theoretical — and spiritually experienced — frame of reference for the profession of religious ministry.

Contemporary Professionalization

The managerial revolution, as we have seen, has brought a technological society, and the corporatization of social institutions. It has been accompanied by professionalization of the clergy and the church. This contemporary kind of professionalization has had significant effects on both.

1. *Erosion of the sense of "special calling."* The increasing emphasis on ministry as a profession, in the midst of a professionalized society, has led to an erosion of the line between the ministry as a "special calling" and all other professions. The tendency has been to apply a generalized professional frame of reference, applicable to all professions. Similarity to and identification with other professions has been emphasized, rather than the difference. This has been expressed in a number of ways:

a. *Academic professionalization* has led to application of the same modes of thought to seminaries, the church's "professional graduate schools," as to all other such professional institutions. Seminary accreditation, which must eliminate theological consideration because of its interdenominational nature, has focused exclusively on academic and professional standards. The identity of professors is established academically rather than ministerially. Professional academic societies, such as the Association for the Scientific Study of Religion, and the Religious Research Association, derive their standards and procedures from the academic world rather than the religious world. They consider this necessary in order for the society to be "professionally respectable."

b. *Professional societies* within the clergy profession itself follow the model developed by secular professions. Prior to the modern era of professionalization of the clergy, there was no need felt for such associations. The church itself was the equivalent of a professional association for the clergy. This is still the case for the majority of the clergy, but not for ministerial specialists. For these, societies such as the Association for Clinical Pastoral Education, the American Association of Pastoral Counselors, the Military Chaplains Association, and others, are non-church related. They follow a professional rather than ministerial model. More recently, the Academy of Parish Clergy follows this model for non-specialized professional parish clergy.

c. Professionalization has led to an *increased emphasis on salaries, working conditions, and job-related benefits*. The professional perspective has gradually shifted from "responding to a divine initiative" toward "marketing a professional service." As this has happened, negotiation between the professional and the recipients of the professional has not only lost its earlier stigma, but has been valued and encouraged. Especially in the church bureaucracies, it has come to be regarded as a positive virtue to advertise a position publicly and receive applications from interested persons, rather than following the classic conventions of the "call." This attitude is increasingly applied to the filling of parish vacancies as well. Lists of available pastorates are circulated by central bureaucracies, and those

The greatest placement crisis, however, has been experienced in those churches which have traditionally depended on a fairly direct perception of the guidance of the Holy Spirit, in both the congregation seeking a pastor, and the minister seeking a place to perform ministry. The terminology used signifies the way the process is regarded. Both the offer of employment and the document embodying its conditions have been formally labeled a "call" in these denominations.

The oversupply of clergy is a critical problem in many denominations. The greatly increased number of women enrolled in theological seminaries has not been accompanied by a reduction in the number of men. Already there is a surplus of seminary graduates in some denominations. One study, looking at these factors, projects that in the Episcopal church, if current trends continue, there will be one priest for every lay member by the year 2004! Other mainline denominations are not far behind.

A relationship between ministerial professionalization and the oversupply of clergy would be difficult to demonstrate conclusively. The extent to which the perspective of religiously motivated persons is that of "choosing a profession" and acquiring the associated professional skills, rather than struggling, often reluctantly, with a sense of compelling call, may well be a factor, however. Another factor may be the academic professionalization of seminaries. To maintain professional academic standards in their faculties, to provide professionally acceptable libraries and facilities, and simply to operate in a society of highly corporatized institutions, seminaries *require* large enrollments. They must attract students. It is no longer possible to operate a "professionally respectable" institution with a few students, taught by a few skillful and experienced (but not academically credentialed) ministers as faculty. In keeping with this need for students, many seminaries no longer give special attention to the sense of calling or the spiritual gifts of students. With some justification from church polity, they consider the spiritual qualifications to be concerns of the ordaining body. They limit their own area of concern to the academic.

"Organizational Techniques" Unique to the Church

To point out all these aspects of professionalization and their effects on both the clergy and the churches is not to call for an end to professional standards, a lowering of academic requirements, a devaluation of professional skills, or a return to the "good old days" when the process was seen simplistically as simply receiving the call and preaching the gospel. It is, however, a call for renewed attention to the *validity of the church's own gifts* and to the transcendent dimension of the minister's professional qualifications. It is a call for a sense of proportion, for recognition and utilization of the special characteristics of the church which make it unique among human organizations.

Human relations skills, managerial skills, specialized degrees, clinical experiences, and the application of computer technology to the ministerial placement process are organizational techniques of the managerial age with a legitimate place in the church. But certain comparable practices growing out of the church's unique organizational characteristics have an equal claim to be labeled (perhaps crassly, but justifiably) "organizational techniques." They have an even greater claim to legitimacy, based on the test of time.

If the special relationship of the Holy Spirit to the church is taken seriously as an *organizational* reality, then the special *call* of the Holy Spirit, to those chosen for leadership in that organization needs no explanation or apology. The experiencing, and the utilization, of such a call can be regarded as a "management technique" entirely appropriate to an organization which recognizes and depends on the special managerial role of God, as Lord of the church. It is not to be regarded as a special sort of esoteric experience, permissible in its place but having no place in the down-to-earth area of professional standards. It *is* a professional standard, central to an organization with this sort of uniqueness.

With regard to the issue of power — a very real one for all organizations — the concept of power by the Holy Spirit is central to the church's view of itself as an organization. If this kind of power is taken seriously, then the endowment of a "called" clergy with special gifts of the Spirit, which must be combined with academic acquisition of special knowledge and skills for complete professional qualification, also becomes an "organizational technique" which the church employs out of its uniqueness.

The divine calling, as a mark of leadership and a source of

power, is not an individualistic experience. The Holy Spirit moves in a special way on the corporate church, in confirming and validating the call. Ordination, whether conferred by bishop, church court, or congregation, is a corporate working of the Spirit through the church. In the same way the "call" to minister in a particular congregation is simultaneously both individual and corporate. The special role of the Holy Spirit in the congregation employing a minister is also an "organizational technique," unique to the church as a special kind of organization, but real and potent if the doctrine of the church is taken seriously. It can be invoked and utilized through such other unique "organizational techniques" as prayer, worship and sacraments.

This does not, of course, imply that organizational techniques derived from the humanness of the church rather than its transcendent dimension — computerization, skilled personnel work, and appropriate organizational structures — do *not* have a rightful place. They do. But the church is not *only* a human organization. Authentic professionalism in the church must give to these unique organizational techniques their full and rightful place.

Church Bureaucrats: Managers in Denominational Organizations

It is in the denominational bureaucracies that the impact of management science has been most strongly felt since the advent of the managerial revolution. Are church bureaucrats the concern of local congregations and pastors? Decidedly so, since they are the agents of the church at large, which is made up of congregations and pastors. No one has a more direct stake in the bureaucracies.

Denominational agencies, both regional and national, provide a natural setting for the application of management techniques in church organizations. The mission agencies, particularly, exhibit nearly all the characteristics of other bureaucracies which employ managers. Identification of goals may be difficult, since they must come from the church at large. Pluralistic goals may be required. However, the mission agency (as distinct from the church) can undoubtedly be regarded as a goal-seeking organization. The four basic elements which orthodox managerial theory says managers of service organizations may manipulate in solving problems and reaching goals are all present. Budgets, personnel, organizational structures and technologies are all available to managers of mission agencies. Like most managers, they are responsible to an outside authority — the constituency of the church — usually represented by a board. They exist to achieve the goals of that outside authority, goals which are theoretically set by the church itself, through its official governing structures. Clearly, then, denominational mission bureaucracies are appropriate arenas for managerial theory and techniques.

The compatibility of theology of the church with the assumptions of management theory, however, remains a relevant concern. The effects of corporatization and professionalization, and the impact of the voluntary nature of the church, must be examined theologically, even in the bureaucracies. Thus church bureaucrats must look at the *appropriateness* of those techniques in the church. They must practice selectivity, utilize only those managerial techniques that are compatible with Christian assumptions, and give full weight to the special organizational techniques which grow out of the church's uniqueness.

Bureaucratic managers are employed professional experts. Special attention must therefore be given to forms of accountability which will ensure these managerial accommodations to the uniqueness of the church. Problems of accountability are often focused in the financial area. So large does the financial issue loom in the current church organizational picture that it calls for extensive treatment, and the next chapter will be devoted to examining the relationship between organizational funding and stewardship. Other aspects of the accountability issue, however, will be examined here.

Control of Bureaucrats by the Church at Large

Bureaucracy, of course — as we have seen in earlier chapters — can exist at every level of the church. There are local church managerial professionals and bureaucratic organizations, just as surely as at regional and denominational levels. Bureaucracy is least likely to become unresponsive and organizationally dangerous in the local church, since the control by the Christian community is direct and immediate. The values of rational organization, professionalism, and the use of managerial techniques, so long as all this takes place within the context of discriminate judgment and theological sensitivity, may be readily realized by leaders of congregations. Distortions and overextensions can be recognized and corrected by the involvement of the members.

It may be assumed also that regional denominational bureaucracies are more directly controlled by the Christian community than are those at the national level, since they are closer to the local churches and under more direct observation. It is an arguable proposition that the regional bureaucracies — staffs of state conventions, dioceses, annual conferences, and presbyteries — are the *center* of denominational action at the present time. There has been a massive power shift away from the national denominational bureaucracies. Since the regional trend in denominational mission became clear to perceptive observers in the early sixties, many of the most able and best trained managers in the service of the church have migrated to the regional staffs. They show little interest in invitations to join national bureaucracies. Budget increases in regional jurisdictions have in many cases matched the decline in support for national organizations. Regional staff increases have been matched by decreases at the national level.

Even though regional bureaucracies are in continuing contact with local churches, the control mechanism is somewhat limited by the fact that they are primarily in contact with *ministers*, rather than the people in the pew. Ministers, by and large, are more likely to support trends toward professionalization, bureaucratization, and corporatization in the church than the laity. Ministers are far more likely than the laity to participate in governing courts and councils, and thus to identify with "the establishment." Ministers typically attend all meetings of presbyteries, quarterly conferences, and diocesan conventions. Even in those denominations with strong lay participation in governmental structures, the average lay Christian is rarely a delegate (never if not a church officer), the average minister always.

Further, clergy are more aware of the total denominational system — the larger whole — than the laity. They move from congregation to congregation in the course of a ministerial career. They stay abreast of denominational policy and developments. They are part of seminary networks. Even in those denominations with congregational systems of government, the *larger denominational unit rather than the local church forms the real base of operations for the minister*. This fact is an essential element in the glue that holds connectional church systems together. The minister, therefore, often belongs to the "manager group" in church organizations. The minister, furthermore, is far more likely to have received training and participated in various managerial processes and techniques current in the church than is the lay person.

Some lay members do share with ministers the managerial viewpoint with regard to church activity. A few of the laity, because of a high level of church involvement, are frequent delegates to presbyteries and conventions. For this reason, and because active involvement is often combined with the "right" perspective, they are frequently selected by clergy-dominated groups to serve as lay representatives on regional or denominational committees and agencies. Once "initiated," these active lay leaders are likely to be called on for management-related services repeatedly. They become, in a volunteer sense, "church professionals." They continue, of course, to reflect a lay perspective which counterbalances that of the clergy. It should be said in fairness that in most instances they try earnestly to represent the views of the much larger lay group which relates exclusively to the local church and views the church almost entirely in local terms. But they frequently share with ministers the "managerial viewpoint."

In spite of these limitations, the continuing contact of the regional bureaucracies with local churches is a major plus in insuring their responsiveness to and control by the Christian community. And if responsiveness to the Christian community on the part of managers is viewed as a form of faithfulness to the essential nature of the church — as is the viewpoint of this book — then the regionalization of mission which has taken place in all the mainline denominations in the final third of the twentieth century may be interpreted as the work of the Holy Spirit.

Because of the limitations, though, regional bureaucracies need to be subject in some measure to the same deliberate controls, exercised by local congregations, which the national bureaucracies need even more urgently. Several aspects may be noted:

1. *The most essential element is recognition of the importance of control of bureaucracies by church members.* The Holy Spirit may, and undoubtedly does, move directly upon bureaucrats. But it is in the corporateness of the church that the leadership of the Spirit is most reliably experienced. Bureaucrats are the servants of the whole church.

It is characteristic of a professionalized society that recipients of professional services are trained to be "good clients." The cured, as they leave hospitals, are congratulated on being "good patients." "Good students" are those who cooperate with the system, not those who challenge educators. The acceptance of professional judgment in diagnosis of needs, in prescription of the best way of filling those needs, and in evaluation of the service rendered, is ingrained in our society. No less with professional managers than with any other professional, no less in churches than in any other organization, we are trained and conditioned to respect professional directions.

As a church bureaucrat I have been a frequent observer of Presbyterian General Assemblies. The commissioners to a General Assembly (equally divided between clergy and laity) are decision-makers chosen to be representative of the denomination. But it has been my observation that most lay members called upon in a Standing Committee to make a decision (regarding a Christian Education curriculum, for instance) find themselves in an unequal contest with professional expertise. They will discover initially that the proposal upon which they are acting probably *came from* the denomination's professional managers of its Christian Education program. In considering its merits, they will listen to anyone who asks to testify, but will naturally attach greatest weight to the *expert opinion* of the same professionals who made the proposal. In voting they will, in the absence of some overwhelming reason to the contrary, follow the *recommendation* of those same experts. Such is the weight of professional expertise in our society that some lay members, whose own experience with the same curriculum in the local church has been negative, will nevertheless follow the expert advice in voting affirmatively! "Who am I to disagree with these professionals? I must be wrong!"

The church is a voluntary organization. Whatever it does denominationally or regionally must reflect the convictions of those in whose name it is being done. Leaders may lead, but only to the extent that they are in touch with membership, and are able to bring the membership along in whatever new directions are being followed. This is true not only sociologically, but theologically, for the priesthood of all believers places the Christian relationship with God not in the hands of experts, but in the hands of all.

It is part of the uniqueness of the church, as an organization, that its strength and its wisdom lie *not in its experts, but in the action of the Holy Spirit on its corporate wholeness.* Because the presence of the Spirit and the corporateness of the church are directly experienced by church members primarily in the local congregation, it is through the collective wisdom of these local churches that the church at large must be directed.

The control of the denominational bureaucrats by the local churches and their representatives, then, is not only organizationally desirable, but theologically essential in the unique organization that is the church. Acceptance of this responsibility on the part of the membership at large, even in the face of all pressures to simply follow the professionals, is the first step.

2. *Control by the local churches operates primarily through the governmental structures of the church.* Bureaucrats work for agencies that are responsible to the governmental structures. As we have noted earlier, however, experiments in turning governmental structures into mission agencies, making legislative decisions on managerial matters regarding the work of the agencies, have not been notably successful. It is only in the broad policy arena, therefore, that local churches aware of their responsibility, exercise control through governmental structures.

3. *Financial support of denominational bureaucracies is inevitably related to the question of control,* and properly so in light of the doctrine of stewardship. Managers, in the nature of things, prefer that funding come without controls. Fidelity to the commands of Christ regarding responses to the claims of the gospel, however, required involvement of the givers in the work done with their gifts. We shall examine this aspect of the

relationship between membership and bureaucracy in some detail in the next chapter.

4. *In pluralistic denominations, consensus groups supporting particular forms of mission and witness have an important role to play* in exercising control over the bureaucracy. Whether these groups are homogeneous local congregations or broader groupings, whether organized sodality groups or informal coalitions, their direct concern and involvement with those particular aspects of mission to which they are deeply committed is a significant element in the relationship of membership to bureaucracy.

5. *A final factor has to do with career patterns for bureaucrats in the church.* Most of the classic forms of bureaucracy have provided for and encouraged career bureaucrats. Except for the Roman Catholic curia, churches rarely have done so. As we have noted, the parish clergy image has been so dominant among church professionals that even after a lifetime of staff service, clergy bureaucrats still prefer to think of themselves as ministers first, and bureaucrats second.

This is undoubtedly a healthy thing. The dominance of professional expertise, at the expense of corporate participation, would certainly be facilitated by a corps of professional church bureaucrats. *De facto* development of a small corps of managerial professionals (made up of those who stay on and on, shifting from job to job to avoid term limitations) may be unavoidable. Adherence to the basic clergy model, however, places limits on its dominance and permanence.

One of the most practical concrete steps that can be taken to limit dominance of career bureaucrats is the establishment of limited terms of service. This is particularly important for top managerial positions but preferable for all agency bureaucrats. Some loss in continuity and experience results from the imposition of term limits. The loss is outweighed, however, by the benefits of fresh ideas and a continuing inflow of people fresh from local church experience. Professionals who are occupying positions in the bureaucracy generally oppose such limitations, suggesting that term limits make it impossible to attract the "best people" to the positions. Experience of the churches, however, is otherwise. Certainly this is the case if *leadership* is to be combined with managerial functions in the bureaucracy. To expect that career bureaucrats can be leaders of the church is almost a contradiction in terms. Practically as well as theologically, it is necessary that the local church perspective be injected into the bureaucracy at frequent intervals.

★ ★ ★

Management techniques can be tools of the church — even tools of the Holy Spirit. But leadership, not management, is the greatest need of the church. As a voluntary organization, expressing its belief in voluntarism theologically in terms of the faith response to grace and the priesthood of all believers, the church at large does not readily take to "management." While management techniques may certainly be employed, the professional/managerial model ill fits the pastor of the local congregation. Professionalization of the clergy and of clergy systems in the church brings benefits, but also dangers. The uniqueness of the church — its transcendent dimension — provides the basis for an authentic professionalism.

Denominational bureaucracies are not the church, but are agencies controlled by it. As such, they adapt more readily to the management model than do local congregations. But even here, the uniqueness of the church must significantly affect management. It is the responsibility of local churches to establish the kind of accountability which will ensure the preservation of that uniqueness. Organizational funding is a key element in such accountability, and we will examine it in depth in the next chapter.

Chapter Ten

Stewardship: Responding to God's Call Versus Organizational Funding

Martin Marty, in an article on the way in which denominations are "surviving the 70's," summarized the contemporary fiscal crisis in the churches:

While per capita giving increases in most churches each year, the gains do not keep up with horrendous inflation. This factor leads hard-pressed congregations to keep funds close to home, and the bureaucratized church bodies have had to cut staffs and programs as a consequence. At the same time, people have chosen to favor regional and even more local expressions of faith. This choice has inspired them either casually to drag their feet or willfully to withstand some of the appeals from "headquarters." So denominations are curiously caught between the ideology and spirit of ecumenism and the practice and spirit of localism.[1]

Many social and environmental factors are undoubtedly at work in the funding crisis. The extent to which reliance on managerial techniques is also a factor would be difficult to estimate. Yet there is good reason to believe that it is one factor.

Church organizations, like all other organizations in this complex society, require funds to operate. But organizational funding, as seen from the managerial perspective, is radically different in concept from Christian stewardship, which has traditionally been the source of church money. The two appear to be on a collision course.

Stewardship

In Christian stewardship, the source of funds and the goals achieved by their use are integrally related. The basic Biblical image of the steward is the starting point. Possessions (including even abilities and skills) are entrusted to the steward by a master, and used in the master's behalf. As translated into the dynamics of Christian giving, stewardship is an expression of Christian commitment, a response to God's gift. "We love because he first loved us" (I John 4:19). The experience of God's gracious love, through Christ, in the Biblical paradigm, leads to an awareness that everything we have is God's gift, entrusted to us as stewards, and to a desire to respond to that grace.

The basic response to the experience of God's grace is a response of action, doing something, the giving of one's life in some measure. The gospels are full of accounts of people who *did something* in response to God's love experienced in an encounter with Christ. A tax collector left his job to become a disciple. A group of fishermen dropped their nets and responded to an invitation to become "fishers of men." On the other hand, a rich young lawyer, seeing that the gospel required a radical commitment, was unable to accept it. But those who were truly touched by the encounter responded, not only the apostles, but many others.

A poor widow gave everything she had, even though it was only two small coins. A healed blind man joined the crowd of followers. Mary Magdalene went home for a jar of expensive ointment, and washed Jesus' feet. Joanna and Susanna provided for the disciples out of their means. The healed Gerasene demoniac went out and proclaimed to everyone what

184

Jesus had done for him. Martha cooked and entertained, as many other unknown people must have done for the needs of Jesus and the disciples to be met. Zaccheus made restitution to everyone he had defrauded, and gave half of everything he had to the poor. Long before there were organizational goals, the church began with people who *responded to Christ's love by doing something*.

Some of the people performed physical acts. Others gave money for particular needs, or in other ways shared what they had. But there was no essential difference between the two kinds of response. Each person did something, direct and personal, in a specific concrete situation. The Christian doctrine of stewardship *has never been willing to divorce the stewardship of money from the stewardship of life*. Both are responses to God's love. Giving of money is simply an action response of a particular kind — one form of giving one's self, sometimes a substitute form of personal involvement.

Response is both an individual and a corporate act. The experience of God's love comes to the individual person, but always as part of a community. The special gift of the Holy Spirit, foreshadowed by Pentecost, was a gift to the church. Even in the context of community, however, God's love is experienced by individual persons. Response with an act of love, a service, a deed done, or a gift of money, is always a personal response, even though the act may be done in concert with others as part of a community.

Acts done together in pursuit of shared goals, however, are corporate responses. The giving of money to do things corporately that cannot be done individually or by direct action is uniquely a corporate form of response. But whether individual or corporate, stewardship is personal action response to a particular experience of God's grace, in a particular situation.

Organizational Funding

Organizational funding belongs to a different order of things. Management requires funds, but its processes are focused primarily on the *use* rather than the *source* of funds. Budget, as we have seen, is one of the elements which the manager may manipulate in providing a service, along with personnel, technology and organizational structure, and

185

material if needed. The budget, however, underlies all these elements except organizational structure. Personnel, technology and material, all translate ultimately into funds. In gross oversimplification then, it may be said that management of an organization takes funds and uses them to reach goals. The source of the funds is irrelevant to this basic managerial process.

This is not to say that getting the funds is unimportant to management. A considerable measure of management expertise may be, and usually is, devoted to insuring an adequate source of money. In business and industry, profit is the "bottom line" — the goal toward which management efforts are directed. Among private non-profit enterprises, the raising of funds is frequently a major goal of managerial efforts. College and University presidents, for instance, are sometimes chosen for their fund-raising abilities.

But even when acquiring funds is the goal, the basic managerial process is unchanged. The goal, and certain *operating funds* to be used in reaching the goal are givens. The managerial task is to convert the operating funds into budget, personnel, technology, and an organizational structure. These variables are manipulated as needed to reach the goal. Managerial *use* of the funds to achieve the organizational goal is divorced from the *source* of the funds, even when the raising of funds or making of profits *is* the goal.

When this management model is applied to church organizations, difficulties arise. To divorce the giving of funds from the act the funds are intended to produce, *to remove the giver from indirect participation in a known act through his or her gift, is to take the act of giving out of the category of Christian stewardship.* If organizational funding is to be Christian stewardship, a high level of giver participation in and identification with the goals is required. Only such identification can keep it in the category of an expression of Christian love in response to an experience of Christian love.

Corporatized Fund-raising

Corporatized fund-raising for non-profit organizations is a highly developed technology. With today's sophisticated methods and efficient management, almost any reasonable amount of money can be raised for almost any reasonable cause.

If Grace Church in Farmington should set out to erect a memorial plaque to St. Simeon Stylites in the middle of its sanctuary, the money could be raised. It could be raised despite the fact that Simeon Stylites had nothing to do with Grace Church despite the fact that ninety-nine percent of the members of Grace would not have the slightest idea who he was; and even if the other one percent knew that the only thing he did was to sit on top of a pole in the middle of a desert for thirty years! A memorial plaque to somebody in a church is a "good cause," and enough money could be raised for a marble plaque, with alabaster angels and solid gold lettering.

The money-raising activities of an agent of the Pallottine Fathers in Baltimore, given wide publicity by the news media early in 1978 when he was indicted for fraud, provide an illustration. Tens of millions of dollars were raised for "Christian work overseas," although less than 3% of the money was actually used for that purpose. The money came through a highly sophisticated fund-raising operation from people who had no real knowledge of what was being done with it.

The case is not unusual. Vast amounts of money are contributed by the public to questionable causes. The secret of organizational fund-raising is twofold. First, people will give small amounts to almost anything that sounds good, if they are asked. Enough people have a hard enough time saying "no" that they will give a little bit, even if they neither know nor care about the way the money is used. This was the Pallottine secret. Second, the appeal must touch the right motivations. These include not only the charitable impulse but the philanthropic tradition of Americans, peer pressure, social duty, status and prestige and income tax deductions in varying situations. Beyond small gifts from large numbers, an appeal to the appropriate motivations can bring in much larger amounts from carefully selected donors. Armed with these basic principles, public fund-raising is nothing more than a managerial problem: the utilization of technology, personnel, organization and budget to reach the established goal.

While the basic good will of the American people is a major element, not to be slighted, these are the principles upon which United Fund campaigns and the fund-raising activities of the corporatized voluntary organizations are based.

Giving in America, a massive study of American voluntary

giving conducted from 1973 to 1975 by the Commission on Private Philanthropy and Public Needs, noted that "for much of recorded history, the church served as the main motivator and institutional channel of philanthropy . . . The course of modern giving, however, can be seen largely as a process of secularization and institutionalization outside of organized religion."[2]

As religiously motivated giving has been replaced by corporatized fund-raising, overall giving has declined. Philanthropy has not kept pace with the growth of the economy, and, according to the Commission report, in constant, uninflated dollars, it has fallen off absolutely in recent years. From 1969 to 1974, it declined from 1.98 percent to 1.80 percent of the Gross National Product. Decline in religious giving in itself accounts for a sizeable percentage of the overall decline. Religious contributions slid from 49.4 percent of all giving in 1964 to 43.1 percent in 1974.[3]

There is reason to believe that these trends, which have accompanied the "managerial revolution," are an outgrowth of its organizational assumptions. Again quoting the Commission report: "Philanthropy has, for the most part, patterned itself after its corporate and governmental counterparts. It has become bureaucratic, safe, and more conservative and less willing to take risks than the relatively inflexible government to which it is so closely related."[4] Dr. Frances T. Farenthold, a member of the Commission and currently president of Wells College, commented that "the phenomenon of the United Way arose from the desire of corporate management to control the solicitation and disbursement of charitable funds" . . . and, she adds, the system of payroll deduction used in United Way campaigns "approached taxation in its mechanical and not always subtle, coercive technique of raising and allocating funds."[5]

Fitting Stewardship and Organizational Funding Together

A collision between organizational funding and Christian stewardship is least likely to be a problem with regard to the funding of the program of the local congregation, precisely because the local congregation is the environment in which most Christians experience God's grace. Stewardship of life, through active response and direct participation in ministries of teaching, witnessing and serving, will be a reality where persons experience the presence of the Spirit. And stewardship of money, enabling believers to do cooperatively things they are unable to do individually, will also be present as a corporate experience of the Spirit. Such congregations need not be concerned about the dangers of managerial techniques.

There are congregations, however, which engage in "corporatized fund-raising" rather than stewardship. And this is likely to be true in direct ratio to the level of professionalization, sophisticated technology requiring the services of experts, and managerially-imposed programmatic unity present — the level of "corporatization," in other words.

A triumph of fund-raising technology is a chapter on "New Approaches to Financial Life" in a book, almost totally devoid of theological or Biblical content, on *Vital Church Management*. The chapter begins with "nine basic qualities which characterize a successful every member canvass" — not one of which so much as mentions the concepts of Christian commitment, stewardship, or response. It is pure technology. Next there is a step-by-step outline, day by day, form letter by form letter — all the necessary techniques. It could be used with equal "success," and without changing a word, by the Society of Atheists.[6]

Such fund-raising in itself has nothing to do with stewardship. Those congregations that depend on skillfully managed Every Member Canvas drives, utilizing subtle forms of pressure to obtain relatively small pledges from large numbers of people, are to that extent engaged in corporatized fund-raising rather than stewardship. Extreme examples, however, are rare. Local congregations are generally saved from the extremes of professionalization by the fact that members of the congregation, who approve the budget, are at least minimally engaged in a corporate process of response to the Spirit.

But the saving grace of involvement is *not* always a factor in regional and denominational church budgets. It is a supportable hypothesis that one of the reasons denominational bureaucracies have fallen on such hard times financially is that they have settled for *fund-raising* rather than *stewardship*. The radical decline in contributions to mainline denominational mission agencies is, as we noted earlier, a well established trend. Staff reductions, declining budgets and continuing financial struggle are commonplace. The reason may be a "United Fund" approach to professionally organized, managerially unified, and bureaucratically implemented denominational mission program. Church members, mystified as to what is going on and suspicious of bureaucracies in general, may simply be giving small amounts to a presumably good cause carried out by agencies whose names they can't remember anyway because of frequent restructure!

Goal-seeking and Organizational Funding

Reliance on organizational funding rather than stewardship comes about when church organizations think of themselves primarily in terms of the goal-seeking model. In orthodox managerial thinking, the governing principles *proceed from the existence of organizational goals, rather than from the act of giving.* When goals are the starting point, and the reaching of those goals is the sole organizational purpose, the principles which govern organizational funding follow naturally:

1. Because the goals are the starting point, and management exists to achieve the goals, and because organizational funding is necessary to goal achievement, the emphasis is on *raising the money needed to achieve the goals.* This means that the source of the money is relatively unimportant (so long as it is not immoral, unethical, or out of keeping with the standards of a church organization). Money from foundations or governmental sources is sought along with money from church members. Funding is simply a means to an end, and the emphasis is on the end, namely, achieving whatever the established goals are.

2. Since allocation of funds to reach established goals is a managerial function, *the less outside interference there is in the way the funds are spent, the better.* Management, therefore, prefers a situation in which givers simply give money "to the church," trusting the managers to spend it wisely and in the best interests of the organizational goals. Member involvement in the way management spends the money would be at best discouraged and at worst regarded as "interference."

3. With organizational funding as the mode, management adopts a *"public relations" approach in its fund-raising relationships with the membership.* This means putting the best foot forward. It means emphasizing those things which the membership readily

supports, in order to "raise money" for a wide range of worthwhile organizational purposes. In a church organization, any level of deceit in such a public relations effort would be unacceptable to management, but a certain amount of manipulation of image does frequently enter into the public relations picture.

Nowhere is this more apparent than in the area of denominational overseas mission activities. It is generally conceded by most knowledgeable church people that the end of colonialism, the independence of third world nations and the establishment of independent national churches in Third World nations (as the product of earlier missionary work) has significantly changed the character of denominational overseas mission. In an earlier day missionaries went where they chose, to preach, evangelize and plant churches. Today they work in partnership with, and often under the direction of, indigenous national churches. Where once missionaries themselves were bearers of "mission," they are now simply agents in carrying out a mission directed by national churches. Once the emphasis was almost entirely on personal evangelism ("converting the heathen") and on works of compassion as a means to evangelism. Now the emphasis is likely to be on self-development of communities, social change, or the institutional needs of the young church.

But givers of money for overseas mission work are often responding to a sense of the imperative to share the blessings of the gospel with those who are now unreached. They are likely to be shaped by images formed in an earlier day. They respond more readily to a simplistic depiction of "the preaching of the gospel to unreached natives" than to the complexities of Christian witnessing through overseas community self-development and social change, or the institutional priorities of an overseas denomination. So management, without intentionally deceiving, selectively reports and depicts those aspects of overseas mission that are most likely to bring a monetary response. The result is that the public relations money-raising picture of overseas mission and the realities of what is going on in overseas mission may be quite different.

The result is not stewardship, but organizational fund-raising.

Stewardship as an Organizational Technique

If the church insists that stewardship be the basis of its organizational funding — the starting point and the theological perspective which sets the limits — a different set of principles emerges:

1. Because of the nature of stewardship as Christian response, *the act of giving has priority* over the act of mission carried out with the gift. The starting point is the experience of grace and response to it, rather than predetermined goals which are to be funded by the stewardship process. The distinction may be a subtle one, but it is all-important. If the organizational goals are the starting point, stewardship becomes nothing more than fund-raising — a means to an end.

2. The direct relationship between the Christian response — the act of giving — and the action that results from that Christian response — the act of mission — must be maintained. This means that the goals must be the *givers' goals*.

3. Because of the diversity inherent in Christian unity, because response to God's grace is the starting point, and because the goals must be the givers' goals, a broad range of responses and consequently a *broad range of goals* reflecting the pluralism of the church must be expected.

4. In reaching the goals, *full communication must be maintained with the givers,* who are the indirect "doers." Constituency involvement must be encouraged, rather than discouraged, even though it hampers the management process.

This means that the stewards — those who are responding to particular challenges and not the managers — determine mission. It does *not* mean, however, that challenges cannot be presented, planning and coordination cannot take place, or annual budgets cannot be used. The context of Christian response includes not only the *awareness of God's love* calling for expressions of human love, but also *awareness of needs* through which human love can be expressed. The perception by the Samaritan of the wounded man beside the road; the awareness of the need of Jesus and his disciples for food and shelter, the presence of the poor, the sick, the hungry, the unreached, are as much a part of the context of stewardship as is the experience of grace which motivates the Christian to respond. Good church managers will see that the needs and challenges are presented.

They remain, however, challenges which call forth response. The act of response remains the beginning of stewardship.

A funding program for the local church which takes seriously the doctrine of stewardship and implements the principles outlined above must have as its foundation the interrelationship of stewardship with other aspects of the life of the Christian community. Response to God's grace through commitment of life and money follows from an *experience* of God's grace. A community which facilitates that experience, through the preaching of the word and celebration of the sacraments, Christian fellowship and nurture, is the vital foundation. Since the purpose of this book is to examine organizational technologies, we will not elaborate further on these aspects of Christian community, other than to note the necessity of their presence.

Congregational Maintenance

The need to provide these basic aspects of Christian community in the local congregation, however, is the starting point. It is the context which, along with the experience of grace, calls forth response. *Provision* for ministry of word and sacrament, for Christian fellowship and nurture, is the first requirement for continued existence of the congregation. Direct action responses, which express the stewardship of life — participation in congregational leadership, teaching, contribution of time and talent in volunteer services of all kinds — are likely to be focused in this area. The core of the congregation's corporate response through the less direct activity of contributing funds is also focused here. Provision, in one form or another, for a building and its maintenance, a ministerial staff and its maintenance and materials for a program of Christian nurture, are central to maintenance of the congregation itself.

In most congregations, this is an area in which *full consensus of all the members* is most likely to be achieved. If not — if the congregation is unable to agree on provision of physical facilities, staff and materials for a program of congregational nurture — it is in serious trouble!

Congregational Outreach

The traditional two-track system of funding, which separated the "current expenses" for congregational maintenance from "benevolences" for congregational outreach, had a sound organizational basis. The maintenance of an institutional base is a necessary foundation for outreach. In addition, separate categories make it possible for a congregation to gauge its own spiritual health by measuring the level of its outreach alongside the level of its institutional maintenance.

Elimination of the traditional separation through the adoption of a "one mission" concept has increasingly been the trend in recent years. It has had a theological as well as a practical rationale. A church pays (from "current expenses") the salary of a pastor who, in the name of the congregation, engages in acts of evangelism and works of compassion locally. Both theologically and practically, this is no less a form of "outreach" than the payment of the salary of a missionary who engages in the same kinds of activity in Zaire. Similarly, the bringing of a child of church members into the fellowship of faith, through the congregation's own program of Christian nurture, is no less a form of outreach than a mission Sunday School in Appalachia. The measuring of a congregation's spiritual health in terms of outreach versus current expenses tends to assign an unwarranted second-class status to such important forms of service as Christian education.

It is probable though that the major reason for adoption of "one mission" unified budgets has been managerial rather than theological. Organizational principles have required it. The unfortunate result has been to *turn mission choices over to budget makers*. This has meant separation of the act of giving from the act of mission, separation of the responder to God's grace from the act of human grace the response initiates. It has been a move away from stewardship toward organizational funding. As imprecise and fallible as the line between a congregational nurture budget and a congregational outreach budget may be, it is still a useful line. The weight of theological concern must be in the direction of retaining stewardship as the mode of Christian giving.

The most important organizational reason for preserving the two categories grows out of the unity with diversity which is characteristic of the church. We noted above that the provision for the nurture and fellowship of the congregation itself is the area in which full consensus is most readily achieved.

Awareness of needs calling forth Christian response takes place readily within the congregation.

In outreach, however, diversity of response is more likely to be present. The range of needs and challenges beyond the immediate congregation is so great as to be almost infinite. Any group of Christians can respond only to a relatively small number of them. Each group must set its own priorities. But there is not always agreement as to what they are. Ever since New Testament times, "God has appointed in the church first apostles, second prophets, third teachers, then workers of miracles, then healers, helpers, speakers in various kinds of tongues" (I Cor. 12:25) — each feeling that the particular claim to which he or she is responding has priority.

a. *Consensus congregations.* We have noted earlier that even in pluralistic denominations, local congregations are often self-selected consensus groups. General agreement on particular outreach challenges that have strongest claim on the particular congregation is not difficult under such circumstances. A social-action oriented congregation will have broad backing for outreach activities which enable members to become directly involved, in actions as well as through their gifts, in influencing legislation and working for social change in areas of discrimination and injustice in their community. An evangelically-oriented congregation will have broad backing for planting new churches in the area and for local ministries stressing evangelism in prisons, college campuses and other institutions.

b. *Pluralistic congregations.* Not all congregations are self-selected consensus groups, however. Some consciously seek to maintain internal diversity and all, presumably, are open to any sincere Christian. Consensus congregations can become pluralistic through changing neighborhoods, or other environmental changes over a period of time. A realistic look at the nature of voluntary church organizations and the historic mission pluralism of the church — or, to put the same phenomena in theological terms, at the doctrines of the priesthood of all believers, and of stewardship as response to the believer's experience of God's love and perception of challenges — will lead such a congregation in the direction of a pluralistic outreach program.

Smaller consensus groups within the congregation can

provide for a range of direct responses in Christian action and also for promotion of a range of challenges calling for indirect responses in the giving of money. The congregational management — made up of the professional staff carrying out directions of the formal structures of congregational government — can consciously encourage such a range of mission consensus groups. Generally speaking, however, such groups will provide themselves in a congregation. All that is required of management is acceptance and coordination.

Acceptance of the legitimacy of mission pluralism is the necessary basis for a planned program of pluralistic mission responses. An all too common pattern in pluralistic congregations is one in which representatives of various mission perspectives ("factions") struggle within the session, vestry or board of stewards on a win-lose basis. In one such congregation I observed, each faction jockeyed for parliamentary victories in session meetings. The minister was allied with the social action faction, which was usually dominant. Eventually the church became a consensus congregation through the subtle "psychological excommunication" of the evangelical faction. Each departure was publicly deplored, and accompanied by earnest protestations that "we urge you to stay (and see things our way)!" But only one "way" was permitted.

Planned pluralism of congregational outreach is difficult to achieve, since it requires full acceptance of *different* responses that may even, at times, seem mutually contradictory. Yet it is illegitimate only from the modern organizational/managerial perspective. When unity *with diversity* is affirmed, it is entirely legitimate. It may be the only way a congregation consciously choosing pluralism as the truest expression of what it means to be a church can remain pluralistic.

A college president, active in denominational affairs and disturbed by the "politicizing" of the church represented by win-lose battles, has called for such conscious pluralism at every level. There are three alternatives for the local congregation, says Dr. James H. Daughdrill of Southwestern College at Memphis. One is for various congregations in a city to "specialize" (self-selecting consensus groups). A second is to choose the least common denominator, middle of the road, which offends no one but lacks vitality. He continues:

There is a third choice — to declare some areas of the church's work as Social Action/Ecumenical and others as Evangelical/Small Group. Then once a year, *and this is important,* get every church member, including those who may just want to audit, to declare a major!

At every level, the church could be enriched by using the energies of its various groups. This, in Daughdrill's words, would rechannel energies from old struggles to new outlets consistent with their differing needs, interest and Christian vocations."[7]

The consensus groups, which sometimes *are* local churches, which sometimes are found *within* local churches, which sometimes are wider groups within denominations or across denomination lines, are a key element in corporate mission activity. We have seen in an earlier chapter how these groups have formed and re-formed throughout church history. They have sometimes been officially encouraged by official church structures, sometimes discouraged, and sometimes coopted into the official structures. Except when the congregation or the denomination is a consensus group, attempts to direct them by managerial control of mission activity have not been successful.

James Gustafson has rightly seen that the complexity of the consensus-forming process within the churches is related to God's presence within the church. It grows out of the perception of consensus groups that, however flawed and limited their response may be, they *are* responding to God's grace.[8] He suggests that it is a function of leadership to give guidance to the consensus-forming process, and certainly Christians look to their leaders for proclamation, teaching and interpretation. But this leadership role is quite different from the managerial role.

Any managerial stance that starts with an assumption as to what direction mission or witness should take, and seeks to manipulate or bend consensus groups in that direction, will probably lead only to the formation of other consensus groups. In his fascinating treatment of the church as an organization (which is labeled "a theoretical argument"), Hugh F. Halverstadt points to a way to "manage consensus groups." His basic assumption is that the church *must* be corporatized and managed in order to have an influence on "the social business of corporatized America." He understands clearly the pluralistic and voluntary nature of the church and its difficulty in setting organization-wide goals. But he seeks to provide a way in which this can be done in spite of the difficulty. He calls (1) for Christians to organize themselves for institution-wide consensus building; (2) for conscious employment by Christians of organizational structures and processes to specify concrete institutional objectives; and (3) for "consensus management" to organize for a "social power base." He sees this achieved through caucusing and negotiating, through a process of forming coalitions and bargaining between coalitions. The application of this model requires the use of OD — a "long range effort in constructive problem-solving, team-building, conflict management, data-feedback, skill training, and change in organizational design."[9] Few have articulated so clearly a management perspective on how consensus groups within the church might be recognized, rather than ignored, in seeking to establish and achieve unified goals.

The lessons of history, however, as well as the theology of stewardship as response, make the achievement of such a grand design unlikely. It is the experience of the church thus far that consensus groups cannot be so managed. It may also be the conclusion of a theology of stewardship as personal response to God's grace that it should not be.

Support of Denominational Mission by the Local Congregation

Denominational nurture and mission programs, whether at the national level or the level of regional judicatories, can exist only with the financial support of local congregations, since *the congregation is the only place where stewardship takes place.* Denominational mission is the area in which the principles of "organizational funding," described at the beginning of this chapter, are most likely to have replaced the principles of stewardship.

In theory, denominational programs exist only as cooperative activities of Christians in local churches, who are expressing a corporateness larger than that experienced in the congregation. Denominational agencies are channels for forms of Christian response which cannot be carried out locally. Since stewardship only takes place in the local church, it follows that only local congregations can ensure that stewardship (rather than organizational funding) governs what takes place at denominational and regional judicatory levels.

Church bureaucrats at these denominational levels are of necessity managers. Even if chosen for specialized expertise in some particular field, such as Christian education or overseas mission, they are expected to be managers of programs in their professional specialties. They are goal-oriented because they are employed to achieve specific goals. They are removed from the level at which stewardship takes place, functioning in organizations which have become highly corporatized. They are chosen, more often than not, for their managerial expertise. Their role is to carry out programs in behalf of others.

This is in essence a managerial role. It should be assumed that such professionals will have a managerial perspective. Unified budgets subject to managerial controls, flexibility in managing those budgets, and as little outside interference as possible are, in the nature of things, their preference. Their reasons are not selfish; they can genuinely do a better job of management under such circumstances. When they testify, as experts, before church courts and conventions, they can be expected to give such opinions. If they did not, they would be remiss in their managerial duties.

Congregations should not expect managers to have the congregational stewardship perspective on budgets and funding. Maintenance at all church levels of this perspective *is the responsibility of the parish clergy and the pew.* If the funding principles based on an understanding of stewardship as response to God's grace are to be the basis of corporate responses at denominational levels, the responsibility of the local congregation is clear. This applies both to the consensus congregation and to the pluralistic congregation. It includes:

a. *Insistence on a direct relationship between the act of giving and the act of mission* which is funded by the giving. Giver involvement is much harder to provide in denominational mission programs than in those of the local church. But the sense of personal involvement can be achieved. It requires (1) awareness of the nature of the challenges being addressed; (2) full knowledge of the way in which programs are being implemented; and (3) familiarity with the results. This kind of relationship is more than mere communication. The believer, in the act of giving, participates as part of a corporate group in a particular action response to the claims of the gospel.

b. *Insistence on accountablility,* through the appropriate church government structures. This includes:

(1) Management accountability, as expressed in the use of funds in such a way that they become the kind of action response the corporate body of givers intended. It is also expressed in the following of policies determined by the responsible governing body.

(2) Theological accountability, which means faithfulness to the theological intention — the sense of vocation — of various corporate bodies of believers whose stewardship responses are being carried out. As we have noted earlier, the bureaucracy is not the place for theological prophets who wish to lead the church in pioneering directions. Managers manage in behalf of someone else; they achieve someone else's goals. The prophetic role on the other hand is part of the leadership role, one of persuasion, of leading corporate groups in pioneering directions. Program managers who are theologically accountable only to their own Biblical interpretations or visions of what mission ought to be, rather than to the corporate groups they represent, are not prophets. They are manipulators.

(3) Stewardship accountability, which involves a consciously pluralistic approach to mission in pluralistic denominations, in order to provide for and to carry out the full range of responses to the gospel. Only local congregations, where stewardship takes place, can insist through the governing structures on this kind of accountability. Managers in the bureaucracy, to a far greater extent than leaders in local congregations where the pluralism of stewardship responses is actually present, are nearly always inclined on principle to seek unity of mission.

There is an idea abroad that for "the pew" to seek to influence bureaucrats in the way mission is carried out with funds contributed from the pew shows "lack of trust." The solution sometimes proposed by OD consultants is to "build trust." Countless hours and dollars have been wasted in designing "trust-building strategies" and conducting "trust-building exercises" in the belief that once "trust is restored" people in the pew will turn their backs and permit the experts to manage mission without interference.

Such a solution reflects corporate funding assumptions

rather than stewardship assumptions. It fails to recognize that the giving of money is a form of personal commitment, an action response to an experience of grace. If stewardship is the church's "fund raising technique," it is not only the right but the duty of congregations to require stewardship accountability from denominational managers. To insist on such accountability is not lack of trust. It is theological fidelity.

Insistence by local congregations on all these forms of accountability on the part of regional and national level church bureaucracies takes place through the regular structures of church government, which in all Protestant denominations involve some kind of representative body. It also takes place through the specific kinds of stewardship responses to which the congregation contributes.

Selective support of those forms of corporate nurture and outreach to which the givers feel challenged to respond, and in which they feel involved, is not often favored by the program managers in the bureaucracy. They are committed to a unified budget and a one mission concept, and they are likely to regard such selective support as "witholding of funds" from the unified budget. But the basic difference, once again, is between the managerial viewpoint and the stewardship viewpoint.

A generalized stewardship response, which gives to the church itself rather than to particular kinds of Christian action, is certainly not only possible but commonplace. But the more generalized it becomes, the further stewardship of money is separated from stewardship of life and the closer it comes to "organizational funding." Specific responses, far from being a "withholding of funds," are the most direct form of stewardship.

Denominational Funding Models

In seeking managerial accountability from the denominational bureaucracies, pastors and concerned laity at the congregational level, where stewardship takes place, can encourage the adoption of denominational funding models which incorporate the principles discussed above. In a pluralistic denomination, any such model would have two aspects. It would provide support from the entire denomination for those basic functions having broad consensual support from the entire membership (corresponding to the maintenance of basic ministry functions at the congregational level). And in faithfulness to the doctrine of stewardship as action response, it would provide for flexibility and diversity in those corporate outreach functions on which there are differences of opinion.

(1) One possibility would be *a two-track voluntary giving model.* Such a model would provide for one track of voluntary giving to a unified denominational program budget. This unified budget would support all generally agreed-on nurture programs and maintenance services in full. It might also support, at a basic level, outreach functions representing a full range of mission responses regarded as valid by the denomination's governing body. A second track would permit Christians to "choose a major" in stewardship. It would provide for voluntary selective giving by congregations or sodality groups. Such funds would go directly to particular forms of mission they feel called to support, thus providing a sense of participation. All such second-track giving would be *in addition* to the basic budget support provided for *each* outreach function by first-track gifts.

Such a model, which is not greatly different from the pattern used by some denominations today, recognizes the validity of the unified budget and corporatized approach to mission through the first track. There is a large consensus group within mainline denominations which supports a corporatized approach to mission. This consensus group represents "public Christianity" primarily, but includes an increasing number of "private Christians" as well.

It affirms corporatized mission in the belief that only a unified denominational witness, often in cooperation with the unified witness of other denominations as well, can significantly affect society. *The key to the success of such a corporatized track is the removal of the perception that the denomination's corporatized mission program is the captive of any single party or group in the church.*

The model can only work if managers do not engage in a budgetary "shell game." The "shell game" budget compensates for additional voluntary giving to a particular form of mission by withdrawing undesignated funds from that cause and giving them to another which has less voluntary support. This kind of "equalization" has a great deal of *managerial* justification if the assumption is that decisions regarding the level of budgetary support for various forms of mission should be made by the experts (or by "the church" in the form of approval of budgets prepared by experts). It does not, however, have a *stewardship* justification, if stewardship is understood as action response. It is perceived by those with this perspective as an attempt to frustrate their stewardship.

The key is a conscious pluralism in the basic program. This model accepts and even encourages consensus groups or sodalities dedicated to the promotion of particular forms of outreach commanding a high level of believer commitment. With its second track, it guarantees the channeling of supplementary funds to the causes for which intended.

(2) Another possibility is *an assessment plus voluntary giving model.* Many denominations provide for some kind of tax, or assessment, often on a per capita basis, to cover basic costs of denominational maintenance. In my own Presbyterian Church, U.S., a General Assembly per capita apportionment, separate from benevolence or mission contributions, covers costs of the annual meetings of General Assemblies, offices and operations of its elected officers, and certain other minor functions included in an "Office of General Assembly."

The kind of model proposed here would substantially increase the number of basic regional and denominational maintenance functions so supported — including such things as denominational Christian education and youth programs, resources in such fields as evangelism and church development, and provision of various support services. All *outreach* programs, however, would be supported entirely from direct giving to particular functions. Supporters of each such form of mission outreach would become *de facto* denominational sodality groups.

This model would make support of basic denominational maintenance and nurture functions the responsibility of all members, inherent in membership itself. But outreach activities carried on at the denominational level would operate entirely as the corporate response of those who feel themselves called to participate. It would thus reflect fully the stewardship of life and money as expressed in the local church.

Practical difficulties of some magnitude would be encountered in making decisions as to which functions would come under the category of denominational maintenance, to be supported by assessment, and which would be regarded as mission outreach, to be supported entirely by voluntary giving. The lines between maintenance and mission are never clearcut. Politicized denominations could anticipate maneuvering by various interest groups to be included in one category or the other. It would be essential that those functions included in the maintenance category have broad consensual support from the entire denominational constituency. Yet combination models with both assessment and voluntary giving have worked reasonably well in some church systems, and with clear definitions of maintenance and outreach as a starting point, it is probable that an expanded use of the assessment model offers real possibilities.

* * *

Both of the models proposed above for denominational agency funding assume that the corporatized unified budget, which has been utilized by many of the mainline denominations in the era of corporatized mission, has failed. That failure stems from the fact that corporatized unified budgets have been based on managerial, rather than stewardship assumptions.

Nowhere has the dissonance between management and theology had more critical effects than in the area of funding. As useful as they are, *goals* cannot provide the starting point for the funding of Christian mission. The starting point is the *response* of the Christian to the experience of grace. Stewardship must be the "management technique" on which the organizational funding of the Christian church is based.

Chapter Eleven

Evaluation: Is God Well Served by What We Are Doing?

"That was a fine sermon this morning, Pastor."

"The Sunday School is simply not meeting the needs of the Junior Highs."

"Something is wrong with our Community Help Center. Nobody is using it."

"Johnny loves the Youth Fellowship. The Robertsons are doing a great job as adult advisors."

All these statements are evaluations. Evaluation in the church is certainly nothing new. It simply means making judgments, positive or negative, about particular persons or activities. It is inherent in human relationships and enterprises. People have engaged in evaluation, and acted on their conclusions, as long as there have been people. But they have done so in a highly personal, haphazard, hit-and-miss way. One of the most useful organizational technologies brought into the church from the managerial world is *planned* evaluation. It makes the process as fair and rational as possible by making it a formal and impersonal, rather than informal and highly personal, process.

The use of evaluation in the church, however, is somewhat different from its use in business management, and this difference has not always been clearly understood. Theologically, the evaluation process may be seen as a form of accountability to the church's true nature. The church lives in organizational tension between its humanness — the characteristics it holds in common with all other organizations — and its uniqueness, derived from its transcendent dimension and experienced in the presence of the Holy Spirit. The purpose of evaluation in a church organization is to ensure the accountability of its humanness to its uniqueness.

Accountability to the Holy Spirit is not a concept easily translated into a management technique! On one occasion, shortly after I assumed my present denominational responsibilities, I received an invitation from a pastor friend to speak at a congregational supper. The letter described the program planned, and then spoke of the speech: "We want to add a spiritual note to what will otherwise be a pretty relaxed evening. Perhaps you can tell us about your work in the Office of Review and Evaluation." It was an awe-inspiring thought — the idea that a description of the process of evaluation could add a "spiritual note" to anything! But at a deeper level it reflected what ought to be a theological truth. We have repeatedly described the uniqueness of the church in terms of the presence and activity of the Holy Spirit. And we have suggested repeatedly that the presence of the Holy Spirit is a *corporate* experience of the church in this sense. For most Christians, the experience takes place in the local congregation, the "natural habitat of the Spirit." If this is true, then accountability of the church to the Holy Spirit takes the form of accountability of organization to the membership, of bureaucracy to the pew. Such a position reflects faith that despite temporary aberrations, over the long haul the Holy Spirit will move and God's will be done through the corporate whole.

The necessity of this kind of accountability is understood in terms of another theological insight, having to do with human sin. One prominent theologian, serving as a consultant to the Office of Review and Evaluation of the Presbyterian Church, U.S. in a project aimed at developing theological criteria for evaluation, made a cogent comment. He noted that the office was one of the few aspects of the denomination's national agency restructure reflecting a theological rather than a purely organizational principle. He cited in the list of "Organizational Principles" underlying the originally proposed structure, the call for "an office of review and evaluation, independent of the rest of the structure, responsible to the General Assembly." He labeled this an organizational expression of the doctrine of sin. The sense of sin, he suggested, has classically been expressed in human structures in the form of checks and balances, or separation of powers. The American founding fathers, he said, understood the reality of sin clearly, and cited it explicitly, in providing for three co-equal branches of government as checks on each other. He pointed to the failure to take the doctrine of sin seriously as a major problem with management science in church organizations, and to the existence of such an office as a theological necessity.[1]

Evaluation, like MBO and other organizational technologies, has reached fad status in contemporary organizations. It is often undertaken as a matter of standard organizational practice, without any clear concept of why it is being done or any significant use of its results. Particularly is this true with regard to evaluation of meetings, conferences, consultations, seminars and workshops of various kinds. The distribution of an evaluation instrument to be filled out by the participants at the end of the event is routine managerial practice. All too often, however, the results are simply filed. When a series of regularly scheduled meetings is undertaken, the first two or three evaluation instruments may be carefully studied and used in refining the process. But once it becomes routine, the use of such evaluation instruments tends to be continued as a matter of course, with little or no attention given to outcomes. In an era of ubiquitous conferences and workshops, the hours spent filling out forms, the reams of paper used, and the space occupied in filing cabinets, must stagger the imagination of God, who alone knows the quantities involved!

Other kinds of evaluation also are sometimes done on a *pro forma* basis, simply because evaluation is an accepted part of managerial technology. Performance evaluations of people in church organizations, for instance, are likely to be highly superficial and laudatory. Church people have difficulty in dealing with their professionals in other than a laudatory way. (The most common exception is a situation in which an informal and *sub rosa* decision has already been made that the person concerned should leave the organization, and the evaluation then becomes a mechanism providing a formal basis for termination!)

Contemporary churches tend to be overloaded with a plethora of managerial activity and organizational wheel-spinning. Vast amounts of money and energy are spent on administrative and bureaucratic maintenance functions. Any formal evaluation process which does not have a clearly defined purpose, or the results of which will not be used in a clearly understood and purposeful way, should be immediately scrapped. But evaluation which is carefully planned and faithfully used has much to contribute to the church, theologically as well as practically.

Profit and Nonprofit Evaluative Models

Churches use two different evaluative models — and not always with awareness of the difference between the two. One comes from the business world. Business management tends to see evaluation as integral to the process of making management decisions. It is part of a continuing "closed loop" (circular) process that includes planning, programming, implementation, evaluation of results, leading to revised planning, further implementation, more evaluation, etc. As such, evaluation is a management tool, used in pursuit of organizational goals.

The second model comes from non-profit organizations, and particularly government. In this model, the evaluation process is independent of operational management, and it serves a "watchdog" purpose. Classic examples have been the Inspector General function in military organizations, and the General Accounting Office (GAO), which is a creature of Congress, providing purse string evaluation of executive agencies. The bureaucratization of society in our times has brought a proliferation of social programs, often vast in scale. While sometimes carried out by private non-profit agencies, they are primarily governmental programs. They are concentrated in the health, education, and social welfare fields, and are aimed in various ways at human betterment. Whether public or private, they share common features, one of which is the separation of operational management from the source of funding. The program itself is carried out by employed professionals — managers and specialists — and the funding comes from outside the agency (often from government grants, even in the case of private agencies).

Money-providers need to know if the funds are well-spent and the programs are effective. Program evaluation of social welfare programs has therefore been a burgeoning field. In contrast to most aspects of contemporary management theory and technology, much of current research and development of evaluation techniques has come from the non-profit sector. The major books, journals and research reports focus on evaluation of health, education, and social welfare programs rather than on business.[2]

Denominational bureaucracies have adopted both models. Those denominations that have taken over the business model have placed their evaluative offices in the mission agencies, where they are responsible to program executives. This model has tended to combine evaluation with research, which is also a tool of managers.

But even though it is preferred by agency managers, the business model has not proved particularly useful in church bureaucracies. It tends to concentrate on workability and results. Such evaluation, which shows why a particular enterprise does or does not make a profit, is an extremely important decision-making tool for managers in a profit-oriented business. But mission programs, as we have seen, tend to be carried out for ideological rather than pragmatic reasons. Churches engage in certain activities "because it is right," rather than "because it works"; because it is part of God's purposes, rather than because it brings results. In denominational bureaucracies which have adopted this model, evaluation offices have not been given a high priority by management. Perhaps for this reason they have often been ineffective. In fiscal crises they have suffered severely.

The independent evaluative model has been adopted by other denominations. These include the United Methodist Church (through its General Council of Ministries), the American Lutheran Church (which has a Standing Committee on Program Review, with employed staff), and the Presbyterian Church, U.S. In these instances the evaluative agencies are unrelated to the program agencies whose work is evaluated. They report directly to denominational governing bodies. The Presbyterian Church, U.S. Office of Review and Evaluation prepares annually a comprehensive "Program Audit" for the denomination's General Assembly.

Independent evaluation agencies had prominent roles in the contemporary crisis of corporatized denominational organizations. It has been an era of high frustration with mission agencies, and their perceived unresponsiveness to constituencies. But it is also an era characterized by a very high level of dependence on professionals. The evaluative agencies have provided the only professionals offering independent analysis and a counterbalancing voice to that of the program professionals. The level of dependence on the evaluators has probably, therefore, been much greater than it would have been in a less crisis-prone period. They have provided an extremely useful mechanism to assist denominations in dealing with their crises.

Only in a reasonably large bureaucratic organization is such a separate office of professional evaluators a possibility. However, assignment of an independent evaluative function to a committee of nonprofessionals representing the church at large is an approach well adapted to the nature of church organizations. It has been usefully applied in regional jurisdictions, and is especially applicable at the local church level.

The two models — the business model which makes evaluation a tool of management, and the independent agency model — serve different purposes. They correspond roughly to the two types of evaluation known by professionals as "formative" and "summative." Formative evaluation takes place while the activity being evaluated is still going on. It is intended to influence the process by determining in midstream what is working and what is not, and intervening with recommended changes. Summative evaluation in its purest form determines how effective something has been after it is completed. While not necessarily confined to programs that are already completed, it is more distant from actual operations than formative evaluation. Its major effect is on *future* plans and policies rather than current operations.

Church evaluative units that follow the business model, under the direction of operational management, are likely to engage primarily in formative evaluation. Those that follow the independent model, reporting to the church governing body or policy makers rather than the managers, are likely to engage primarily in summative evaluation.[3]

Types of Evaluation

There are three distinct kinds of evaluation, each with its own techniques and uses. One type is *process evaluation*, which is most commonly applied in connection with particular meetings, conferences, or workshops, but also at times with longer term projects. It focuses primarily on whether the process used is effective in bringing about the desired result. A second type is *program evaluation*, which deals primarily with outcomes of particular programs rather than processes used. The third type, *personnel evaluation*, focuses on the performance of the people involved in organizations and programs. Each kind has its own problems and techniques.

Process Evaluation

It has become commonplace in bureaucracies and informed organizational circles to employ or appoint a "process observer" or "process consultant" for meetings, for particular projects involving a series of meetings, and for other organizational activities. Whether a paid professional or an unpaid member of the group, the observer is expected to have some measure of expert knowledge of processes used to reach objectives, and particularly of the dynamics of groups. It is his or her role both to advise the participants as to what process will be most useful for each task and to evaluate the effectiveness of processes being used, often recommending changes when a particular process is non-productive.

When a professional process consultant is employed by a church committee or task force charged with responsibility for a particular project, the role is a crucial one. The consultant knows what process will be most useful in bringing about a particular desired outcome. The ideological stance of the process consultant, then — and in church circles he or she is sure to have one — becomes an important element. Perhaps one reason for the popularity of process consultants in contemporary church circles is the usefulness of this particular tool as a political control mechanism, in the shaping of outcomes of group endeavors. The combination of a skillful chairperson and a well-chosen process consultant can, *almost without exception,* control the outcome of group projects.

This is by no means intended to suggest that process consultants are usually biased. Certainly most of the professionals make every effort to be impartial, and to confine their role to suggesting methods rather than shaping goals. Even those who substantially influence the outcome generally do so out of the highest motives, believing that a particular outcome is in the best interest of the church. But expertise in the group process is a powerful tool. Participants in groups often fail to realize how susceptible they are to manipulation. But experts used solely for impartial advice and evaluation rather than for manipulation are extremely helpful.

Process professionals are often expert on, and committed to, particular techniques and methods. They have a tendency to evaluate process in terms of this professional commitment — to evaluate in terms of whether or not the group conforms to the professional standards of the expert. This tendency needs to be balanced by emphasis on the usefulness of the *outcome* as seen by the ultimate consumers or beneficiaries, as a standard by which to measure the process. Process evaluation, therefore, nearly always depends partially on some form of questionnaire filled out by participants in the conference, meeting, or workshop.

It is a characteristic of group dynamics that for participants in a small group who become genuinely involved, the experience is nearly always exhilarating. A closeness, a feeling of sharing, a sense of group accomplishment, and an emotional high can result. It nearly always does in a well-run group. This is a major reason for the fad status enjoyed by various kinds of sensitivity, encounter, therapy and growth groups which focus on the group experience itself rather than a group task. Persons become "hooked" on groups, and receive a great deal of emotional support and personal satisfaction from various groups in which they participate. It becomes necessary, then, to separate out this "group exhilaration" factor in seeking to evaluate a process by assessing the reactions of participants. Unless the group has "bombed," participants nearly always "feel good" about the experience when it is over. Evaluations based on participant reactions at the end of the experience need, therefore, whenever possible, to be balanced by less emotionally-loaded and more detached evaluations at a later date and by uninvolved persons.

With a minimum level of training, a volunteer "process observer," with a list of specific things to watch for and a prescribed method of recording observations, can assist in making a meeting or series of meetings in a local congregation more effective. Such observations should always be fed back to the participants in the meeting, to make the results useful. In combination with some simple evaluation instruments to measure results, this is probably all the process evaluation required in most situations. Even this limited form of evaluation should be used only for those meetings or projects in which there is a recognized need for process improvement.

Program Evaluation

Program evaluation enables a congregation to make judgments about the effectiveness of particular activities. In business and industry where profit-making is the motive, and generally in governmental and social welfare undertakings as well, the reason for undertaking the program is in terms of anticipated results. Evaluation of the results is therefore the central element in the usual assessment of program success or failure.

Uniquely in church organizations, however, motivation for engaging in particular forms of activity may be ideological. Particularly when the activity is seen as stewardship of life and money, understood as response to God's grace, the results may seem almost irrelevant. Evangelism, for instance, has been interpreted by some as the *proclamation* of the gospel, in word and deed, commanded of Christians quite independently of whether or not converts are made as a result of the proclamation. The test, according to this view, may be seen solely in terms of whether or not authentic proclamation takes place. It is assumed that the making of converts is the work of the Holy Spirit, not of the proclaimer. Program evaluation in terms of the *results* of such activity can be useful to the church, since results do affect the organization. It is useful, however, in a far more limited sense than would be the case in an organization which engaged in activity only because of the results.

To move the process of program evaluation beyond an assessment of results, and take into consideration spiritual and ideological factors is difficult. The planners of a recent denominational mission consultation, when shown the design for the evaluation of the consultation, asked that an additional question be added. "How do the Consultation results fit with the interpretation of mission in Scripture?" A substantial use of "Scriptural witnessing" had been included in the consultation plan, and the planners felt that this element should have been included in the evaluation. It was only possible, however, to obtain participant reactions to the effect on them of the scriptural witnessing, since the "interpretation of mission in scripture" is a highly ideological judgment, not readily quantifiable in an evaluation design. Evaluation in terms of faithfulness to the transcendent nature of the church is, however, quite central to the whole purpose of evaluation in church organizations. It is important, therefore, that even though they are difficult to quantify for measurement, the place of elements such as use of Scripture, and others of the church's traditional means of appropriating the power of the Holy Spirit (which have been referred to elsewhere as "spiritual techniques") be included in the evaluation design.

As suggested at the beginning of this chapter, the closest approximation of testing the faithfulness of the church to the Holy Spirit is to be found in testing the faithfulness of programs to the intentions of the corporate whole. This is readily done by informal methods in the local congregation. It can be done, in the form of constituency surveys, by regional and denominational agencies. As flawed and fallible an instrument as constituency surveying may be, it is probably the best evaluative instrument available to the church.

Personnel Evaluation

Churches have long had difficulty in evaluating people.

Christian injunctions to charity, forgiveness (seventy times seven times if necessary) and turning the other cheek have rightly been applied by church people in their dealings with those they have employed full time in church work. Further, the doctrine of the ministerial call has long excluded the clergy from the category of those simply "hired to do a job." To the extent that a minister's calling is authentically the action of the Holy Spirit, resulting in dedication of life, clergy performance may genuinely be in large measure a matter between the minister and God.

An additional factor has been the concept of "ministry" itself (which has been applied not only to the professional clergy, but to all those employed in church service — musicians, administrators, secretaries — and to the services of the laity as well). Ministry is serving others. It is called forth by love, not money. Ministry, in this sense, is paid for, but cannot be "bought."

Finally, the authority relationship (in the spiritual realm) which has traditionally existed between minister and parishioners, the shepherd and the flock, has been a factor. While strongest in those denominational traditions emphasizing the office of priest and the apostolic succession, the concept of the clergy as set apart for a leadership role, answerable only to God in the realm of faith and conscience, has, even in free church traditions, given to the clergy an aura of untouchability not easily amenable to a process of performance evaluation. For all these reasons personal evaluation has not been an area of emphasis in church circles.

Secular bureaucracies, however, have long taken performance evaluation for granted. Since modern church bureaucracies have been modeled after secular bureaucracies, such personnel evaluation first entered church organizations through denominational agency staffs. The process of "professionalization" which we examined in an earlier chapter, has gradually changed the concept and style of professionals throughout the church. There is increasing emphasis everywhere on a wide range of professional skills, on salaries commensurate with performance and responsibility, on negotiation over working hours and conditions and bargaining about conditions of employment. This change has naturally been accompanied by growth in performance evaluations of parish ministers, who are now perceived at least in part, as "selling their services" to congregations.

But personnel evaluation in the church should not be seen simplistically as a triumph of secular professionalism over Christian charity. The concepts of love in human relationships, of "ministry" as the mode of employed service in the church, and of Christian calling remain valid and may even need greater emphasis in today's professionalism. Far from negating evaluation, they should be the *basis* of evaluation in church organizations. Love not only forgives and turns the other cheek; it also corrects failures, fosters growth, and sets high standards. The concept of ministry implies giving one's best. The doctrine of Christian calling involves the congregation as well as the minister; it implies that *the Holy Spirit can and does work in ongoing assessment of a fruitful and growing relationship*, not just in the processes leading to decision to enter or sever a pastoral tie. Evaluation can be an expression of these dynamics unique to the church as well as those of professionalism.

As with other managerial techniques, personnel evaluation takes place in the tension between the human and transcendent organizational dimensions of churches. It calls for full utilization of the "spiritual techniques" in combination with those having management sources. Evaluation of the performance of persons *does* take place, informally if not formally, haphazardly if not in a planned way. Even those church people with a strong sense of the nature of the call to the ministry, its service dimension, and the priestly responsibility to God alone, still "like" or "dislike" the minister. And much that takes place in the local church is affected by these informal evaluations. The value of formalizing a process which is already informally present lies in the addition of justice, fairness and rationality — qualities in which church organizations should have a special interest. In a local congregation personnel evaluation is probably best handled by a committee of the congregation's governing unit — the session, vestry, or deacons. There must be a significant role for the senior pastor in the case of all other staff. The purposes for which the evaluation is undertaken must be understood in advance both by the evaluated minister (or other professional) and the congregation which the governing body represents. If this is not the case, it will almost inevitably be perceived by the minister as a threat, and by the congregation as a weapon.

Properly handled, performance evaluation benefits *both* the minister and the congregation. A summary of its purposes from both perspectives would include the following:

(1) *Mutual clarity regarding expectations.* What does the congregation expect of the minister, and what does the minister expect of the congregation? Whether or not a "job description" is the proper vehicle for clarifying such expectations is a moot point. In bureaucratic systems, job descriptions tend to limit the way the job is performed. They become ends in themselves, assuming an importance far beyond their basic purpose as a tool. Certainly church organizations should not seek to "fence in" the Spirit, or the freedom of minister and congregation to respond to the Spirit. But some clear and current description of what is expected is a useful starting point for an ongoing evaluation process. It may take the form of a brief job description, combined with a statement of current professional goals.

(2) *Measurement of growth, development, and changing expectations,* for the mutual benefit of minister and congregation. No person and no pastoral relationship remains static. Growing congregations, enlarged staffs, changing neighborhoods, experience, and continuing education of ministers, all change the equation. But congregations and ministers may continue to operate out of images formed years before, when the pastoral relationship was first established. Needed salary adjustments, changes in working arrangements, and in minister's and congregation's perceptions of each other, can all be accommodated through a regularly scheduled assessment process.

(3) *Feedback* to the minister as to how the congregation views the ministry, and to the congregation as to how the minister views its activity. The minister's knowledge of congregational reactions is an important element in his or her own program of continuing education, professional development, and growth toward greater maturity in ministry. It permits periodic mutual assessment of the pastoral relationship itself. Most important of all, it is theologically significant as a testing of faithfulness to the leading of the Holy Spirit, as mediated through the congregation.

The term "performance evaluation" is probably preferable to "personnel evaluation." The emphasis should be on job performance of the minister, rather than on personal attributes and characteristics. Personal qualities are examined, are accepted or rejected, before a call is extended or employment takes place. It is not relevant to ask, "Does the minister have a loving, pastoral heart?" as part of a periodic assessment. That question should have been answered at the time of employment. From then on, the question is, "Does the minister, with whatever pastoral heart he or she possesses, carry out effectively the pastoral duties mutually expected?"

A common mistake in ministerial performance evaluation is to concentrate exclusively on those organizational and professional aspects of performance which are in some degree measurable, leaving out entirely the spiritual or transcendent dimension. Such an evaluation surrenders to organizational technology and is indistinguishable from that of a manager in a secular non-profit organization. It is unfair to the transcendent dimension of the church as an organization, and to the minister as one called of God. Spiritual growth is hard to measure; so is the effective employment, both in personal life and in organizational leadership, of the "spiritual technologies" which are uniquely entrusted to the church. But it is a tragic mistake to omit this central element. Here again, the church lives in tension between its human and transcendent organizational dimensions, and neither must be neglected.

Evaluation Methods

Most evaluations, whether of process, program or performance, use two methods. One is objective measurement (in the sense of being impersonal or non-subjective), and the other is personal judgment. *Evaluations usually are based far more on personal judgments than impersonal measurement.* That fact should be recognized and accepted.

1. *Objective measurement.* Truly impersonal measurement can take place only in quantitative terms. A certain amount of quantification is possible and desirable in evaluation. It is common for the literature on the evaluation process to emphasize goals that are (1) clear; (2) specific; (3) measurable; and (4) behavioral. With such goals, measurement of the degree to which they have been reached is a reasonably

non-subjective process. If the goals were not clear to the organization, the evaluator may be urged to begin the evaluation process by achieving specificity about them.[4]

A congregation's plan to "conduct three Christian Education workshops, each of two days duration, each attended by fifteen participants," is such a measurable goal. If three workshops are indeed conducted, each does indeed last two days, and each is indeed attended by fifteen participants, the measurable goal has been achieved. An evaluation based on quantitative measurement would so state. But such an evaluation would be able to make no statement about the quality of the workshops and of their results.

The term "objective measurement" is sometimes applied to the use of opinion sampling procedures which are developed and carried out according to standards of statistical reliability. This, however, may be a misnomer. No matter how objective the *process* of measurement, what is being measured in such instances is collective personal judgments.

2. *Personal judgments.* Most evaluation processes, including *all* that assess quality rather than quantity, depend on personal judgments. Planned and formal evaluation differs from unplanned and informal, *not* in eliminating the personal element, but in broadening the base of judgment, specifying the criteria on which judgments are made, and seeking fairness and justice in making and reporting the judgments. Personal judgments are likely to enter the evaluation process in three ways:

a. *Personal judgments by interpreters of the data.* Evaluators, professional or non-professional, are usually selected on the basis of perceived objectivity, and as little personal bias as possible is a prime qualification. They may collect data from a wide range of sources. Yet, because evaluative data must be interpreted to be useful, the result inevitably reflects the personal judgments made in so doing. This fact needs to be recognized, no matter how objective and professional the evaluators seem to be.

b. *"Expert" personal judgments, by professionals.* Professionals in the field are likely to be much better informed about programs, and better qualified to make judgments than anyone else (in the sense of professional background and familiarity). Professional assessment therefore has a major role in most evaluations. Since the number of professionals is likely to be fairly small, data are often gathered in personal interviews, as distinct from written survey instruments, and may therefore have greater depth and breadth.

Professional judgments, however, are likely to be made on the basis of the expert's own professional standards. Further, they are likely to be biased because of the heavy investment professionals naturally and properly have in their field of professional expertise. Particularly is this the case when the same professionals who are responsible for a particular program have significant input into the program's evaluation. (They usually do, since to leave out the persons who know a program best and have the heaviest investment in it would seem unfair to them.) There is inherent risk, however, when the same professionals identify needs, prescribe the solutions, and evaluate the results.

c. *Collective personal judgments from the people in the pew.* We have noted repeatedly that for reasons connected with the uniqueness of the church, the most important source of evaluative judgments is the pew. For most Christians the local congregation is the natural habitat of the Holy Spirit. Professional experts complain that survey data from the entire membership of a congregation, or a whole denominational constituency, represent a "least common denominator" kind of collective personal judgment. They are right. But it is also the fairest sort of collective judgment, in that the element of personal bias found in opinions expressed by individual persons disappears. Where the group is large, a survey of a relatively small percentage of total membership according to certain professional procedures enables evaluators to acquire such collective personal judgments, with a statistically predictable level of reliability.

Evaluative Criteria

A carefully designed evaluation process seeks to minimize the subjectivity inherent in the large role played by personal judgments, by *specifying the criteria* on the basis of which those personal judgments are to be made. To ask, "What is your opinion of this congregation's 'Meals on Wheels' program?" will bring a wide range of responses and provide no way of knowing the basis of judgment. But to ask, "What is your opinion of the

'Meals on Wheels' program as a response to the commandment to love your neighbor?", or to ask, "What is your opinion of the 'Meals on Wheels' program in terms of its impact on the problem of hunger in this neighborhood?" is to specify the criterion on the basis of which judgment is to be made.

Judgments by professionals, as we have seen, are likely to be made in terms of their professional standards. But since professional standards and stances are likely to vary widely specification of criteria on which judgments are asked is necessary even with experts. It is still more important in dealing with public opinion, since large populations represent such a wide range of knowledge, familiarity, and emotional responses to various programs. It is perhaps most important of all for the evaluators themselves, the interpreters of data, to specify the criteria used in making their judgments. Otherwise the results may be seriously misinterpreted by users of the evaluation.

Specification of criteria is not easy in evaluations in church organizations. Ideological or faith-related criteria are almost always involved in personal judgments by Christians. Because of the pluralism — and even polarization in the case of mainline churches with diverse membership — personal judgments about particular programs may be vastly different, depending on the "public" or "private," "liberal" or "conservative," social activist or evangelical stance of the responder. Different experiences of God's grace, and perceptions of the challenge of the environment, naturally result in different reactions to what is done. Even specification of the criteria does not completely overcome this problem, but it does make the data somewhat more reliable.

"Baptizing the Process"

Evaluation is a highly human, limited, and management-oriented technique. The role of a sovereign God is setting goals for the Christian community, the role of the Holy Spirit in the achievement of God's purposes through the church, the personal and organizational empowerment derived from commitment to the Lord of the church — all these organizational processes are well beyond the reach of human evaluation. Yet they are so inextricably interwoven with the church's human activity and accomplishments that to leave them out of the evaluative context is unacceptable.

A sense of the limitations of the evaluation process is a good starting point. Final judgments are to be made not by evaluators, or even by the church itself, but by God. Penultimate judgments should be made, however, by the church rather than by professional or non-professional evaluators. The implied spirit of every evaluation ought to be something like this: "We are able to make certain assessments of the evangelism program of this congregation. In terms of quantitative measurements, certain forms of witnessing have taken place, a certain number of persons have been reached to some degree, and a certain number of persons have been added to the membership of the church. In terms of personal judgments regarding its effectiveness, professional judgments are thus and so; the opinions of the members of the congregation, insofar as we have been able to measure them, are thus and so. We have made every effort to evaluate its faithfulness to God's purposes. But only God knows the level of personal response reflected by the participation of members of the congregation in the program; only God knows the persons who have been truly reached and in what ways; it is the action of God that has brought the results we have been able to measure. The value of the program, therefore, whether or not it should be continued, and in what form, is essentially a theological rather than a managerial decision, in which the evaluation report can only play one small part."

The tension between human and transcendent elements in church organizations makes evaluation particularly important. More than most management techniques, it is a theological necessity. Yet because the standards and criteria must reflect that transcendent dimension of the church, it is harder than most managerial tools to translate into a clearly defined "technique." So the full utilization of "spiritual technologies" by all those engaged in evaluation activities — participation in the study, prayer, word and sacrament of Christian community — is an essential element. This alone can make it a Christian technique.

Chapter Twelve

"Baptizing" Other Management Techniques

Baptism is the sign of entry into the church. It signifies recognition of the Lordship of Christ, and acceptance of the standards and obligations of Christ's Kingdom. In a figurative sense, we have been proposing the "baptism" of management techniques brought into the church. The key elements in adopting these techniques are derived from the baptism metaphor. First, there must be recognition that the Lordship of Christ has priority over the assumptions of management. Second, the standards of the Kingdom must be applied as they are used.

We have looked in some detail at three management techniques with special significance for the church: leadership, stewardship, and evaluation. Each has important theological implications. There are a number of other techniques which, while less significant theologically, also have applications in church organizations. In this chapter we will examine three — goal-setting, Management by Objective (MBO), and organizational restructuring — that have been widely adopted and utilized by local congregations as well as church bureaucracies.

We will also look at the church renewal (or "congregational revitalization") movement, a product of the church itself rather than of management, but one utilizing organizational technology — a prime example of "baptizing management techniques."

Goals and Goal-setting

In church circles, the most ubiquitous weapon in the management consultant's arsenal is goal-setting. It approaches the status of being the all-purpose management technique. Nearly every local church renewal or organizational consultation process undertaken under the guidance of a management expert is almost sure to include goal-setting as its primary element. In fact, it is often just about all that happens in such projects!

Goal-setting as a management technique is based on some organizational assumptions, which we examined in some detail in Chapter Four. These include assumptions (1) that organizations exist to reach goals; (2) that their goals can be articulated, agreed on, and accepted by the entire organization; and (3) that the resources of the organization can be focused in a coordinated way on the achievement of the goals.

We noted in that chapter some problems in applying the goal-seeking paradigm to churches. First, there is a real question as to whether churches *fit* the orthodox managerial assumption that organizations exist to achieve goals. There is a strong stream of classic church doctrine which sees the church as existing simply to *be* the church, with goal-seeking activity as derivative and secondary. Second, even though purposeful activity by Christians has always been present, the "goals" of this activity have often been thought of as set by God, rather than by the church as an organization. Finally, the pluralism of the church has made agreement on unified goals exceedingly difficult.

The tension in which the church exists, between its human and transcendent dimensions, is apparent here as well as elsewhere. It exists for God's sake, to carry out God's purposes. But it is an organization of humans who must, in response to God's grace, be in mission, and, therefore, it *can* be seen in goal-seeking terms. The first step in "baptizing" the goal-setting process is to place it in the context of this tension. The tension is missing from management's assumption. It comes from adding the church's own transcendent assumptions.

With this perspective, there are real values in such a process:

1. Churches, like other organizations, can fall into a pattern of going through familiar motions, engaging in non-purposeful activity simply because "it's always been done that way." They devote their energies mainly to the preservation of the *status quo*, with no sense of joy, of excitement, of movement or accomplishment. Such congregations need to think through their reason for existence. They need clarity about their purpose in carrying out the kinds of activity in which they are engaged. Identification and adoption of specific goals can help by restoring to such congregations a sense of meaning, of accomplishment and excitement.

2. Goal-setting provides a means of making congregations mission-conscious. The maintenance tasks for preservation of the Christian community and nurture of its members are important. However, such necessary congregational maintenance can consume so much time and energy that it is easy for a church to become self-centered and inward-turning. The exercise of examining and articulating goals can bring to the consciousness of such a congregation the need for sharing, for serving, for witnessing — for turning its attention outward beyond itself in response to God's grace.

3. Congregations sometimes face particular challenges — whether vaguely sensed or clearly seen — but are at a loss as to how to proceed in addressing them. Goal-setting can be an orderly way to examine the challenge and begin to meet it. Trinity Church is in a racially changing neighborhood. St. Johns confronts a community of big old houses, converted to boarding houses and rundown apartments, occupied largely by lonely elderly people who survive on small Social Security payments. Central Church faces a declining membership and a dearth of leadership. Such conditions can exist for years

without perceptible change on the part of the church, until some specific event gets things moving. Goal-setting can be that event.

The technique for goal-setting, as used in the church, is fairly commonplace. The small group process is an important tool, and skill in group facilitation is a key qualification for the leader or consultant. Goal-setting may involve either the entire congregation or a select committee of leaders. The process will generally begin with a study of the congregation and its environment. Demographic and sociological characteristics, congregational resources, strengths, and weaknesses, the nature and needs of the community, all will be assessed.

With these data, participants in the goal-setting process are often divided into small groups for a brainstorming exercise. They are encouraged to surface all their hopes, dreams, and visions of the future of the congregation. The mass of information so acquired will then go through a narrowing-down process. Similar pieces of data will be collated. Frequency of mention will be noted for clues as to how widely shared a particular goal may be. Wording will be refined. This can be accomplished either by recycling the material to the same groups that produced it or moving it from group to group. Another way is to assign the refinement process to a smaller executive or steering group, the final product being tested by the larger group of participants.

From these two sources — analysis of the church and its environment, and the hopes and dreams of its members — a list of specific goals will be produced. They may be subjected to a process which enables the participants to place them in order of priority. The writing of the end product is nearly always handled by a selected few, but it is tested by the whole group.

Finally, the goals so set are assigned either to task forces or groups organized specifically for the purpose of carrying them out or to existing organizational units. Plans are then developed for implementing them.

Pluralism and Goal Setting

Local congregations are often self-selected consensus groups, and in such groups goal-setting works well. In pluralistic congregations, goal setting is sometimes seen as a technique for bringing about unity of purpose. Such a hope nearly always turns out to be an illusion. A unified goal *reflects* congregational unity; it does not create it. Forced agreement on a single set of unified goals, whether by parliamentary victories of a majority or by wording so vague and general as to encompass multiple interpretations, can be destructive rather than constructive.

The dynamics of small groups are such that a temporary agreement can often be forged. Group pressure, the urge to conform, and the power of the experience itself, all help to bring this about. Agreement can be reached, and the members can achieve an emotional "high" in the process of reaching it. Such an experience has sometimes been ascribed by Christian groups to the work of the Holy Spirit, bringing unity to a diversified group. The power of the Spirit to do so cannot be discounted by anyone who takes seriously the Lordship of Christ in the church. However, caution is in order. Group dynamics has demonstrated again and again the power of small groups to forge similar unity in secular groups dealing with secular issues, achieved with a similar emotional "high." Any skilled process person can create such an experience; but to do so, calling it the work of the Spirit, may be presumptuous. The test comes in the *maintenance* of the unity once the group experience is over and the emotional high has receded.

Pluralistic goals, achieved by various internal consensus groups, may be far more productive than managerial unity, artificially achieved through a manipulated process, but not supported once the process is over. A variety of goals will permit particular groups of Christians to respond to particular challenges by which they are moved. In such a process, the Spirit may forge unity out of the congregation's diversity.

The church's own organizational assumptions always have priority over management assumptions. The goals of the congregation are never just the hopes and dreams of its members, but God's purposes for that congregation. And God's purposes are received, not "set." They are divined through some of the church's own "spiritual techniques," which can be integrated into congregational goal-setting:

1. Every goal-setting exercise ought to involve, as a starting point and major element, *intensive* study of and reflection on the scripture. Beginning a meeting with prayer and devotions is not enough. Ten percent Bible study and ninety percent human technology is a questionable reflection of priorities. Openness

to all those ways in which God communicates purposes to the church must be quantitatively as well as qualitatively prominent in the design. It is an awesome responsibility to "set" goals which are presumed to be the goals of the Holy Spirit. For the church, goal setting is listening.

2. Studies of the social and demographic make-up of the congregation and community, and of environmental influences and challenges, both locally and worldwide, may be an exercise in stewardship. It is the *combination* of the experience of God's love, and the experience of challenge and need from the environment, which calls forth Christian response.

3. The "hopes and dreams" of the people of the congregation may play an important part in the process. But the formulation of the hopes and dreams should at least be as much an exercise in prayer as a "brainstorming" exercise. The process can be deliberately structured for this purpose.

4. Assignment of goals to Task Forces or committees may be in the context of personal dedication and commitment, which can be symbolized in a special service of commitment.

Management by Objective

All too often congregational goal-setting is the focus of management efforts, and *achievement* of the goals is left to take care of itself. MBO has value as a goal *achievement* technique.

The basic purpose of the technique is to enable organizations to reach particular goals by breaking them down into specific, concrete "objectives" to be met in specific increments on a specific time schedule. It is a planned, orderly way of going about reaching goals.

An illustration might be found in a congregation's goal to increase its membership by twenty persons within three months. Let us assume that such a goal is adopted on March 1. Each objective is achievable by carrying out specific tasks on a specific time schedule.

Goal: To have increased the congregation's membership by twenty persons by the end of May (three months).

Objective 1: To have completed preparation for the membership drive by the end of March (one month), through:

          (a) Organizing eight groups of home callers,

(b) Dividing the community into eight areas, assigned to the groups of callers,

(c) Training the callers to describe the church's fellowship and invite unchurched persons to visit the congregation.

Objective 2: To have identified at least thirty-two active prospects by the end of April (second month), through:

(a) Calls within the month by each group in at least twenty unchurched homes,

(b) Encountering by each group of at least four interested responses,

(c) Inviting each interested person to be the guest of a team member in attending a service of the church.

Objective 3: To have at least twenty persons make decisions to unite with the church by the end of May (third month), through:

(a) A follow-up call by a minister on each of the persons responding affirmatively to a visit to the worship service,

(b) Inviting each person who has responded affirmatively to the worship service to attend, as the guest of a team member, an activity of the community of believers which might meet that person's particular needs.

(c) Scheduling a church membership class in which at least twenty of these interested persons will enroll.

Such a breakdown into specific tasks on a specific time line does not ensure reaching the goal. It does, however, make it possible to pin down the point of failure, and to take timely corrective action. MBO provides opportunity for a kind of *managerial supervision* which is based on the achievement of mutually agreed-on objectives, rather than direct oversight. It enables the supervisor and the persons having responsibility for reaching the objectives to agree in advance on a time schedule and checkpoints. It provides for mutual exchange of information and guidance at the time the checkpoints (or "milestones") are reached. Within that context, it permits a considerable measure of autonomy in reaching the objectives. Supervision becomes a matter of "coaching" the subordinate who has responsibility, rather than personal assumption of responsibility by the manager.

It should be noted that the managerial frame of reference may not be entirely applicable to the relationship between a pastor and the volunteer groups within the church which have undertaken particular goals. "Supervision" may be more appropriate to relationships within a professional staff, where the senior pastor does actually have managerial responsibility, and to relationships in church bureaucracies, than to the work of the congregation itself. However, mutual agreement in advance on goals and milestones does permit periodic mutual checking on progress, mutually acceptable coaching, and orderly goal achievement. MBO also provides a basis for *evaluation*, both of program and of persons, in terms of what is being done. While the means used are not irrelevant to such an evaluation, the focal point is the reaching of agreed-on objectives. Attention is directed not toward personal qualities, but toward performance effectiveness.

Some overly-enthusiastic MBO advocates may seek to force every aspect of the church's life into the goal achievement format: to set goals in the creation of a sense of Christian community, in the worship and devotional life of the congregation — to "program the Holy Spirit." When carried too far, this can intensify a tendency to see the church entirely in terms of organizational goal-achievement.

MBO is quintessentially a "management" approach. All its philosophical assumptions are those of management, which we have examined earlier in some detail. From the theological perspective, it has all the dangers we have noted: of humans assuming a role in a church organization which properly belongs only to God, of inadequate attention to human fallibility and sin.

MBO focuses so directly on goal achievement that the danger of seeing the church exclusively in terms of the organizational goal-seeking model, without the balancing tension of the transcendent dimension of the church, is enhanced. Indeed, it is precisely this tendency in congregations where the practices of management have been efficiently implemented that has led those with a strong concern for the spirituality of the church to reject it entirely. The church is seen as "just another organization" engaged (very efficiently) in doing good.

MBO can, indeed, be a useful tool in certain areas of the church's life. Whenever the corporate response of the whole community, or of particular groups within it, takes the form of undertaking a particular project, its possibilities should be examined. Its basic approach — that of breaking down major goals into manageable objectives to be achieved on a realistic timetable — is extremely helpful for such projects. As a basis for managerial supervision, and for performance evaluation, it is useful within the professional staff of the church.

Its dangers to a church organization can probably best be avoided by a liberal use of those "spiritual technologies" which the church has traditionally employed in carrying out its purposes. The power of the Holy Spirit in goal achievement is integral to the church's basic organizational understanding of itself. The efficacy of prayer, the strength in the corporateness of the life of the community, the collective guidance and direction through study and reflection, the empowerment that comes through worship and the sacraments — all these, seen as *organizational* techniques, given to the church by its sovereign Lord as means of achieving God's purposes for the church, can "baptize" MBO.

Organizational Restructuring

Prior to the advent of the managerial age, changes in the structure of organizations and institutions came infrequently, slowly, and often reluctantly. But if organizations are "deliberately constructed to seek specific goals," it makes sense to adjust the way they are constructed as frequently as necessary to make goal achievement more effective. From the managerial perspective, structure in an organizational system is one element to be "managed," along with budget, personnel and technology, in bringing about the desired result.

Organizational restructuring has therefore become commonplace in modern business, governmental and public service organizations. A whole range of managerial processes within organizations — leadership, decision-making, communication, planning, evaluation, as well as the actual organizational arrangements for implementing these processes — are hindered or facilitated by the organizational structure. A whole range of structural models — from the pyramidal structure of the classic bureaucracy to new "matrix" structures and highly flexible "coalitional models" — has been developed to facilitate particular kinds of leadership, decision-making, planning, communication, and control. Numbers of church people have become familiar with the process of restructuring to improve organizational functioning. This is particularly true of the middle classes who populate the businesses, service industries, and the governmental, educational and public service bureaucracies that are the prime consumers of organizational theory — and who are most likely to populate the mainline denominations as well.

Restructure has been common at every level of the church. Rare is the congregation which has not undergone some kind of reorganization in recent years. The purpose, in many instances, has been to make congregational mission the official business of the church's governing structure through a mission-oriented organization. But congregational reorganization has rarely been a major issue. The average person in the pew, hearing the word "restructure," is likely to think of changes in denominational organization.

We are emerging from a period of massive denominational reorganization, both regional and national, which has affected nearly every mainline church. As we have noted earlier, at least ten denominations restructured themselves in the late sixties and early seventies, with the greatest change taking place in the national mission agencies.

Restructure must be seen in relation to the regionalization and decentralization trends we have earlier noted. Some form of structural change, both nationally and regionally, was probably a necessary adaptation to the larger systemic change. If for no other reason, the radically reduced funding of national agencies which accompanied the growth of local and regional mission required organizational adjustment. The denominational restructures, however, were primarily managerial in purpose. They were intended in considerable measure to promote organizational efficiency. They completed the consolidation of program, centralization of planning, and the unifying of budgets already long under way.

In addition to the basic managerial assumptions, there were

some more generalized assumptions that shaped the thinking of church planners and organizational specialists during the heyday of restructuring. One was a widespread assumption that change had become the social and organizational norm of contemporary society. Alvin Toffler's book, *Future Shock,* with its emphasis on the rapidity of change, the instability of institutions, and the necessity of flexibility, was extremely influential during the period.[1] Under the fresh impact of the human potential movement, change and flexibility were regarded as positive values in their own right, by many organizational experts.

A related assumption was that the new structural models, emphasizing flexibility and response to changing needs, were the wave of the future. The aerospace industry, in which the new models had been developed, was the glamor industry of the sixties. Hierarchical organization was identified with traditional authority, inflexibility, and resistance to change.

An instrumental view of the church was also assumed by many in that period, particularly in the liberal establishment that dominated the mainline denominations. "The world sets the agenda" was the catch phrase, reflecting a belief that the church exists for the purpose of responding to society, and that its structures must change as society changes. Finally, as we have noted earlier, goal-seeking assumptions about organizations led to a failure to distinguish between mission agencies and governmental structures. It was assumed that to restructure the mission agencies was to restructure the denomination.

Lyle E. Schaller, in his helpful overview of the denominational restructures that took place in the decade from 1965 to 1974, assumes that "another round" of restructure will come in the late 1970's and early 1980's.[2] The 1972 Plan of Restructure of the Presbyterian Church, U.S. built an assumption of continuing structural change into its organization, with a requirement that its Office of Review and Evaluation make a thorough study of organizational arrangements and recommend changes to the General Assembly every seven years.[3] Even though Schaller gives reasons for his expectation of another round in terms of deficiencies of models adopted in the last round, both expectations probably reflect basic managerial assumptions

233

about the desirability of frequent structural change. It is possible, however, that some of those managerial assumptions of the sixties and early seventies may now be less supportable.

While the experience of restructure was an upsetting experience for some bureaucrats then in the system,[4] those who remained, and the new managers now in the systems (both national and regional) tend to view the results positively. They see the present corporatized mission structures as necessary and effective.

As the church's "managerial class," they are for the most part professionally and ideologically committed to the unification and centralization of program, and to the managerial principles expressed organizationally in the changes.

Generally, however, it must be said that for the people in the pew — the membership at large of the mainline denominations — the era of denominational restructure has left a sour taste. In the first place, restructure was probably oversold to them, as a way of solving deep and frustrating problems with which denominational constituencies were concerned. Second, church members were confused and disgruntled by the disappearance of a familiar order. National agencies with which they had been long familiar were no more. Long-time leaders, identified as symbols of particular programs, departed. Names of agencies changed and changed again. The image of denominational agencies was one of turbulence, uncertainty and confusion. Finally, the restructuring turbulence has provided a convenient handle on which to hang blame for a wide range of grievances and reduced services still being experienced by the constituencies. It may be added that for some, disenchantment with restructure has become a symbol for a much wider disenchantment with organizational and managerial processes, interminable meetings, internal maintenance and organizational wheel-spinning, which seem to them to have been occupying the attention of the church — and particularly its bureaucracies — to the exclusion of discipleship and witness.

Some lessons have emerged from the era of church restructure:

1. The particular form of ongoing organizational structure is probably far less important than many once thought. Restructured organizations generally encounter many of the

same difficulties experienced before — along with some new ones. There is no conclusive evidence that they are dealing with the difficulties any more effectively than the old structures did.

2. Restructure does not change the basic nature of the church and its problems. Despite managerial centralization, church people stick stubbornly to the voluntary principle. Denominational mission budgets have continued to decline, and "one mission" slogans have not eliminated pluralism. The managerial commitment to unified approaches has not dealt adequately with diversification of mission responses within the churches.

3. "Organizational principle" sometimes turns out to be nothing more than organizational fashion. Despite the high level of commitment of the part of human potential-trained managers to collective leadership, such models generally have not proved any more workable than the old ones; they may be prone to be less so. The "flexible organization," "matrix models" and "task group" concepts which became so popular with management and organizational specialists in the sixties were not readily adaptable to fairly stable church organizations.

4. But there is nothing sacred about traditional organizational structures, even in the church, where an assumed sacredness tends to attach itself to anything traditional. Structural change which arises from the *needs of the congregation or the denominational agencies* need not be feared. We have learned in the managerial age that organizational structure *can* be a useful tool in achieving goals.

Organizational structure must reflect *both* major elements in the organizational nature of the church. It must embody the character of the church as the people of God, its relationship to the Lord of the church, and the presence within it of the Holy Spirit. It must also reflect the church's human organizational characteristics and its goal-achievement needs. The view that change itself must be positively valued is no longer so fashionable as it once was. Change in response to changing conditions in the society or the environment has much to commend it, although there is danger in regarding the church as existing solely to serve society and respond to environmental needs. Such response is needed, and systems theory is to be thanked for teaching the church to see its organizational structures as systems, having their place in larger systems. But flexibility cannot be bought at the expense of the church's autonomous responsibility to "be the church," its continuity, its relationship with its eternal Lord, and its own nurture and community needs.

It may be noted finally that management science itself is beginning to give attention to "self-designing organizations," which develop their own structures internally in response to internal requirements, with far less necessity for externally imposed tinkering or managerial manipulation than some have considered necessary.[5] It may be that the historic development of church organizations, out of internal experience and the work of the Spirit, has been an example of such a self-designing organization in the past. And a larger place may need to be allowed for such self-design, as opposed to managerial tinkering, in the future.

Church Renewal

In contrast to goal-setting, MBO, and organizational restructuring, all of which are managerial techniques imported into the church, the cluster of techniques known as "church renewal," "congregational renewal," "parish development" or "congregational revitalization," is a product of the church itself. Yet its methods are so frequently those of management and organizational development that it deserves mention here.

The basic problem with which the church renewal movement deals is as old as the church itself — that of inactive, stagnant, worn-out, non-vital, "dead" congregations. For centuries, the church's method of dealing with the problem has focused on renewal of the flagging spirits of *individual* church members. Revivalist movements, from the Great Awakening of the colonial period to the Billy Graham organization of contemporary America, have all been aimed toward the Christian commitment of individual persons. They have often been described as evangelistic. They seek to bring new converts into the Christian community. But consistently their main effect has been renewal of existing churches. This continues to be true today; several studies show that the greatest effect of Billy Graham crusades is on those who are already church members. Even today, traditionalist evangelical congregations seek renewal through periodic "revivals."

The contemporary church renewal movement is unique in

that it attempts to revitalize Christians *organizationally* rather than individually. In this sense it is peculiarly a product of the managerial age. Certainly no lack of concern about the spiritual health of individual persons is intended. But the method is organizational.

There have been two main channels of church renewal in mainstream Christianity. One has been the small group movement. Closely allied to the human relations movement, with its insights into group dynamics, it seeks to renew the church through the vitality of small groups within the larger congregation. Variously known as "house churches," support groups or fellowship groups, these small groups within congregations have been described and promoted in a prolific literature. For a time, house churches were seen by many as the institutional form for the church of the future.

Some church-related small groups have been virtually indistinguishable from the personal growth groups of the human potential movement. Indeed, the small group movement in the church crested at about the same time as the encounter group movement outside the church. But it would be grossly unfair to see it as nothing more than a religious version of encounter groups. At its best, the small group movement in the churches has depended heavily on New Testament models, for the first churches were all small groups meeting in homes. The New Testament term for Christian fellowship, "koinonia," has been closely associated with the movement, and has given the contemporary church its clearest picture of the reality of the presence of the Holy Spirit in the fellowship of faith. It has been one of the few movements affecting both the evangelical and social activist wings of the contemporary church. Although some of the early excitement has now worn off, its impact on the church seems to be durable.

The second channel has been more explicitly organizational. It has promoted renewal of congregations through a variety of organizational technologies. Those technologies coming out of the human relations movement have been particularly prominent. It relies heavily on goal-setting, conflict resolution, and team building: indeed, most of the church-generated literature on organizational techniques has been written and circulated in the church under the rubric of congregational renewal.

As in the traditional individually-oriented revivalist movement (with the term "revival" itself), the prominence of the life-death metaphor in the church renewal movement is striking. Book titles give an indication. One of the most influential of the early books on small groups in the church was that of Robert Raines, *New Life in the Church*.[6] A book strongly reflective of the Human Relations "OD" orientation is that of James D. Anderson, *To Come Alive! A New Proposal for Revitalizing the Local Church*.[7] The term "revitalization" itself, which along with "renewal" designates the movement, has precisely the same meaning as "revival" — although the context is vastly different.

A word should be said about the "church growth movement," currently strong in the evangelical wing of Christianity. Unlike "church renewal," this is not essentially an attempt at renewal through organizational methods. While emphasizing techniques, and in so doing relying certainly on managerial and organizational approaches, its basic thrust is individual. It produces church growth by the simple and direct method of adding new members to the church. The movement is claiming increasing attention from the mainline denominations, where declining membership is now being recognized as critical.

Other OD Technologies and Management Techniques

A wide range of other management techniques and OD technologies are available, and frequently used, in church organizations. These include such systemic approaches to management as PPBS Systems, which provide a "packaged" method of incorporating major elements of the management process into a yearly cycle. (The initials are used in many organizations, and sometimes translated "Planning, Programming, Budgeting System, at other times, "Program Planning & Budgeting System.") PPBS was first developed in the Department of Defense. It is appropriate to large bureaucracies with multiple elements, which require a high level of coordination to avoid organizational chaos. Its utility in smaller organizations, such as local churches, is less certain. While some kind of annual planning is important, a fairly simple process is probably best in most parishes. The returns from PPBS may not justify the effort required to manage so complex a process.

Adaptability to the voluntary nature of church organizations must also be closely examined. The reason such systems (like that adopted by the United Presbyterian Church as "PBE" — Planning, Budgeting, Evaluation — in the early 70's) have not been notably successful is probably to be found here. It was a management-control model, in a member-control system.

Certain OD technologies derived from the Human Potential movement, such as conflict management and team building exercises, are also frequently employed by churches. We have noted their use in church renewal. These people-oriented techniques have received much affirmation in the church because of their humanization emphasis. Their limitation is precisely that they are "people-oriented techniques" reflective of a management viewpoint that regards "personnel" as one of the variables which may be manipulated in the goal-achievement process. Management has no monopoly on the tendency to manipulate people. People manipulate people without benefit of managerial training, and they always have. Yet a frame of reference which encourages manipulation, however subtly, holds real dangers for the pastor. "People" in a parish must never become "personnel." The differences between leader and manager, as we have seen in an earlier chapter, are real.

There is probably no management technique which is off-limits to the church, unless it is blatantly manipulative or inherently immoral. Yet every management technique needs to be examined with discrimination as to its implications, its effect, and its appropriateness in the community of the redeemed. It can be "baptized" for use in such a community only when organization is seen in the tension of the transcendent with the human, and used together with those long-tested "spiritual technologies" which are the gift to the church of its transcendent Lord.

239

CHAPTER THIRTEEN

THE MOST BASIC ORGANIZATIONAL PRINCIPLE: TRUST THE HOLY SPIRIT

We began this book with a look at the organization-mindedness of the contemporary church. We examined both the church's own organizational heritage, in classical treatment of the doctrine of the church, and the secular sources of the organizational and managerial techniques so popular in the church today.

Against this background, we looked analytically in Part II at some of the most significant factors shaping the church in the managerial age. We examined the basic assumptions of organizational theory and management science about the goal-seeking nature of all organizations, and the results of applying these assumptions to the church. We looked at the voluntary nature of churches as organizations, and the results of applying management methods in such organizations. We examined two pervasive trends of American society in the managerial age: bureaucracy and professionalization; and we looked at the effect of the managerial age on denominations, ministers and congregations.

Finally, in Part III we have been examining practical applications of management theory and techniques in the unique organization that is the church. We have sought in this entire section to think theologically about the use of these techniques in the church, and we began with the theological perspective which sees the presence of the Holy Spirit as both the organizational uniqueness and the organizational power of the church. We then moved on to a pragmatic look at the applications, the usefulness and the appropriateness of specific techniques within this framework. We gave particular attention to organizational leadership issues as they apply to ministers, to funding issues in terms of the doctrine of stewardship, and to evaluation processes in the church setting. We looked finally at some of the most popular applied techniques.

Throughout, we have sought to preserve the very real tension between the unique, transcendent nature of the church, as an organization established by Christ, "managed" by God, and empowered by the continuing presence of the Holy Spirit, and the equally real nature of the church as a human organization, made up of fallible and sinful people, subject to the same human dynamics, problems and needs as all other organizations. In the process, we have been working with two vocabularies.

What About Management Jargon?

On one occasion a colleague, listening as I discussed some of the organizational issues dealt with in this book, dismissed it as a linguistic problem. "What really bothers you," she suggested, "is the management jargon. You don't mind if the church uses all these organizational techniques. You just want to describe them in pious language!"

But on another occasion, a consultant who, though himself a churchman, is vocationally unrelated to the church, took the opposite tack. "Why do you church people insist on using the language of management?", he asked. "The church is a basic 'vital center' of society, with its own assumptions and validity. The issue is not 'goals and objectives,' but 'What needs to be done around here?' " Managerial language, he suggested, can impose its own categories and thereby affect the church's meaning and message. The church ought instead to be offering people its own unique symbols with which to think about their possibilities, he said.

How important is the use or non-use of managerial language in the church? Certainly many of the people in the pew are put off by organizational jargon. The ubiquity of talk about goal-setting, prioritizing, restructuring and evaluating is one factor leading to the plaintive calls from the pew to stop concentrating on management and structure, and "get on with the business of the church."

It is undoubtedly true, also, that managers who communicate in managerial jargon contribute to the professionalization of the church. "Coding" conceals. To the extent that the running of the church becomes a technological mystery, understood only by the experts, the essential nature of the church as the community of the faithful has been distorted.

Yet it is the contention of this book that language is not the real issue. It is the *substance* of managerial assumptions, the theological *implications* of organizational technologies, the "*faith*" of a managerial age, that matter. Clearly there are managerial techniques that have been and will continue to be useful to the church. To use managerial terms while employing these techniques, so long as the terms are understood by the church — as many of them are in this managerial age — may make for clarity. These are the terms invented to convey the precise meaning intended. A theology of human responsibility calls for the use of all appropriate human learning and skills in the service of God's kingdom, including human terms.

But words are symbols. If the talk is *too* managerial, the reality also may be out of proportion. We have returned repeatedly in this book to the tension in which the church lives, between the transcendent and the human, the mysterious communion and the down-to-earth institution.

To neglect either of these dimensions is to distort the reality of the church as an organization. To deal with the church *only* as a theological, transcendent, "spiritual" entity — as Christian theology has done through much of history — is unrealistic.

The human, organizational realities are there, and to ignore them or refuse to deal with them is to leave them to solve themselves. Often they have done so in ways which are destructive and self defeating, as an ecclesiastical history all too full of bickering, sectarianism, "holy wars" and power struggles demonstrates. But to deal with the church as if it were *only* a human organization, to be managed like any other human organization, is to reduce it to just that: another human organization. There is real danger that the ascendence of organizational and management theories and techniques in this managerial age has moved the church too far in that direction.

Both dimensions are real, and the church neglects either at its peril. It lives in tension between the two. Management techniques have their place in this kind of church; Christians have an obligation to study them, try them, select those that are most appropriate, call them by their names, and use them well. But whenever there is doubt, the real priority of the church is not in question. Its ultimate loyalty is to the Lord of the church, and its transcendent nature is its greatest prize.

The Holy Spirit in Organization

The Holy Spirit is God present in the church and in the world. The gift of the Spirit to the church is unique; God is present in the church in a special way. The purpose of this book has been to suggest that it is impossible to take such an understanding of the church seriously without making *trust in the Holy Spirit the church's most basic organizational principle*. Everything that enhances this trust and enables the Spirit thus to work through the church is valid. Everything that conflicts with it must be discarded.

Control is always a central organizational issue. What an organization is and what it does can ultimately be seen under the rubric of control. For the church, *God is in control.* We do not manage the Holy Spirit. We do not plan the Spirit. We do not budget for the Spirit. We do not establish goals for the Spirit. We do not program the Spirit. For the Spirit, like the wind, "bloweth where it listeth" (John 3:8 KJV).

This does not mean that we have no obligation to manage, to plan, to budget, to program those aspects of organizational life which *have* been entrusted to our control. As Christians responsible to God, we must. But we cannot manage it all and

243

we are false to the church and her Lord when we try. This means that it is unnecessary for us to *try* to plan and program everything. The Church can probably get by with *a good bit less attention to organization and management* than has been given to these matters in recent years. All processes do not have to be designed. Everything does not have to be structured and continually restructured.

To fly planes, an airline must be managed. It must procure equipment, train pilots, devise schedules, coordinate routing, computerize reservations, fuel the planes, maintain the runaways, clean out the compartments — a whole host of administrative and maintenance and support tasks, all of which are essential. Without this planning, management and maintenance, the airline could not possibly transport passengers and freight. When it begins to neglect them, the whole system begins to go downhill. It may be far-fetched to suggest that an airline could become so wrapped up in developing better planes, rearranging the seats, devising new schedules, and providing ever more sophisticated computerized booking systems that it neglects to fly the planes! Yet some are suggesting that this is precisely what has been happening to the church. And while the analogy is overdrawn, the accusation may not be so far from reality as we might wish.

Balance is essential. Trusting the Holy Spirit does not mean *neglecting* management and maintenance. Trusting the Spirit means, among other things, counting on the Spirit to *provide* good managers, to *redeem* organizational techniques, to *work through* Christian people in bureaucracies — even through their manipulations, their politics, their organizational tinkering. But it always means to recognize that God is the *ultimate* manager.

The church does not have much in the way of a "theology of organization." Even less does it have hymns to organization. But one of our failures, perhaps, has been the failure to recognize that even the most exalted of our hymns can have organizational meaning:

> The Church's one foundation
> Is Jesus Christ her Lord;
> She is his new creation
> By water and the word;

244

From heaven he came and sought her
To be his holy Bride;
With his own blood he bought her,
And for her life he died.

The following article created a great deal of interest when it first appeared in the July 6-17, 1977 issue of *Christian Century*. Now it provides a very specific backdrop for the work that has emerged. The book is much more than an elaboration of this article, but the central concerns here give many helpful clues to certain implications of the book.

PLURALISM AND CONSENSUS: WHY MAINLINE CHURCH MISSION BUDGETS ARE IN TROUBLE

The 'unified' approach to missions promoted by national church bureaucracies is collapsing because of the failure to take full account of the fact that churches are voluntary organizations.

THE GOOD NEWS was headlined in an October 1976 news release: "Increased Church Giving Reported by National Council of Churches." The average member in 42 denominations gave a record $137.09 to the church in 1975. The bad news was tucked away three paragraphs down: when adjusted to 1976 dollars (to compensate for inflation) the average 1975 contribution was worth only $85.04 — *down* almost 1 percent from the 1974 similarly adjusted average contribution of $86.09.

It was not a one-shot decline. A 1975 study of philanthropic giving in the U.S. found that giving to churches has been declining steadily for years. An overall drop in philanthropic giving — both in proportion to the gross national product and absolutely in constant, uninflated dollars — is accounted for almost entirely by decreased giving to religious organizations. Between the years 1964 and 1974, religious contributions dropped from 49.4 percent to 43.1 percent of the total *(Giving in America: Toward a Stronger Voluntary Sector* [Commission on Private Philanthropy and Public Needs, 1975], pp. 70-71).

This trend, distressing enough in itself, is further complicated by a shift in the way churches have been allocating their declining revenues. More and more money is kept and spent by local congregations. More and more of what is left after the congregation meets its own needs is kept reasonably close to home, in the diocese, presbytery, state convention or conference. The once-powerful central denominational headquarters have fallen on hard times.

A 1975 study conducted by the Office of Review and Evaluation of the Presbyterian Church, U.S., showed that within that denomination, when three factors are combined — the effect of inflation, the larger share kept by the local church, and the larger share sent to regional units (presbyteries) — the real income of national church agencies is less than half of what it was ten years ago *(Minutes of the 116th General Assembly* [Presbyterian Church, U.S., 1976], p. 117).

Organizational restructurings have been endemic within the major denominations. The urge to restructure grows out of a number of factors — not least the churches' infatuation with "organizational development" and an optimistic hope that structural change can solve deep-rooted problems. But far more than the reorganizers have realized, they may have been responding to increasing financial pressures, which in turn are symptomatic of some deeper changes. There is increasing evidence that these changes may signal a major shift in the pattern of American church life.

The Corporatizing of America

American society is characterized by what sociologist Ted Mills has called "creeping corporatism" (" 'Creeping Corporatism' vs. Rising Entitlements," *Harvard Business Review*, November-December 1976). The individual American has less and less opportunity for personal initiative and for impact on his or her environment. Nearly all major social structures have in this century become huge, technologically sophisticated, bureaucratic entities. They appear to have taken on a life of their own, independent of the collective will of those who organized them, support them, or make up the membership.

The self-evident model is government. Whether anyone or anything — a president, an administration, a political movement — can assume real control of the federal government and significantly change its inexorable course became a hotly debated issue during the 1976 presidential campaign. Many citizens have given up; they are resigned to a government so massive, so powerful, so self-perpetuating, that it is impervious to the will of voters, or even presidents.

But government is not the only social structure that has become corporatized. Businesses, labor unions, military services, educational institutions, professional societies, charitable organizations — even farms — have followed the same course. And churches are no exception. In part, the process has been a function of sheer size. American social structures are characteristically big. They are made up of — or deal with — huge numbers of people, sums of money, quantities of goods.

Bureaucratic organization is not inherently evil. As Max Weber, the pioneer sociologist who first described the characteristics of bureaucracies, pointed out, they are designed to make organizations rational and just through written rules fairly applied to all and through standardized procedures. They are organized to achieve goals, to operate efficiently, and to base internal policies on merit and competence rather than capricious favoritism (*The Theory of Social and Economic*

Organization [Oxford University Press, 1947], pp. 324-340). But perhaps for these very reasons, bureaucratic organizations are less responsive to individuals than to internal rules and "standard operating procedures."

Advanced technology is another characteristic of corporatized social structures. Ever larger numbers of people are bureaucratically managed, controlled or serviced ever more efficiently by sophisticated electronic data processing. More important, the corporatized structures appear to be relatively impervious to attempts to influence or change them.

The Search for Self-Fulfillment

But as Mills points out, alongside the creeping corporatism — and at least partially in response to it — a countervailing trend has developed. Americans are looking ever more insistently for personal satisfaction. Sociologist Daniel Bell has referred to a "revolution of rising entitlements," characterized by a search for personal control, a loss of respect for authority, and an insistent egalitarianism. The capturing of this mood may have been the most important clue to the winning of the U.S. presidency in 1976 by a relatively unknown governor of a southern state.

The focal point of the revolution of rising entitlements is the self. The movement has been called the "new narcissism." Cults and therapies for the self-centered, devoted to self-development, self-fulfillment and self-actualization, have popped up like mushrooms, finding fertile ground even in churches. Varieties of formalized "assertiveness training" have surfaced. Numbers of community political groups have recaptured local schools from educational bureaucracies. Priests' organizations have issued challenges to Roman Catholic bishops. "Rightsmanship" is practiced by minorities and other groups who have felt themselves to be oppressed: women, blacks, Chicanos, Indians, homosexuals, ethnics. Separatist movements grab headlines, win elections or launch revolutions. The traditional American order is reversed as "smallness" becomes more treasured than "bigness." A century-old population trend is reversed, as people leave the cities and rural areas become the growth centers. Urbanologists call for planned shrinkage. A Ralph Nader becomes a folk hero, and E.F. Schumacher's book *Small Is Beautiful* becomes a cult bible.

It is in the context of a society dominated by these two movements — huge bureaucratic organizations in collision with a mood of personal assertiveness — that what is happening to the churches must be seen. Mainline Protestant churches have become as corporatized as any other major social structure. National-level bureaucracies have suffered forced attrition in the past few years, but regional structures have been growing, and the bureaucratic spirit extends even to the staffs and the newly elaborate organizational set-ups of local congregations.

Classic Patterns of Mission and Giving

It is helpful to remember that the corporatization of denominations has *not* significantly affected what was historically the basis of their existence as churches. Forms of church government have remained relatively unchanged. Bishops, presbyteries and associations have carried on their traditional roles as guardians of faith and order. Conflicts have been adjudicated. The clergy have been called, ordained and disciplined. Theological standards have been debated.

Corporatized structures have been developed to produce and market the "product" of church life: "Christian mission." Christian faith has always led to some kind of action: nourishing the Christian community, spreading the faith, teaching the young, feeding the hungry, healing the sick, challenging evil, changing society.

For most of Christian history, this kind of missional activity has been *voluntary* and has taken place *outside* the formal church governmental structures. Voluntary missional activity has always depended on activists who do the work, and money-givers who support it. The historic pattern has been one in which the activists, with the approval of church authorities, have gone directly to the members to arouse enthusiasm, enlist support and collect funds.

The Roman Catholic Church developed admirable structures for carrying out these missional activities in the various lay and priestly religious orders. These have been permitted to be self-governing internally. Teaching orders, missionary orders, charitable and serving orders could focus on their own particular missional interests, and they have had free access to church members to develop support and collect funds.

The Protestant equivalent of the Roman Catholic order, as a

250

structure for voluntary mission activity, has been the voluntary association. Most early mission associations were not formally related to churches, and their support was inter-denominational. William G. McLoughlin, in tracing the history of Protestant philanthropy, notes that in the early years the American population was so over-whelmingly Protestant and the climate of social thought so pervaded by a religious tone that it is impossible to separate public from Protestant philanthropic efforts. In the 18th century, the multitude of charitable societies had no nationwide pattern. "Virtually all were local in origin and function, and a large percentage of them were denominational in origin and backing," says McLoughlin. In the 19th century the most significant change was the gradual development of statewide and national societies. They were interdenominational, and they came to be dominated by laity, rather than by the clergy who often founded them ("Changing Patterns of Protestant Philanthropy, 1607-1969," in *The Religious Situation 1969*, edited by Donald R. Cutler [Beacon, 1969], pp. 538-614).

Even the most "churchly" forms of mission — religious education and the spreading of the gospel at home and abroad — developed under nonchurch auspices. The history of the nondenominational Sunday school societies and foreign mission societies is well known. As denominationally related committees and boards began to replace the independent societies in the latter half of the 19th century, to provide programs of publication and education, foreign and domestic mission, they remained separate from church governmental structures. They were largely autonomous groups within the denominations, cultivating their own constituencies, raising their own funds with denominational cooperation, and carrying out their various kinds of mission.

The Flaw in the Unified Budget

Over a period of years, denominational governing structures have gradually assumed more and more control over the formerly autonomous mission agencies. Various activities have been drawn together into "one mission." Unified budgets have been stressed. Agencies have been discouraged from going directly to the people to raise money for particular causes.

251

Denominational bureaucrats have been given control of the allocation and spending of funds.

The development of corporatized denominational structures is a 20th century phenomenon. It did not reach full flower until after World War II. It has promoted a generalized "mission of the church" and has brought holistic planning, trained specialists, and overall coordination by skilled managers. At its best, this approach to mission has been impressive indeed. It has achieved a breadth of planning, a level of efficiency, a utilization of specialized expertise, and a concentration of efforts unequaled in previous church history.

Corporatization of mission has paralleled the flowering of the ecumenical movement. Unified budgets have included substantial support for "ecumenical agencies." These agencies in turn have developed their own bureaucracies. Corporatized mission of mainline Protestant churches is probably best symbolized by its skyscraper monument in New York city, the Interchurch Center at 475 Riverside Drive. But corporatized mission began to collapse even before it was fully developed. Funds began to dry up even before corporate headquarters buildings were paid for, and bureaucracies began to shrink even as "priority strategies" proliferated. The collapse was probably due chiefly to one basic flaw: the failure to take full account of the fact that *churches are voluntary organizations*.

The Power of the Purse String

To say that churches are voluntary organizations is not to deny their special character as the Body of Christ, established by God through the work of the Holy Spirit. It is not to claim that they are *only* voluntary organizations. Theologically and transcendently, they are far more. But *humanly* speaking (which is another way of saying "sociologically"), they are clearly voluntary organizations. Membership is entirely optional. Financial support comes from voluntary contributions. The level of participation is up to the individual member. Churches are groups of like-minded persons, banded together by common consent to achieve common goals.

Corporatized organizations are by nature unresponsive to the individual's search for control over his or her environment. They often devote a great deal of bureaucratic attention to

252

responsiveness, but their programmed attempts to be personal — computer-printed solicitations addressed to Mr. Board O. Education and mechanically typed form letters automatically signed with "Warm personal regards" — come across as phony, and are as likely to enrage as to placate the frustrated recipients. And voluntary organizations are highly vulnerable targets for rage and frustration.

Most corporate structures are implacable. Taxes are as inevitable as death. One can only sigh and submit when the last appeal procedure confirms the original ruling by an officious GS-6 that one is ineligible for a benefit, or when the insurance company insists that the fine print excludes one's own kind of accident. It is easier to pay the bill, even if it is incorrect, after the 12th computer-printed threatening note. But there is one exception to the helplessness of persons facing corporate giants. In *voluntary organizations* individuals can make their impact felt, through the *power of the purse string*.

All major voluntary organizations have to some extent been corporatized, and some have done so without suffering loss of income or incurring constituency distrust. In general, those that have not suffered fall into one of two categories: (1) organizations that limit their efforts to one narrowly defined field, with a specialized appeal and a special-interest constituency (for example, the American Cancer Society or the Boy Scouts), or (2) organizations that depend on small contributions from large numbers of people who contribute out of generalized goodwill or employer pressure, and who are not deeply concerned about what happens in the organizations. United Fund or Community Chest drives capitalize on this dynamic, and some of the agencies so supported go their own way, relatively independent of the desires of the "volunteers" who support them but know little about them. The fund-raising effort itself reaps the benefits of highly corporatized efficiency, and most of the gifts are given without much sense of personal involvement.

Pluralism and Consensus

The mainline churches, in contrast, are inclusive and pluralistic. They cannot focus their endeavors narrowly, since the missional interests of the members cover a wide range of activities, some of them mutually contradictory. Furthermore, their members care deeply. In this respect, they cannot be regarded only as *human* voluntary organizations, since the motivation behind their missional activities — and the deep caring — has transcendent sources.

The "mainline" denominations are sometimes described as liberal, but they are not so much liberal as pluralistic, since all of them include within their membership a wide range of social, ethical and theological perspectives. (The acceptance of pluralism may in itself, of course, be a "liberal" attitude.) More conservative denominations, in contrast, operate with a high level of internal consensus. Dean M. Kelley, in his perceptive analysis *Why Conservative Churches Are Growing* (Harper & Row, 1972), ascribes the relatively prosperous state of these denominations to their focus on a historically indispensable function of religion, that of giving meaning to life. He also credits the strength of their commitment and discipline, and their strictness.

Dean R. Hoge, in an extremely helpful book on the present status of mainline Protestantism, *Division in the Protestant House* (Westminster, 1976), does much to illuminate the absence of consensus and its effect on mission in these denominations. He points to the presence of two basic theological parties. Building on the work of Martin E. Marty (*Righteous Empire: The Protestant Experience in America*) and David O. Moberg (*The Great Reversal: Evangelism vs. Social Concern*), he calls these "Public Protestants" and "Private Protestants," and then adds an additional insight: that the striking characteristic of the contemporary situation is the "collapse of the middle" — the absence of a large group of moderates to bridge the two extremes.

Supporting theory with empirical analysis, Hoge shows that the two parties differ strikingly in their mission priorities. The Public Protestants — theologically liberal, socially optimistic, and reflecting the scientific humanist world view of the contemporary university — place the highest priority on issues of national social reform, injustice, and local social problems. They are least interested in personal evangelism — locally, in the United States and overseas. The priorities of Private Protestants — theologically conservative, pessimistic about the possibilities for social change, and reflecting the classic evangelical Christian world view — are exactly opposite. They are most concerned about personal evangelism and least concerned for social action (Hope, pp. 74-91). When consensus exists that a particular task should be undertaken, any religious group, large or small, will have little difficulty doing it, and that it is done through a corporatized structure will arouse little or no resentment.

The Southern Baptists, a large denomination, can for two reasons maintain massive denominational missional activities without the level of financial backlash experienced by mainline churches. First, a remarkably high level of consensus exists, for a denomination with few controls or sanctions. There is generally a high level of strictness and internal discipline in the local congregation, but very little at other church levels. Nevertheless, the rapid growth of the denomination in a period when mainline churches are declining has added members who share a similar theological and social perspective, and the system is held together by this consensus. Second, the missional activities are supported directly by congregations which back particular enterprises, with no attempt by a denominational structure to exercise central control over the congregation's allocation of funds. The Foreign Mission Board is supported directly by those who believe in and contribute to foreign missions. It is the classic Protestant pattern of a voluntary association within the denomination to carry out a particular kind of mission activity.

Internal Groupings and Shared Commitments

Lon L. Fuller, in an insightful analysis of voluntary organizations, has shown that two basic principles hold such organizations together: shared commitment and a legal principle — a constitution, by-laws, established existence. (Acknowledgment of the lordship of Christ and experience of the transcendent dimension of church life would be the basis of the shared commitment, but also one of the most important elements of the "legal principle" in church organizations.) Both principles, says Fuller, are present in almost all voluntary organizations. Such organizations tend to move from the first principle to the second (the "routinization of charisma," in Weber's analysis). Organizations dominated by the first principle — shared commitment — cannot tolerate internal groupings. But when dominated by the legal principle, voluntary organizations not only can tolerate but in fact need internal groupings based on deeply shared commitment ("Two Principles of Human Association," in *Voluntary Associations*, edited by J. Roland Pennock and John W. Chapman [Atherton, 1969], pp. 3-23).

Internal groupings are often provided within pluralistic denominations by local congregations, which tend to be relatively homogeneous. The voluntary-association principle is strongly at work as persons choose a congregation with which to affiliate; they usually select a like-minded group. While some diversity is present in every congregation, knowledgeable church people in any city can identify particular local churches as "liberal" or "conservative," "missionary-minded" or "social activist." Individuals with strong convictions can make their presence felt in the congregation; as a last resort they can (and often do) move their membership to a more congenial congregation.

The difference between consensus denominations and pluralistic denominations is illustrated by the two most recent schisms in American Protestantism. In 1973 a group of congregations left the Presbyterian Church, U.S., to form the Presbyterian Church in America. The schism had been resisted for years by the pluralistic Southern Presbyterians, with a series of compromises, study groups and movements aimed at reconciliation. The 1976 schism in the Luthern Church-Missouri Synod grew out of the opposite dynamic. It was in effect initiated by the denomination's hierarchy through disciplinary steps and the application of sanctions, in an effort to resist pluralism and to maintain the Missouri Synod's historic high level of consensus.

In voluntary organizations, a highly corporatized central structure is not likely to work unless a clear consensus exists. Reasonably unanimous commitment to a single set of goals, clearly understood and generally supported, is the *sine qua non*. It is a curious anomaly in American church life that it is precisely those inclusive, pluralistic denominations without a clear consensus which have gone furthest in corporatizing their denominational structures!

Coming to Terms with Voluntarism

Churches enjoy an enormous advantage over other voluntary organizations in that they are not *just* voluntary organizations.

256

They are the beneficiaries of a huge reservoir of commitment *to the church* — not because of its agreed-upon goals, not because it is a well-run organization, not because it meets all its members' needs, but because it *is* the church, divinely established, the Body of Christ on earth. Predictions in the volatile '60s that the institutional church would wither away proved to be extraordinarily wrong-headed. The churches are here to stay.

But that does not necessarily mean that corporatized denominational mission structures are here to stay. If the foregoing analysis is correct, they are in serious trouble. Many Christians will continue to give simply to "the church" — whether or not they agree with denominational priorities — out of a generalized sense of loyalty and commitment to the transcendent Lord of the church. The now well-established trend in funding, however, is sure to continue. Three things seem clear:

1. In the society at large, the collision between the corporatization of social structures and the revolution of rising entitlements will not soon be resolved. Voluntary organizations are caught in the middle. Frustrated people cannot affect significantly what is done with their taxes, but they can and will affect what is done with their gifts.

2. The classic Christian pattern of *voluntary* missional activity, through relatively independent agencies, is a long-standing one, and one that has never been repudiated by much of Christendom. It has remained the basic pattern in the Roman Catholic Church, and in much of Protestantism, to the present. Only the "mainline" Protestant denominations have fully corporatized their mission activities.

3. Corporatized missional structures present special problems for inclusive pluralistic churches. Such denominations tend to be held together by the legal principle rather than by shared commitment to particular activities. They may be forced toward a more thoroughgoing missional pluralism.

In light of these factors, it is probably not possible for church bureaucracies to continue to view their deteriorating financial situation as a temporary one, sure to be reversed as soon as the recession is over, when "trust is restored," when the efficiency of their frequently restructured organizations has time to take effect, or when they can "get their message to the people." Nor, in pluralistic denominations, are consultations on the mission of the church, study groups, or more effective goal-setting processes likely to bring about the kind of shared commitment on which a single approach can be based.

What, then, is the answer? The radical solution would be to dismantle the superstructures and return to a simpler pattern, in which like-minded persons group themselves together outside church structures to do whatever they feel called to do in response to the demands of the gospel. Denominational structures would be devoted to issues of faith and order alone. Missionally, to choose this solution would be to opt for pure voluntarism.

This may be the direction in which the forces of history move us, if present trends continue. There is a good bit of evidence that it *is* happening in the area of overseas missions. Nearly every mainline denomination has significantly reduced its number of overseas missionaries. The total in six major denominations dropped from 4,548 to 3,160 between 1958 and 1971 (Kelley, p. 10). In that same period, however, the number of missionaries sent out by independent, generally evangelical groups has increased substantially. In a number of instances, missionaries dropped from the rolls of mainline denominations have simply shifted to independent sponsorship and continued to work in the same country. While hard figures are lacking, it is quite probable that the overall number of American missionaries in overseas areas has not dropped at all. But the pattern has been shifting to one of nondenominational voluntarism.

Toward a Genuine Pluralism

For today's corporatized denominations, a return to pure voluntarism in missional activity is not likely. Less radical solutions are probably desirable. They are dependent on a recognition that *in voluntary organizations, missional activity must reflect the missional will of the members.* In the absence of the shared commitment which might result from denomination-wide consensus, a voluntary organization needs smaller consensus groups — internal groupings of people with shared commitment. In church organizations, such groupings must form the base for voluntary mission activity.

One possibility is a return to the earlier pattern of a variety of mission agencies within the denomination, each cultivating and appealing to its own constituency with denominational approval and cooperation, and carrying out its own mission. This pattern, which as we have noted is still normative for some religious bodies, would be decentralized and highly voluntaristic, although denominational identification and relationship would be retained.

However, such a full surrender of the advantages of a unified approach to mission is probably not necessary. A coordinated denominational mission, carried out by integrated mission agencies, may still be possible in a pluralistic denomination, if its basis is *affirmation of rather than resistance to the pluralism of the constituency.*

A centrally planned and administered missional structure often turns into a denial of pluralism. It assumes that "everyone will agree with me if I can just get the message across to them." It tends to seek its solutions in the direction of better goal-setting and prioritizing processes. It tends to assume that the "priorities of the church" can be set by mustering a 51 percent majority in the governing body or, even worse, by manipulating the formal passage of a missional objective that has the real support of a minority of the constituency.

A genuine pluralism, with a variety of activities freely supported by a variety of constituencies, held together not by political victories but by mutual acceptance, must be the direction of the future. There are plenty of data to demonstrate that voluntary funding is effective (1) where there is a freely gathered consensus on doing a particular task, and (2) where what is done reflects the intentions of the donors. A denominational program which sets out to affirm rather than resist the pluralism of the constituents would probably include most of the following elements:

1. Acceptance of the existence, within the denomination, of a variety of consensus groups, each with its own missional priorities and goals.

2. Integrated planning of a full range of mission activities, substantively as well as nominally responsive to the intentions of various groups of donors.

3. Integrated promotion by the denomination of a full range of mission activities, together with acceptance of promotion by consensus groups of their own mission goals.

4. Full utilization of the widespread Christian commitment to the church itself, which leads to generalized giving to the whole mission of the church by many, but with full acceptance also of designated giving to particular causes.

5. A guarantee that all designated contributions go to the cause designated.

6. A willingness for the constituency to affect the missional priorities through its designated giving, without the kind of ecclesiastical shell game which compensates for increased giving in one area by shifting an equivalent amount of nondesignated money away from that area.

7. An intention to serve the needs and reflect the concerns of *all* groups within the constituency.

Such an approach involves some loss in the area of a unified approach to mission, and some surrender to the constituency-at-large of decision-making functions now exercised, perhaps with greater efficiency and better planning, by church bureaucrats. It does however, take seriously the nature of the church as a voluntary organization, and it offers some hope of defining a useful missional role for central denominational headquarters.

The imperative to respond to the Word of grace with concrete actions is perceived by different Christians in different ways. The guidance of the Holy Spirit is never easy for the church to discern, and it may be that the voice of the Spirit speaks in a variety of ways in these times.

NOTES

Notes, Chapter One

1. Brochure, "Management Skills Workshops Designed Especially for Smaller Church Pastors," sponsored by the JSAC Church Development Task Force (1976).
2. *The Christian Century,* July 7-14, 1976.
3. Report of Rev. Thomas E. Engle, Metter Presbyterian Church, Metter, Georgia, To Savannah Presbytery, August 8, 1978. Quoted by permission.
4. Sermon by Dr. James B. Forbes at Presbyterian Church, U.S. Mission Consultation, Montreat, N.C., February 2, 1978 (quotation transcribed from tape recording). Quoted by permission.

Notes, Chapter Two

1. The discussion which follows is based on: Karl Barth, *The Faith of the Church,* trans. Gabriel Vahanian (New York: Meridian Books, 1958) and *Church Dogmatics IV: The Doctrine of Reconciliation* (New York: Charles Scribner's Sons, 1956); Gregory Baum and Andrew Greeley, eds., *The Church as Institution* (New York: Herder and Herder, 1974); Waldo Beach, *Christian Community and American Society* (Philadelphia: Westminster, 1969); John Bright, *The Kingdom of God* (Nashville: Abingdon-Cokesbury, 1953); Orlando E. Costas, *The Church and Its Mission: A Shattering Critique from the Third World* (Wheaton, Ill.: Tyndale House, 1974); James M. Gustafson, *Treasure in Earthen Vessels* (New York: Harper and Brothers, 1961); Hans Kung, *The Church,* trans. Ray and Rosaleen Ockenden (London: Burns and Oates, 1967); Donald Miller, *The Nature and Mission of the Church* (Richmond: John Knox

Press, 1957); Paul S. Minear, *Images of the Church in the New Testament* (Philadelphia: Westminster, 1960); Jurgen Moltmann, *The Church in the Power of the Spirit,* trans. Margaret Kohl (New York: Harper and Row, 1977).

2. Minear, *Images of the Church in the New Testament.* Three of these major images, People of God, Creation of the Spirit, and Body of Christ, are the categories under which contemporary theologian Hans Kung discusses "the fundamental structure of the church." (See *The Church,* p. 144ff).

3. John Bright, *The Kingdom of God,* is a classic work which treats the whole biblical teaching about God's people under this rubric.

4. Moltmann, p. xiv.

5. Kung, p. 121.

6. C. Ellis Nelson, "The Habitat of the Spirit," Commencement address, Princeton Theological Seminary, May 1977. Quoted by permission.

7. Moltmann, p. 311; also Kung, p. 120.

8. Westminster Larger Catechism, 17.

9. Westminster Larger Catechism, 15.

10. James D.G. Dunn, in what is surely the definitive contemporary treatment of *Unity and Diversity in the New Testament* (Philadelphia: Westminster Press, 1977), has documented this extensively. He examined both the content of New Testament writings and the various manifestations of New Testament Christianity. He found "a fairly clear and consistent unifying strand which from the first marked out Christianity as something distinctive and different, and provided the integrating centre for the diverse expressions of Christianity" (p. 371). But he also found the range of diversity to be very great. A genuine pluralism has thus been inherent in Christianity from the beginning.

11. Albert C. Winn in conversation with staff of the Office of Review and Evaluation, Presbyterian Church, U.S., Atlanta, GA, Jan. 25, 1978.

12. Franz-Xaver Kaufman, "The Church as a Religious Organization," in *The Church as Institution,* eds. Gregory Baum and Andrew Greeley (New York: Herder and Herder, 1974), pp. 77-82.

13. Andrew M. Greeley, *The Denominational Society: A Sociological Approach to Religion in America* (Glenview, Ill.: Scott, Foresman and Co., 1972), pp. 81-83.

14. Max Weber, *Theory of Social and Economic Organization,* trans. A.M. Henderson and Talcott Parsons, ed. Talcott Parsons (New York: Oxford University Press, 1947); and Max Weber, *Sociology of Religion,* trans. Ephraim Fishoff (Boston: Beacon Press, 1963).

15. Gustafson, *Treasure in Earthen Vessels.*

Notes, Chapter Three

1. James Burnham, *The Managerial Revolution* (New York: The John Day Co., 1941).

2. Jacques Ellul, *The Technological Society*, trans. John Wilkinson (New York: Random House, Vintage Books, 1964). For an illustration of the "engineering" approach, see Benjamin Schwartz, "The Rousseau Strain in the Contemporary World," *Daedalus* 107, no. 3 (Summer 1978): 193-208. It is Schwartz's thesis that Rousseau added a "moralist strain" to the engineering/technological approach to the human condition which dominates modern history.

3. George C. Lodge, *The New American Ideology* (New York: Alfred A. Knopf, 1975). Lodge sees a shift from traditional American (Lockean) values to "communitanian values." The society of these communitanian values is dominated by large organizations headed by managers.

4. Peter F. Drucker, *Management* (New York: Harper and Row, 1973), pp. 1-6.

5. Ted Mills, " 'Creeping Corporatism' vs. Rising Entitlements," *Harvard Business Review* 56, no. 6 (November-December 1976): 6-8.

6. Adam Yarmolinsky, "The Professional in American Society," *Daedalus* 107, no. 1 (Winter 1978): 159.

7. Michael Novak, "The Religious Consciousness of the Professional-Managerial Class," *Christian Century*, 10 March 1976, pp. 217-224.

8. Ellul, p. 275.

9. Ivan Illich, *Medical Nemesis* (New York: Bantam Books, 1977) and *Deschooling Society* (New York: Harper and Row, 1971).

10. John McKnight, "Professional Service and Disabling Help" (Paper delivered to the First Annual Symposium on Bioethics of the Clinical Research Institute of Montreal, October 8, 1976). Mimeographed, October 1976.

11. Antoine Mas, *L'Introduction du Machinisme dans le Travail Administratif* (Paris: Dunod, 1949), quoted by Ellul, pp. 11-12.

12. Westminster Confession, Chapter II.

13. Max Weber, *Theory of Social and Economic Organization*, trans. A.M. Henderson and Talcott Parsons, ed. Talcott Parsons (New York: Oxford University Press, 1947), pp. 324-340.

14. This summary of Weber's analysis of characteristics of rational organizations is based in part on discussions in Amitai Etzioni, *Modern Organizations* (Englewood Cliffs, N.J.: Prentice-Hall, Inc., 1964), pp. 50-54; and Peter M. Blau and Marshall W. Meyer, *Bureaucracy in Modern Society*, 2nd ed. (New York: Random House, 1971), pp. 18-23. The underlined phrases are Weber's, *Theory of Social and Economic Organizations*, pp. 229-230. Weber describes other characteristics of bureaucracies, but these four are the most important.

15. Charles B. Perrow, *Organizational Analysis: A Sociological View* (Belmont, Calif.: Brooks-Cole Publishing Co., 1970), p. 50; pp. 50-91 contains a discussion of "non-bureaucratic" models and the bureaucratic tendency that affects all organizational models. For a recent discussion of a "coalitional model," see Jeffrey Pfeffer and

Gerald R. Salancik, "Organizational Design: The Case for a Coalitional Model of Organizations," *Organizational Dynamics* 6, no. 2, (Autumn 1977): 15-29.

16. Robert C. Worley, *A Gathering of Strangers* (Philadelphia: Westminster Press, 1976), pp. 34-37.

17. Perrow, pp. 90-91.

18. Worley, pp. 67-88.

19. Alvin J. Lindgren and Norman Shawchuck, *Management for Your Church* (Nashville: Abingdon, 1977), p. 34; the diagram also shows a Boundary and a Feedback Loop.

20. Theodore Erickson and Mineo Katagiri, "A Systems Approach to the United Church of Christ," prepared for UCC Task Force on Staffing for Mission. Mimeographed 1974.

21. See Orlando E. Costas, *The Church and Its Mission: A Shattering Critique from the Third World* (Wheaton, Ill.: Tyndale House, 1974).

22. Kurt Lewin and Paul Grabbe, "Principles of Re-education," in *The Planning of Change,* eds. W. Bennis, K. Benne and R. Chin (New York: Rinehart and Winston, 1962) pp. 56-64. The sketch of the Human Relations movement on the following pages is based on a more detailed history of its development in the author's doctoral dissertation: Richard G. Hutcheson, Jr., "An Examination of the Value System Reflected by the Sensitivity and Encounter Group Movement in Adult Education, 1950-1970" (Doctoral Dissertation, The American University, 1971).

23. Hutcheson, "Examination of the Value System," pp. 79-86. Abraham Maslow's book, *Toward a Psychology of Being* (Princeton, N.J.: Van Nostrand Co., 1962) became almost a bible for the movement.

24. Charles Y. Glock and Robert N. Bellah, eds., *The New Religious Consciousness,* (Berkeley, Calif.: University of California Press, 1976), p. 98.

25. Leland P. Bradford, Jack R. Gibb, and Kenneth D. Benne, *T-Group Theory and Laboratory Method* (New York: John Wiley and Sons, 1964), p. 1; also p. 118.

26. Hutcheson, "Examination of the Value System," pp. 197-249.

27. W. Warner Burke and Harvey A. Hornstein, *The Social Technology of Organization Development* (Fairfax, Va.: NTL Learning Resources Corp., 1972), pp. 40-41.

28. Philip Lesly, *The People Factor: Managing the Human Climate* (Homewood, Ill.: Dow Jones-Irwin, Inc., 1974).

29. H. Newton Malony, "Toward a Theology for Organizational Development," *The Christian Ministry* 6, no. 4 (July 1975): 19-24. (Originally a paper prepared for the Conference on Religion and the Human Sciences, Washington, D.C., 1973).

30. As late as 1976, sociologists Glock and Bellah published the results of research on *The New Religious Consciousness,* covering the human potential movement and a wide range of related religious and

quasi-religious movements.

31. Hutcheson, "Examination of the Value System," pp. 304-345.

32. Peter L. Berger "A Call for Authority in the Christian Community," *Christian Century*, 27 Oct. 1971, pp. 1257-63. Berger's *A Rumor of Angels* (Garden City, N.Y.: Doubleday and Co., 1969) was an early landmark in the recovery of transcendence after the excesses of radical theology in the sixties.

33. Abraham Maslow, *Eupsychian Management* (Homewood, Ill.: Richard D. Irwin, Inc. and Dorsey Press, 1965).

34. Alvin J. Lindgren and Norman Shawchuck, *Management for Your Church* (Nashville: Abingdon, 1977), pp. 79-100.

35. Drucker, *Management*, p. 441.

36. Drucker, *Management*, pp. 430-442; see also Drucker, *Managing for Results* (New York: Harper and Row, 1964).

37. Dale E. McConckey, *MBO for Nonprofit Organizations* (New York: AMACOM, Division of American Management Associations, 1975), p. 171 ff.

38. Terminology — the use of such terms as "mission," "goal," "objective," "priority goal," "measurable objective," — is not standardized and is often confusing. As used by most managers, the term "goal" is more general while the term "objective" more specific and measurable, although some use them in precisely the opposite sense, with broad objectives and specific, measurable goals.

Notes, Chapter Four

1. Paul M. Harrison, "American Baptists: Bureaucratic and Democratic," *Christian Century*, 5 April 1978, p. 354.

2. Janet Harbison Penfield, "Presbyterian Prognosis: Guarded," *Christian Century*, 15 Feb. 1978, p. 160.

3. Amitai Etzioni, *Modern Organizations* (Englewood Cliffs, N.J.: Prentice-Hall, Inc., 1964), p. 3.

4. Charles Perrow, *Organizational Analysis* (Belmont, Calif.: Brooks/Cole Publishing Co., 1970).

5. Peter Drucker, *Management* (New York: Harper and Row, 1973), p. 46.

6. *The Proposed Book of Confessions of the Presbyterian Church in the United States* (Atlanta: Materials Distribution Service, 1976). The Presbyterian Church, U.S., did not adopt the new declaration of faith as a formal confessional standard of the denomination. The 1977 General Assembly did, however, adopt it "as a contemporary statement of faith, a reliable aid for Christian study, liturgy, and inspiration" *(Minutes* of the 117th General Assembly, 1977, p. 168).

7. *Proposed Book of Confessions*, p. 204. It does become clear from reading the citations that those from the Scripture are considerably more directly relevant than references to the classic confessions, which tend to be quite general in applicability. For instance, the reference to

the Geneva Catechism cited in the section on the church's mission to strive for justice is to questions on the Ten Commandments. The scriptural references, however, are voluminous and directly relevant.

8. Karl Barth, *The Faith of the Church,* trans. Gabriel Vahanian (New York: Meridian Books, 1958), p. 147.

9. L.K. Anderson, Letter to the editor, *Presbyterian Outlook,* 9 Jan. 1978.

10. Earl H. Brill, "The Episcopal Church: Conflict and Cohesion," *Christian Century,* 18 Jan. 1978, pp. 41-47.

11. John R.W. Stott, *Christian Mission in the Modern World* (Downers Grove, Ill.: Intervarsity Press, 1975), p. 12.

12. Dean R. Hoge, *Division in the Protestant House* (Philadelphia: Westminster, 1976).

13. Martin E. Marty, *Righteous Empire: The Protestant Experience in America* (New York: Dial Press, 1970).

14. David O. Moberg, *The Great Reversal: Evangelism vs Social Concern* (Philadelphia: Lippincott, 1972).

15. Hoge, pp. 74-91.

16. Lon L. Fuller, "Two Principles of Human Association," in *Voluntary Associations,* eds., J. Roland Pennock and John W. Chapman (New York: Atherton Press, 1969), pp. 3-23.

17. Dean M. Kelley, *Why Conservative Churches Are Growing* (New York: Harper and Row, 1972).

18. Alice Murray, "Stemming the Church Membership Drop," *Atlanta Journal-Constitution,* 8 Apr. 1978, quoted with Mr. Schell's permission.

19. See the *Open Letter,* publication of the Concerned Fellowship of Presbyterians (the denomination's evangelical wing), March 1978. The 1978 General Assembly added comments modifying some of the wording, but left the product relatively intact. The document was then sent to the Presbyteries for comment, and to the General Assembly Mission Board for formulation of specific program recommendations — a compromise solution which postponed battles about specific goals until some future date.

20. This account is my personal analysis, and should not be confused with any official denominational report or position on the consultation. I was instrumental in making the recommendation which led to conducting the consultation, and my office was in continual liaison with the planning task force throughout its life. My office prepared a major report that went to the consultation as part of its agenda, and I bear as much responsibility as any other single person in the denomination for the consultation and its outcome. The analysis is not intended as a reflection on any other person who participated, for all of whom I have the deepest respect and affection. It is intended only as a case history of the way a particular managerial assumption, state of mind, and process (which I have in the past advocated as staunchly as anyone in American

Protestantism) appears to have worked out in this instance.

Notes, Chapter Five

1. Max Weber, "The Protestant Sects and the Spirit of Capitalism," in *From Max Weber: Essays in Sociology,* eds. Hans Gerth and C. Wright Mills (New York: Oxford University Press, 1946); Ernst Troeltsch, *The Social Teachings of the Christian Churches,* trans. Olive Wyon, (New York: The Macmillan Co., 1932); many others have elaborated the typology. H.R. Niebuhr added the denomination as a middle ground in America. Becker added a fourth, the cult. J.M. Yinger suggested six types: the universal church, the "ecclesia," denomination, established sect, sect, and cult. The basic typology has been generally accepted, however, and Andrew M. Greeley has called it the only significant sociological theory concerning religion as an organization. Andrew Greeley, *The Denominational Society* (Glenview, Ill.: Scott, Foresman and Co., 1972), p. 73.

2. Greeley, *Denominational Society,* p. 79.

3. See, for instance, Michael Novak, "The Meaning of 'Church' in Anabaptism and Roman Catholicism: Past and Present," in *Voluntary Associations,* ed. D.B. Robertson (Richmond: John Knox Press, 1966), pp. 106-107.

4. Jurgen Moltmann, *The Church in the Power of the Spirit,* trans. Margaret Kohl (New York: Harper and Row, 1977), pp. 289-386.

5. Theodore Erickson and Mineo Katagiri, "A Systems Approach to the United Church of Christ," Mimeographed, 1974.

6. Dale D. McConkey, *MBO for Nonprofit Organizations* (New York: AMACOM, 1975), p. 197; Cecily Cannan Selby, "Better Performance from 'Nonprofits,' " *Harvard Business Review,* 56, no. 5 (Sep-Oct, 1978): 92-98.

7. Peter M. Blau and W. Richard Scott, *Formal Organizations: A Comparative Approach* (San Francisco: Chandler Publishing Co., 1962), pp. 43-55; David L. Sills, *The Volunteers* (Glencoe, Ill.: The Free Press, 1957); G. Wayne Gordon and Nicholas Babchuk, "A Typology of Voluntary Organizations," in *The Government of Associations,* eds. W. Glaser and D. Sills (Totowa, N.J.: The Bedminster Press, 1966), pp. 24-28.

8. Amitai Etzioni, *A Comparative Analysis of Complex Organizations* (New York: Free Press of Glencoe, 1968), pp. 4-6.

9. Alexis de Tocqueville, *Democracy in America,* 2 vols. (New York: Alfred A. Knopf, 1976), 2:106.

10. Max Weber, *Theory of Social and Economic Organization* (New York: Oxford University Press, 1947), pp. 324-386.

11. Paul M. Harrison, *Authority and Power in the Free Church Tradition* (Princeton, N.J.: Princeton University Press, 1959); Hugh F. Halverstadt, "The Church as Organization" (Doctoral dissertation, Northwestern University, 1973); Peter M. Blau and W. Richard Scott,

Formal Organizations: A Comparative Approach (San Francisco: Chandler Publishing Co., 1962), pp. 27-39.

12. Robert C. Worley, *A Gathering of Strangers* (Philadelphia: Westminster Press, 1976), p. 31.

13. Worley, pp. 34-66.

14. William G. McLoughlin, "Changing Patterns of Protestant Philanthropy, 1607-1969," in *The Religious Situation: 1969*, ed. Donald R. Cutler (Boston: Beacon Press, 1969), pp. 538-614.

15. William L. McBride, "Voluntary Association: The Basis of an Ideal Model and the Democratic Failure," in *Voluntary Association*, eds. J. Roland Pennock and John W. Chapman (New York: Atherton Press, 1969), p. 202.

16. David L. Sills, *The Volunteers* (Glencoe, Ill.: The Free Press, 1957), p. 23.

17. James M. Gustafson, "The Voluntary Church: A Moral Appraisal," in *Voluntary Associations,* ed. D.B. Robertson (Richmond: John Knox Press, 1966), p. 313.

18. Philip Selznik, "An Approach to a Theory of Bureaucracy," in *The Government of Associations,* eds. Willima A. Glaser and David L. Sills (Totawa, N.J.: The Bedminster Press, 1966), pp. 190-193; Paul S. Ello and Mary D. Wagaman, *Motivating Participation in Voluntary Membership Associations* (Foundation of the American Society of Association Executives, June 1970); and Herbert A. Simon, "The Nature of Authority," in *The Government of Associations,* pp. 123-127.

19. Bernard Bonher, "Bureaucratic Organization and the Volunteer," in *Social Perspectives on Behavior,* eds. Herman D. Stein and Richard A. Cloward, (Glencoe, Ill.: Free Press, 1958), pp. 606-609.

20. Selznik, p. 193.

Notes, Chapter Six

1. James M. Gustafson, *Treasure in Earthen Vessels* (New York: Harper and Brothers, 1961), pp. 37-40.

2. Paul M. Harrison, *Authority and Power in the Free Church Tradition* (Princeton, N.J.: Princeton University Press, 1959), p. viii.

3. Andrew M. Greeley, *The Denominational Society: A Sociological Approach to Religion in America* (Glenview, Ill.: Scott, Foresman and Co., 1972), pp. 79-83.

4. Hugh F. Halverstadt, "The Church as Organization: A Theoretical Argument" (Doctoral dissertation, Northwestern University, 1973).

5. Lyle E. Schaller, *The Decision-Makers* (Nashville: Abingdon, 1974), pp. 82-104.

6. For a Catholic view of this process of provision for voluntary service organizations within a non-voluntary church, see *The Laity Today,* Bulletin of Concilim de Laicis, No. 13-14 (Vatican: 1973); also Michael Novak, "The Meaning of 'Church' in Anabaptism and Roman

Catholicism, Past and Present," in *Voluntary Associations,* ed. D.B. Robertson (Richmond: John Knox Press, 1966), pp. 96-97.

7. William G. McLoughlin, "Changing Patterns of Protestant Philanthropy, 1607-1969," in *The Religious Situation: 1969,* ed. Donald R. Cutler (Boston: Beacon Press, 1969), pp. 538-614.

8. Ralph D. Winter, "Protestant Mission Societies and the Other Protestant 'Schism'," in *American Denominational Organization,* ed. Ron Scherer (Philadelphia: Fortress Press, 1977); also Winter, "The Two Structures of God's Redemptive Mission," American Society of Missiology, 1974. Gustafson (pp. 34-35) has seen the two forms of organization as illustrating formal and informal political processes. He sees the extra church voluntary associations as pointing to the need for denominational institutional forms.

9. David Kuchardsy, "The Year of the Evangelical, '76," *Christianity Today,* 22 Oct. 1976, p. 13.

10. Richard G. Hutcheson, Jr., *The Churches and the Chaplaincy* (Atlanta: John Knox Press, 1975).

11. C. Ellis Nelson, "The Habitat of the Spirit," Commencement address, Princeton Theological Seminary, May 1977.

12. Religious News Service report, *Presbyterian Outlook,* 2 Jan. 1978, p. 3.

13. The 1978 General Assembly of the Presbyterian Church, U.S., refused to adopt a theological paper on the ordained clergy, sending it back for further revision because it did not deal adequately with non-parish clergy specialists.

14. Martin Marty, *Context,* 15 November 1976, p. 1.

15. Harrison, p. 211.

Notes, Chapter Seven

1. Paul A. Mickey and Robert L. Wilson, *What New Creation?* (Nashville: Abingdon, 1977). This book deals primarily with the restructures of five mainline denominations: American Baptist, Episcopal, Presbyterian, U.S., United Presbyterian, USA, and United Methodist. Lyle Schaller refers to ten Protestant denominations that have restructured in the late sixties and early seventies.

2. Ted Mills " 'Creeping Corporatism' vs. Rising Entitlements," *Harvard Business Review* 54, no. 6 (November-December, 1976).

3. "Report of the Special Committee on Church Membership Trends," quoted on cover of *The Presbyterian Outlook,* 24 May 1976.

4. Robert Nisbet, *Twilight of Authority* (New York: Oxford University Press, 1975).

5. *Minutes of the 112th General Assembly, Presbyterian Church, U.S.,* 1972.

6. *Giving in America: Toward a Stronger Voluntary Sector* (Commission on Private Philanthropy and Public Needs, 1975), pp. 70-71.

7. *Minutes of the 116th General Assembly, Presbyterian Church, U.S.,* 1976, p. 117.

8. Earl H. Brill, "The Episcopal Church: Conflict and Cohesion," *Christian Century*, 18 Jan. 1978, pp. 19-47.

9. Dean M. Kelley, *Why Conservative Churches are Growing* (New York: Harper and Row, 1972), p. 10.

10. Arthur J. Moore, "Mission and Organizational Style," *Presbyterian Outlook*, 16 Jan. 1978, p. 7.

11. John McKnight, "Professional Service and Disabling Help," (Paper delivered at the First Annual Symposium on Bioethics of the Clinical Research Institute of Montreal, 8 Oct. 1976). Mimeographed, October 1976.

12. Ivan Illich, *Medical Nemesis: The Expropriation of Health* (New York: Bantam Books, 1977). Also, Paul Starr, "Medicine and the Waning of Professional Sovereignty," *Daedalus* 107, no. 1 (Winter, 1978): 175-194.

13. Lyle E. Schaller, "What Will 1978 Bring?" *Presbyterian Outlook*, 9 Jan. 1978, p. 5.

14. Ivan Illich, *Deschooling Society* (New York: Harper and Row, 1971).

15. *Washington Post*, 10 August 1978, p. A2.

16. Meg Greenfield, "Carter and Compassion," *Newsweek*, 19 Dec. 1977, p. 104.

17. A recent issue of *Daedalus* (107, no. 1, Winter 1978) seeks to assess the changes that have taken place in America since the sixties. The issue is entitled "A New America?" Of its eighteen essays, two (by Adam Yarmolinsky and Paul Starr) deal with professionalization and its effects. While not so radical a critique as those of McKnight and Illich, they point to the same phenomena.

Notes, Chapter Eight

1. Lyle E. Schaller, *The Decision Makers* (Nashville: Abingdon, 1974), p. 82.

2. Paul A. Mickey and Robert L. Wilson, *What New Creation?* (Nashville: Abingdon, 1977).

3. Cary D. Habegger, "Organizational Effectiveness in the Christian Church: A Study of the Survey of Organizations" (Paper delivered at the 1977 annual meeting of the Society for the Scientific Study of Religion and the Religious Research Association, Chicago, October 28, 1977). Based on doctoral dissertation, Rosemead Graduate School of Psychology, 1977.

Notes, Chapter Nine

1. James M. Gustafson, *Treasure in Earthen Vessels: The Church as a Human Community* (New York: Harper and Brothers, 1961), pp. 38-40.

2. Paul M. Harrison, *Authority and Power in the Free Church Tradition*, (Princeton, N.J.: Princeton University Press, 1959), pp. 208-216.

3. Abraham Zaleznik, "Managers and Leaders: Are They Different?", *Harvard Business Review* 55, no. 3 (May-June, 1977): 70.

4. Zaleznik, "Managers and Leaders," pp. 70-75.

Notes, Chapter Ten

1. Martin E. Marty, "Denominations: Surviving the 70s," *Christian Century*, 21 Dec. 1977, pp. 1186-88.

2. *Giving in America: Toward a Stronger Voluntary Sector,* Report of the Commission on Private Philanthropy and Public Needs, 1975, p. 63.

3. *Giving in America,* pp. 70-71.

4. *Giving in America,* p. 168.

5. *Giving in America,* p. 216.

6. Philip M. Larson, Jr., *Vital Church Management* (Atlanta: John Knox Press, 1977), pp. 57-66.

7. James H. Daughdrill, Jr., "Alternative to Politics," *Presbyterian Outlook,* 20 March 1978, p. 8.

8. James M. Gustafson, "The Voluntary Church: A Moral Appraisal," in *Voluntary Associations,* ed. D.B. Robertson (Richmond: John Knox Press, 1966), pp. 315-320.

9. Hugh F. Halverstadt, "The Church as Organization: A Theological Argument" (Doctoral dissertation, Northwestern University, 1973). The quotation is from page 146.

Notes, Chapter Eleven

1. Albert C. Winn (former President of Louisville Theological Seminary and Chairman of the Ad Interim Committee on a New Confession of Faith and Book of Confessions, Presbyterian Church, U.S.) in conference with Office of Review and Evaluation, January 25, 1978. Cited by permission.

2. See, for instance, the journals *Evaluation, Evaluation Quarterly* and Francis G. Caro, ed., *Readings in Evaluation Research* (New York: Russell Sage Foundation, 1971).

3. For a discussion of formative and summative evaluation see John Van Maanen, *The Process of Program Evaluation* (Washington: National Training and Development Service Press, 1973), pp. 3-4. Also Barry M. Stow, "The Experimenting Organization, *Organizational Dynamics* 6, no. 1 (Summer 1977): 3-18.

4. See Van Maanen, pp. 18-30 for such a discussion.

Notes, Chapter Twelve

1. Alvin Toffler, *Future Shock* (New York: Bantam Books, 1970).

2. Lyle E. Schaller, *The Decision Makers* (Nashville: Abingdon, 1974), pp. 102-104.

3. *Minutes of 112th General Assembly, Presbyterian Church, U.S.,* 1972.

4. Denis E. Shoemaker, "Ecclesiastical Future Shock: The Ordeal of Restructuring," *Christian Century,* 14 Mar. 1973, pp. 312-315.

5. See Karl E. Weick, "Organizational Design: Organizations as Self-Designing Systems," *Organizational Dynamics* 6, no. 2 (Autumn 1977): 31-46. See also discussion of "situational theory" in Jay W. Louch, "Organizational Design: A Situational Perspective," in the same issue of *Organizational Dynamics,* pp. 2-14.

6. Robert Raines, *New Life in the Church* (New York: Harper & Row, 1961).

7. James D. Anderson, *To Come Alive! A New Proposal for Revitalizing the Local Church* (New York: Harper & Row, 1973).